THE DEAD SEA SCROLLS

Qumran in Perspective

THE DEAD SEA SCROLLS

Qumran in Perspective

Geza Vermes

With the collaboration of
PAMELA VERMES

Revised Edition

FORTRESS PRESS   PHILADELPHIA

First published in Great Britain by
William Collins Sons & Co. Ltd. 1977

First Fortress Press edition 1981

Library of Congress Cataloging in Publication Data

Vermeš, Géza, 1924–
  The Dead Sea scrolls.

  Bibliography: p.
  Includes index.
  1. Qumran community. 2. Dead Sea scrolls—Criticism, interpretation, etc. I. Vermes, Pamela,
joint author. II. Title.
BM175.Q6V47   1981   296.8′15   80-2382
ISBN 0-8006-1435-6

8558J80   Printed in the United States of America   1-1435

Contents

Preface

If it were known exactly when, in the spring of 1947, the first Dead Sea Scrolls were brought out of Qumran Cave 1, we might have celebrated the thirtieth anniversary of the initial discovery at about the time this Preface is being written. To those of us who have been closely associated throughout the years with these famous documents, and who have become accustomed to speak of the 'recent' manuscript finds, it comes as a shock to realize that the students who listen to our reminiscences not only do not remember the events so familiar to us, but were not even born when Qumran first came to the world's notice.

During the fifties, introductions to the Scrolls appeared in almost every language, but no up-to-date general survey is now available in English. Hence this book in which I intend to re-examine the whole issue in a way that will interest the educated public, but also cater for the needs of university students. Thus the eight chapters are directed to both categories of reader, but the subsequent bibliographical aids are meant primarily for those wishing to specialize in religious and oriental studies, theology and ancient history.

The Qumran library and the Community to which it belonged possess distinctive, even unique, features, but they must also be viewed as integral parts of the larger Palestinian Jewish world of the inter-Testamental age. For this reason I have endeavoured to adopt whenever possible a broad approach to these texts and to the people who stand behind them so as to make them more meaningful and real.

I should perhaps also explain that in describing the life and

Preface

institutions of the sect I have deliberately introduced the terminology current in contemporary Christian religious orders. Expressions such as 'postulants', 'novices', 'the professed', 'the contemplatives', etc., are used analogically in these pages, and have no proper Hebrew equivalents in the Scrolls themselves.

This volume is the outcome of many years of research and reflection. I have learned a great deal from my seniors, E. L. Sukenik, G. Lambert, P. Kahle, W. F. Albright, H. H. Rowley, R. de Vaux, and Sir Godfrey Driver among the dead, and A. Dupont-Sommer among the living. I owe also much to my contemporaries and friends, D. Barthélemy, S. P. Brock, F. M. Cross, J. A. Fitzmyer, J. T. Milik, F. G. B. Millar, J. Neusner, J. Strugnell, E. Ullendorff and Y. Yadin. But *The Dead Sea Scrolls: Qumran in Perspective* is especially the fruit of a continuous dialogue with my wife. Many of her ideas have found their way into the final version, and as always she has helped to improve the manuscript in every way, including the more than occasional re-statement of the substance itself.

The Oriental Institute,   G.V.
University of Oxford   18 April 1977

CHAPTER 1

Discoveries in the Judaean Desert

1 THE DEAD SEA SCROLLS FROM QUMRAN

Thirty years ago precisely, in the spring of 1947 when the Judaean desert was still under British mandate, a young Taamire goat-herd called Muhammad ed-Dhib set out apparently to look for a lost animal and stumbled on a treasure infinitely more valuable to the world at large – a cave containing jars, some broken and others intact, filled with ancient manuscripts.

This chance discovery, proclaimed by W. F. Albright, one of the foremost Palestinian archaeologists of that period, as not merely 'sensational' but 'the greatest manuscript find of modern times', aroused immediate and universal interest which persisted throughout the 1950s and was revived in 1965 and 1966 by means of highly popular Scrolls exhibitions in the United States and Britain. In fact, even after three decades their fascination is still with us.

What is so peculiar about these Dead Sea Scrolls? Why has their appeal to our imagination been so much stronger than that of other major discoveries in the domain of biblical archaeology? After all, the 100,000 Hebrew, Greek, Aramaic and Arabic fragments transferred to Cambridge from the famous depository of old manuscripts known as the Cairo Geniza, by the renowned rabbinic scholar of the turn of the century, Solomon Schechter, have substantially transformed biblical and Jewish studies, and even our understanding of the social history of the Mediterranean countries in the Middle Ages. Yet in contrast to the Scrolls, these have remained the preserve of scholars and connoisseurs. Similarly, there was no general stir of anything like the same magnitude when in 1929 a Syrian ploughshare uncovered in Ras Shamra, the ancient Ugarit, an enormous collection of clay tablets bearing a previously unknown cuneiform alphabetic script, though these Canaanite sources have added vastly to our grasp of early biblical Hebrew and of the poetic and religious imagery of the Old Testament.

The answer in brief is that the Scrolls have fulfilled an age-old expectation in that they are written documents belonging to the Bible or connected with it. They were found not in Egypt or Syria, but in the Holy Land itself. Thus at long last, the land of the Bible, dug and turned over by archaeologists thousands of times in hundreds of places, has given the lie to the thesis, which in my student days still counted as an axiom, that no ancient text written on perishable material such as leather or papyrus could resist the ravages of the Palestinian climate. The Scrolls are a dream that has come true.

Some time in the second half of 1947, the Taamire tribesmen, represented by a Bethlehem cobbler-cum-antique dealer surnamed Kando, sold their finds, in part to the Metropolitan Mar Athanasius Yeshue Samuel, head of the Syrian Orthodox monastery of St Mark in Jerusalem, and in part to Eleazar Lipa Sukenik, the then professor of archaeology at the Hebrew University. The monks of St Mark's were more interested in the monetary value of their purchases than in their scholarly importance. Their hopes, however, met with successive disappointments. A Syrian employee of the Department of Antiquities and a visiting Dominican Old Testament scholar judged the manuscripts worthless. Professor Sukenik, on the other hand, who made his first contact with the Arab Scrolls dealer in the summer of 1947, felt sure that the documents were authentic and, apparently on 29 November 1947, the day of the UN vote creating the State of Israel, acquired for the Hebrew University three manuscripts: an incomplete roll of Isaiah, a collection of hymns resembling biblical Psalms, and an account of an allegorical war between light and darkness.

Two conflicting accounts exist of the events leading to the acquisition of four documents of Mar Athanasius. According to Sukenik, they were shown to him at the beginning of February 1948 and he was granted first refusal by the Metropolitan. The other version is that the first person to declare the Scrolls genuine and old was the acting Director of the American School in Jerusalem, John C. Trever, and that this happened at the end of February. Be this as it may, Mar Athanasius accepted the American bid and gave them the right to publish a complete Isaiah manuscript, a rule book entitled the Manual of Discipline, and a commentary to the Book of Habakkuk. All three texts were immediately photographed by Trever. The fourth, named the Lamech Scroll on the basis of a fragment detached from it, could not at that time be opened. It was not until several years later, when it was under different ownership, that this became known as the Genesis Apocryphon.

Because of the disturbances which accompanied the establishment of the State of Israel, Mar Athanasius decided on a wise, though not quite legal, course of action. He removed his precious property from the danger zone and ultimately took it to the United States, where for years he tried to find a buyer, the price asked for the four manuscripts being a million dollars. In 1954, he was offered a quarter of that amount by a mediator and accepted it. Whereupon the Scrolls, purchased in reality for the Hebrew University, were taken to Israel by Sukenik's son, Yigael Yadin, and since 1967 all seven of them have been displayed in the Shrine of the Book in Jerusalem.

The next phase of the Scrolls story brings us to the beginning of 1949. The location of the cave of manuscripts had been carefully concealed by the Bedouin, but at the instigation of a Belgian officer, Philippe Lippens, serving with the UN Observer Corps, a search was carried out by members of the Arab Legion of Jordan and in late January of that year the site was found. Two archaeologists, G. L. Harding, director of the Amman Department of Antiquities, and the Dominican Roland de Vaux, director of the École biblique et archéologique française of Jerusalem, soon arrived on the scene and subjected the cave to a systematic exploration from 15 February to 5 March 1949.

In one essential respect, their findings were conclusive. Hundreds of manuscript fragments, some of them belonging to the Scrolls already known, proved that the latter came from that particular cave, one situated some eight miles south of Jericho and over a mile inland from the western shore of the Dead Sea. Moreover, non-written archaeological material, pottery, wood and cloth, indicated that the deposit, including the Scrolls, was indeed an ancient one. Unfortunately, however, this pronouncement on the authenticity and approximate age of the manuscripts was at once spoilt by an error and a blunder. The error consisted in identifying most of the jars and bowls as Hellenistic, and consequently in asserting, despite the presence of some Roman pottery, that the manuscripts were concealed in the cave at the end of the second, or at the latest the beginning, of the first century BC. The blunder, which incidentally delayed progress by about two years, was the failure on the part of de Vaux and Harding to recognize or even investigate properly any potential link between the cave and the neighbouring ruins of Qumran. A superficial survey in 1949 led them to identify Qumran as the remains of a small Roman fort from the third or fourth century AD. Later, de Vaux merely said that at that time the ruins 'had not seemed to have any evident connection with the discoveries in the cave'. But when he and Harding set out to excavate Qumran thoroughly in November 1951, the truth became immediately and inescapably apparent. The pottery found in the cave and that buried on the site were identical. Some of it was unquestionably Roman. So the original dating of the manuscript deposit to *c*. 100 BC was proved wrong. Moreover, coins discovered in the debris indicated that the buildings had remained in use until as late as the first revolt of the Jews against Rome in AD 66-70. Indeed, it was during the course of that war that the inhabitants of Qumran had hidden their manuscripts.

In the spring of 1952 de Vaux, who was in the process of completing his first campaign at Qumran, prepared a report for the French Académie des Inscriptions in which he advanced his new interpretation of the archaeological facts and confessed his previous mistakes: '*Je me suis trompé* . . . *Je me suis trompé* . . . *Je me suis trompé* . . .'

During the same period, the Taamire Bedouin were continuing their search for manuscripts, and in February 1952 discovered a second cave in the same area. The fragments it contained were sold by them to the authorities. Father de Vaux and his group followed in their footsteps and in 1952 scored two successes, Caves 3 and 5, and in 1955 another four, Caves 7, 8, 9 and 10. Cave 4, which is literally within a stone's throw of the Qumran site, was overlooked by the archaeologists. The Bedouin found it in the summer of 1952 and in so doing laid their hands on the richest manuscript deposit of them all. Roland de Vaux admits that they noticed cavities in the marl terrace while they were excavating Qumran a few months earlier but says they thought them 'archaeologically barren'. Two further caves were discovered by the Taamires: Cave 6 in 1952, and in 1956 Cave 11 containing several large documents, including a Psalms Scroll and an Aramaic paraphrase of Job.

1956 saw the end of manuscript finds in the Qumran region, and the final season of archaeological excavations at Khirbet Qumran. In addition to the initial dig in 1951–2, there had been altogether four campaigns. During the last two, the search had extended to the area lying between Qumran and Ain Feshkha two miles further south. In 1958, the buildings at Feshkha were identified as a dependency of the Qumran settlement, an agricultural and industrial establishment. But Feshkha yielded no manuscripts; the only written documents found there are inscriptions on a jar and on a stone weight.

Although there was no actual evidence of further Scrolls finds, rumours continued to circulate in Jordanian Jerusalem concerning the existence of other fragments, and even of complete manuscripts remaining in unauthorized hands. But no-one could be sure whether these had any factual basis until 1967. The Israeli victory at the end of the Six Day War enabled Yigael Yadin, who succeeded his father E. L. Sukenik in the Jerusalem archaeology chair, to take possession of the Temple Scroll. This is the largest document, twenty-eight feet (8·6 m) long, to emerge from a Qumran hiding-place, apparently Cave 11. The complete Isaiah Scroll with the sixty-six chapters of the biblical book, measures only twenty-four feet (7·3 m).

The circumstances in which the Temple Scroll was obtained are still unknown. 'I cannot at this stage disclose the way this scroll came into our hands,' Yadin wrote in the *Biblical Archaeologist* in December 1967, 'lest I endanger the chances of acquiring further scrolls.' Another ten years have passed and we are still without an explanation.

To sum up, the chronology of the Qumran discoveries is as follows.

1947   Cave 1 is accidentally found.
1949   Cave 1 is identified and excavated.
1951–6 Five seasons of archaeological work at Qumran.
1952–6 Ten more manuscript caves are discovered.
1955–8 Archaeological search between Qumran and Feshkha.
1967   The Temple Scroll appears.

2 THE MANUSCRIPTS FROM THE BAR KOKHBA CAVES

As early as October 1951, the Taamire Bedouin discovered further caves in the desert and offered Hebrew and Greek manuscript fragments for sale to Father de Vaux. The bargaining with him went on for some months. One of the Arabs, Hassan Farhan, justified the exorbitant price he was asking for a Greek papyrus and other small fragments by the difficulty in obtaining them: the cave was distant from Bethlehem and almost inaccessible. 'As I looked sceptical,' wrote de Vaux in his diary on 8 January 1952, 'he said: "Come and see!" I jumped at the opportunity. Would this be possible? He reassured me. I might perhaps obtain a permit from the Department of Antiquities to employ them legally? He applauded. In that case, I must inform the Director of Antiquities? Hassan consented.'

A party led by de Vaux and Harding reached the caves in question, which lay in Wadi Murabbaat, fifteen miles southeast of Jerusalem and eleven miles south of Qumran Cave 1, on 25 January 1952. The Jordanian police accompanying the archaeologists surprised thirty-four Taamires in the act of rifling the site for further remains but de Vaux took half of them on as honest labourers.

These four Murabbaat caves showed signs of successive occupation from prehistoric times to the Roman era but the pottery, domestic objects, weapons and coins demonstrated that the manuscripts belong to the latter period. The earliest coin found was of Antigonus-Mattathias (40–37 BC), followed by one of Agrippa I dated AD 42–3, three of the procurators of Judaea under Nero (AD 58–9), one of the first revolt (AD 69–70), one of the city of Ascalon under Trajan (AD 113–14), one of Tiberias under Hadrian (AD 119–20), and nine of the second revolt (AD 132–5). There were also three Roman coins, two mentioning the Tenth *Fretensis* Legion stationed in Palestine after AD 70. The third is still unidentified. The main occupation of the site seems therefore to have coincided with the Jewish rebellion under Hadrian, an archaeological deduction fully confirmed by the contents of the manuscripts themselves.

The caves had been visited by Arabs in the Middle Ages. They had left pottery there, textiles, one or two coins, and a few fragments of paper inscribed with Arabic texts, one dating to AD 938–9.

Among the older documents, one palimpsest papyrus is traceable to the eighth or seventh century BC and there were also biblical scraps. By far the most sensational finds, however, are connected with the warrior hero Bar Kokhba, whose complete name and title, Simeon ben Kosiba, prince of Israel, appears frequently. A number of texts deal with legal matters pertaining to that period and the three languages of Jewish Palestine, Hebrew, Aramaic and Greek, are all represented. A few badly damaged Latin papyri dating to the second century AD testify to a subsequent Roman occupation of the caves.

In March 1955 yet another hiding-place was found by an Arab shepherd in Wadi Murabbaat containing a fairly extensive though badly worn roll of the Hebrew Minor Prophets. Earlier, in 1952, twenty-four fragments had also been acquired belonging to a Greek translation of the Minor Prophets. These were said to have come from an unidentified cave in the Judaean desert, but in fact the Bedouin took them from the Israeli sector, as later events were to make plain.

Emulating the successful manuscript hunt in Jordan, Israeli archaeologists initiated in 1960 and 1961 a systematic search of the wadis situated further south in the wilderness between Engedi and Masada and explored caves in Nahal Hever, Nahal Zeelim and Nahal Mishmar. The richest discovery was made in Nahal Hever in what came to be known as the Cave of Letters, where Yigael Yadin, who happened to be leading that particular party, unearthed an important cache of Hebrew, Aramaic and Greek documents from the Bar Kokhba period, some biblical fragments, and a private archive of thirty-five Aramaic, Greek and Nabataean deeds dating from AD 93–4 to AD 132 and dealing with the affairs of a Jewish lady, Babata the daughter of Simeon, and her family. Nahal Hever also yielded thirteen scraps of parchment belonging to the Greek Minor Prophets Scroll mentioned earlier. Its place of discovery is therefore no longer 'unidentified'.

As none of these documents should really be listed under the heading of Dead Sea Scrolls and will not in consequence be analysed in the later chapters, this is the moment to describe and evaluate them briefly.

Among the manuscripts from the Bar Kokhba caves are dated contracts and other writings in Hebrew, Aramaic and Greek which add considerably to our knowledge of Jewish legal terminology prior to the earliest post-biblical law code, the Mishnah (c. AD 200). We now for instance possess an Aramaic acknowledgement of debt, dated to AD 55–6, which contains a clause stipulating that the sum borrowed was to be repaid even in a sabbatical year. To grasp the significance of this, it must be remembered that biblical law demands that in a sabbatical year all debts should be cancelled (Deut. 15:2). Although it was no doubt appropriate in the economical system current before the Babylonian exile, in the first century of the Christian era this statute made it difficult to obtain a loan towards the end of the seven-year cycle. To relieve the periodical credit squeeze, new legislation was introduced, the famous *prosbul* rule attributed to Hillel, the great Pharisaic teacher, whereby a debtor may formally renounce his sabbatical privilege. The Murabbaat papyrus in question (no. 18), dated to the second year of the reign of Nero, corroborates the custom though not the wording as it is codified in the Mishnah (m Shebiit 10:4).

In addition, we now also have a bill of divorce and a marriage contract from the sixth and the eleventh years of Provincia Arabia, probably November AD 111 and February 117 respectively. As for the archive of Babata, this includes her marriage contract, her property deeds, and even her tax return (or *census*), written in Greek, completed on 2 December 127, and sworn before the Roman district official at Rabbath Moab 'by the Fortune (*Tyche*) of the Lord Caesar'. To judge by what is known of her financial affairs it would seem that her declaration was not entirely truthful.

Incidentally, it is worth emphasizing that Jewish legal scribes of the early second century AD used not only Hebrew and Aramaic, but also Greek and even Nabataean, and that the dates given accord with the secular era in force.

The Bar Kokhba texts themselves are of extraordinary historical significance, mainly because the second revolt of the Jews against Rome under Hadrian is otherwise so poorly documented, amounting to a brief notice by Cassius Dio (lxix 12–14) supplemented by occasional and highly tendentious references in rabbinic literature and in the writings of the Church Fathers. The new papyri are too scanty to provide a full record of the war, but they afford valuable insights into various aspects of the rebel government.

With the outbreak of the revolution in AD 132, a new era was started known as the first, second, third and fourth years of 'the liberation of Israel by Simeon ben Kosiba'. The rebels divided the territory held by them into districts and placed them under the command of military governors. They also set administrators or *parnasin* in charge of the civil communities, and these officials, in addition to their normal business, were made responsible for leasing out the land that had formerly belonged to the emperor but had been appropriated by Simeon ben Kosiba. They were expected, furthermore, to co-operate with the military commanders of their region.

Simeon ben (or bar) Kosiba – for such was his name before his admirers re-styled him Bar Kokhba, Son of the Star (= Messiah) and his critics, Bar Koziba, Son of the Lie (= false Messiah) – was a stern man always ready to threaten both his enemies and his own people alike. 'Let it be known to you that I will inflict punishment on you,' he wrote to the inhabitants of Tekoa. To one of his commanders he sent the warning that if he did not obey his orders he would set his 'feet in irons as I did to Ben Aphlul'.

The texts so far released tell us nothing about the hostilities themselves, and the Romans are only once referred to by name, though on a few occasions one finds the term *goyyim*, Gentiles, applied to them. All the localities alluded to – among them Herodium, Tekoa and Engedi – are situated in the Judaean desert, the theatre, according to the rabbis, of the final phase of the war during which Bar Kokhba was himself slain.

This revolutionary government insisted on strict observance of the Jewish religious practices: war or no war, messengers were to rest on the Sabbath, the laws of tithing of agricultural produce were to be maintained, and sabbatical years were to be enforced. One letter from Bar Kokhba to a local commander deserves to be quoted for its sheer irrelevance to the perils of the moment. 'I am sending you,' it tells him, 'two donkeys, and you will despatch two men with them [to the commanders of Engedi] that they pack palm branches and citrons and bring them to you for the camp. You shall send other men from your place [Kiriath Arabayya] to bring you myrtles and willows. Tithe them and send them to the camp.' This probably happened in the autumn of AD 134, when the collapse of the revolution lay only a few months ahead. Yet headquarters needed palm branches, citrons, myrtles and willows, all duly tithed, to celebrate Sukkoth, the Feast of Tabernacles!

Following the last disastrous battle at Bether in AD 135, a few of the surviving Jewish soldiers fled to remote and inaccessible hiding-places in the wadis of the wilderness taking with them their families and a few of their belongings and manuscripts. Once they were inside, however, the pursuing Romans placed guards on the exits of the caves and let starvation take its course. Such a large number of skulls and skeletons was found in one of them that the Israeli archaeologists gave it the name of the Cave of Horrors. One moving witness to a patriot who died consists in a piece of broken pottery with written on it: 'Saul son of Saul. *Shalom!*'

3 THE MANUSCRIPTS FROM MASADA

Masada, an apparently impregnable rock fortress, was built by Alexander Jannaeus (103–76 BC) at the beginning of the first century BC and embellished and enlarged by Herod the Great (37–4 BC). Its fame is due mostly to the bravery of the Zealot garrison which seized it in AD 66 and continued to resist the power of Rome years after the fall of Jerusalem in AD 70. When after a long siege all hope of escape had disappeared, the captain of Masada, Eleazar ben Yair, a descendant of Judas the Galilean, the founder of the revolutionary Zealot party, persuaded his companions to kill themselves rather than surrender. Each man consequently put his own family to death, and afterwards ten were selected by lot to slay the rest and then each other. The survivor was instructed to fire all the buildings before committing suicide. Two women and five children hid and escaped destruction, but when the legionaries eventually entered the fortress they found nine hundred and sixty Jews who had defied them even to death.

This awe-inspiring place was thoroughly and expertly excavated by an international team of volunteers under the direction of Yigael Yadin. The two seasons of digging, October 1963 to May 1964 and November 1964 to April 1965, produced impressive results and considerably improved our knowledge of the history of Masada during the Herodian period and the Zealot occupation. If scholars had not already been spoiled by the Qumran Scrolls, the written documents discovered in the fortress would have been hailed as astonishing. Within the new perspective, they are interesting without being spectacular.

The Masada texts comprise the Bible (fragments from Genesis, Leviticus, and Psalms), the Apocrypha (twenty-six large fragments belonging to the Hebrew Ecclesiasticus or Wisdom of Jesus ben Sira), a small scrap from a sectarian Angelic Liturgy known from Qumran Cave 4, a Hebrew and a Greek papyrus, over two hundred potsherds inscribed in Hebrew and Aramaic, and several Latin papyri left behind by the Romans.

The presence of a Qumran writing in the last Zealot stronghold will be discussed later in connection with the identity of the Dead Sea sect. By contrast with the Qumran library where the manuscripts were exclusively religious by nature, those found at Masada and in the Bar Kokhba hiding-places were of various kinds, though those dating from the Bar Kokhba period itself were predominantly secular.

As an epilogue to the Masada saga, it should be added that the fall of the fortress used to be dated to the spring of AD 73. The end came on the day of Passover, according to Josephus, who tells us further that the conquest was the work of Lucius Flavius Silva. Some twenty years ago, however, two Latin inscriptions were found in Italy implying that this Flavius Silva did not leave Rome for Judaea until some time in AD 73, in which case he would not have had time to travel to Palestine, organize the siege and capture the fortress by Passover of that same year. It is therefore much more likely that Masada fell in AD 74.

Although this emended chronology, which appeared in a learned German doctoral thesis, devoted not to Masada or the Jews, but to Roman senators living between the reigns of Vespasian and Hadrian, was published in 1970, its repercussions did not reach scholarly circles outside Roman history experts until some years later. It did not in any case influence the Israeli celebration in 1973 of the nineteen hundredth anniversary of the heroic end of the defence of Masada.

4 THE FRAGMENTS FROM MIRD

A new type of manuscript material was offered for sale by the Bedouin in the summer of 1952 in the form of Greek fragments from the New Testament (Mark, John and Acts) and the Book of Wisdom belonging palaeographically to the 5th–8th centuries AD. Other Old and New Testament relics (Joshua, Matthew, Luke, Acts, Colossians) were represented in Syro-Palestinian, the Christian Aramaic script and dialect of Palestine. There were also non-biblical Greek texts as well as Syriac and Arabic papyri. According to the Arabs, they came from the Kedron Valley.

A Belgian expedition, led in the spring of 1953 by Robert de Langhe from Louvain University, had no difficulty in establishing that the documents originated in the ruins of Mird, half-way between Bethlehem and Qumran. Known as Marda in Byzantine sources, Mird is the site of the monastery of Castellion founded in AD 492 by St Sabas. Further fragments in Greek, Syro-Palestinian and Arabic were retrieved, including a scrap from Andromache of Euripides.

Needless to say, the Mird texts have no relevance to the study of the Dead Sea Scrolls.

5 THE PUBLICATION OF THE SCROLLS

The universal interest generated by the Qumran discoveries had the effect of expediting the initial stages of the editorial process. Already in 1948 and 1950 E. L. Sukenik issued two preliminary studies in Hebrew, entitled *Hidden Scrolls from the Judaean Desert*, containing extracts from the manuscripts acquired by the Hebrew University (photographs, transcription, commentary) and even from the Scroll of St Mark's, but the American Schools for Oriental Research were the first to publish complete documents. The editors, Millar Burrows and his colleagues, adopted the unselfish policy of releasing their treasures to the world of scholarship without translation or interpretation; thus the large Isaiah Scroll and the Habakkuk Commentary appeared in 1950 and the Manual of Discipline in 1951. Sukenik did the same in the posthumous publication in 1954 of the Scrolls of the Hebrew University (Isaiah, the War of the Sons of Light and the Thanksgiving Hymns). Finally, the best preserved parts of the seventh manuscript from Cave 1, the Genesis Apocryphon, were issued by N. Avigad and Y. Yadin in 1956 with photostats, a transcription of the Aramaic text, and an English and Hebrew translation. So all in all, seven major Scrolls were made available to scholars, and almost simultaneously in translation to all interested readers, within less than ten years of their discovery. For this, the American and Israeli editors and their publishers deserve full credit; it was an achievement probably without precedent.

Unfortunately, similar congratulations cannot be offered to the team in charge of the edition of the fragments collected in the eleven caves. Obviously, it is in general simpler and easier to publish a more or less complete manuscript than a mass of scraps. It would reduce their significance considerably if they were photographed and transcribed without any attempt to piece as many of them together as possible. Father de Vaux, the editor-in-chief of the series, *Discoveries in the Judaean Desert*, went to the other extreme and decided to produce definitive editions providing photostats, transcription, palaeographical and textual study, translation and as full a commentary as possible. This was bound to prolong the venture.

Yet the process started auspiciously. The fragments from Cave 1 were entrusted in 1951 to two young scholars, Dominique Barthélemy and J. T. Milik, and by the autumn of 1952, when I saw them at work at the École Biblique, a substantial part of their task was completed. In fact, the first volume of this sumptuous series was published by the Oxford University Press in 1955.

The trouble began in 1953 with the creation of an international team of editors under de Vaux to cope with the mass of newly acquired fragments. At first, while they actually resided in Jerusalem, the work made good progress, but with the return of these experts to their respective countries (France, England, United States, Germany) the pace slackened. Volume II, devoted to the Murabbaat texts and largely the work of Milik, did not appear until eight years later in 1961, and Volume III representing the Minor Caves, not until one year after that, in 1962.

By that time the politics of the Middle East had become a force to be reckoned with, and the series previously known as *Discoveries in the Judaean Desert* had to be re-named *Discoveries in the Judaean Desert of Jordan*. The next two instalments, Volume IV (the Psalms Scroll from Cave 11, 1965) and Volume V (exegetical fragments from Cave 4, 1968) also appeared under this heading. In 1967, however, all the Dead Sea manuscripts, except the Copper Scroll housed in the Amman Museum, passed to the Israelis when they occupied the old city of Jerusalem during the Six Day War. Volume V was already in the hands of the publishers and was issued in the following year; but after this, all editorial activity came to a halt. It was said that some members of the team refused to publish anything under non-Jordanian sponsorship, but whether or not this was so, the deadlock continued until Roland de Vaux's death in 1971. His successor, Father Pierre Benoit, appears to have found a way to re-launch the venture, and Volume VI, once again entitled *Discoveries in the Judaean Desert*, is on the Clarendon Press's list of forthcoming books. Meanwhile, Milik published in 1976, in a volume separate from this series, the fragments of the Aramaic Enoch from Cave 4.

Israeli scholars in their turn have also lost their original impetus and speed. Neither the Bar Kokhba documents discovered in 1960 and 1961, nor the Masada texts, have yet been published *in toto*, and the edition of the Temple Scroll has been postponed from one year to the next ever since 1967.

The greatest backlog, however, is to be found among the thousands of fragments from Cave 4. J. T. Milik and M. Baillet have, it is said, material sufficient for several volumes ready for publication, but heaven knows when the remaining lots, assigned to other members of the famous international and inter-confessional team *twenty-four years ago*, will appear in print.

On this thirtieth anniversary of their first coming to light the world is entitled to ask the authorities responsible for the

publication of the Qumran Scrolls and the Bar Kokhba documents what they intend to do about this lamentable state of
affairs. For unless drastic measures are taken at once, the
greatest and most valuable of all Hebrew and Aramaic manuscript discoveries is likely to become the academic scandal
par excellence of the twentieth century.*

* Since the completion of the manuscript, Volume VI of *Discoveries in the
Judaean Desert* has appeared containing an archaeological description of
Cave 4 (by Roland de Vaux) and the publication (by J. T. Milik) of
phylacteries, *mezuzoth* (small biblical scrolls affixed to door-posts) and
scraps of Aramaic paraphrases of Leviticus and Job. The Hebrew edition
of the Temple Scroll appeared in November 1977; the English version is
still to come.

Readers interested in the Cairo Geniza and Ras Shamra discoveries may consult P. E. Kahle, *The Cairo Geniza* (Blackwell, Oxford, 1959); 'Genizah, Cairo', Enc. Jud. 16 (Keter, Jerusalem, 1971), 1333–42; S. D. Goitein, *Mediterran Society. The Jewish Communities of the Arab World as portrayed in the Documents of the Cairo Geniza* I–II (Berkeley & Los Angeles, 1967, 1971); A. S. Kapelrud, 'Ugarit', *Interpreter's Dictionary of the Bible* IV (Abingdon, Nashville, 1962), 724–32; J. Gray, *The Legacy of Canaan. The Ras Shamra Texts and their Relevance to the Old Testament* (Brill, Leiden, 1957); G. R. Driver, *Canaanite Myths and Legends* (T. & T. Clark, Edinburgh, 1958).

1 THE DEAD SEA SCROLLS FROM QUMRAN
All the general introductions to the Scrolls contain a more or less detailed chapter on the finds themselves. See below, pp. 231-2. The following dictionary articles include also useful information: 'Dead Sea Scrolls' and 'Qumran' in the *Interpreter's Dictionary of the Bible* (O. Betz, 1962) and its *Supplement* (G. Vermes, 1976); Enc. Jud. 5 (F. F. Bruce, J. Licht, 1971). Cf. further R. G. Boling, 'Twenty Years' Discovery' in D. N. Freedman and J. C. Greenfield, eds, *New Directions in Biblical Archaeology*, (Doubleday, Garden City, 1971). The official editions always provide a descriptive account of the discovery. For archaeological matters the standard work of reference is R. de Vaux, *Archaeology and the Dead Sea Scrolls* (O.U.P., London, 1973).

The main periodicals regularly dealing with the Scrolls are *Biblica, Israel Exploration Journal, Jewish Quarterly Review, Journal for the Study of Judaism, Journal of Biblical Literature, Journal of Jewish Studies, Revue Biblique* and in particular *Revue de Qumrân.*

The first reports on the Scrolls discoveries may be found in the 1948–49 issues of *Biblical Archaeologist* and *Bulletin of the*

American Schools for Oriental Research (articles by M. Burrows, W. F. Albright, J. C. Trever, W. H. Brownlee and Mar Athanasius Yeshue Samuel). The Hebrew University version is given in the two volumes, *Megillot genuzot mi-Midbar Yehudah* by E. L. Sukenik (Bialik, Jerusalem, 1948, 1950).

2 THE MANUSCRIPTS FROM THE BAR KOKHBA CAVES

The main sources are P. Benoit, J. T. Milik, R. de Vaux, *Discoveries in the Judaean Desert* II: *Les grottes de Murabba'at* (Clarendon, Oxford, 1961); N. Avigad, Y. Yadin et al., 'The Expedition to the Judaean Desert', IEJ 11 (1961), 1–81; 12 (1962), 167–262; B. Lifshitz, 'Papyrus grecs du désert de Juda', *Aegyptus* 42 (1962), 240–56; H. J. Polotsky, 'Three Documents from the Family Archive of Babata, *Eretz-Israel* 8 (1967), 46–51; Y. Yadin, *Bar-Kokhba* (Weidenfeld & Nicolson, London, 1971). The Greek Minor Prophets have been edited by D. Barthélemy, *Les Devanciers d'Aquila* (Brill, Leiden, 1963). For the archaeological aspects consult Y. Yadin, *The Finds from the Bar Kokhba Period from the Cave of Letters* (Israel Exploration Society, Jerusalem, 1963).

For a re-evaluation of the historical evidence concerning the Jewish revolution under Hadrian see Schürer–Vermes–Millar, *The History of the Jewish People in the Age of Jesus Christ I:* (Clark, Edinburgh, 1973) 534–67.

3 THE MANUSCRIPTS FROM MASADA

The Masada material is described by Y. Yadin, 'The Excavation of Masada – 1963–4', IEJ 15 (1965), 1–120. It is presented in a more popular form in the lavishly illustrated *Masada: Herod's Fortress and the Zealots' Last Stand* (Weidenfeld & Nicolson, London, 1966). Yadin has also published *The Ben Sira Scroll from Masada* (Israel Exploration Society, Jerusalem, 1965).

For the chronology of the fall of Masada, see W. Eck, *Senatoren von Vespasian bis Hadrian* (Beck, Munich, 1970). Cf. Schürer–Vermes–Millar I, 512, 515.

4 THE FRAGMENTS FROM MIRD

Only a few Mird fragments have been published so far: J. T. Milik, 'Une inscription et une lettre en araméen christo-palestinien', RB 60 (1953), 526–39; C. Perrot, 'Un fragment christo-palestinien découvert à Khirbet Mird', RB 70 (1963), 506–55; A. Grohmann, *Arabic Papyri from Hirbet el-Mird* (Bibliothèque du Muséon 52, Louvain, 1963).

5 THE PUBLICATION OF THE SCROLLS

The following are the definitive editions of Qumran manuscripts.

Cave 1

M. Burrows, J. C. Trever, W. H. Brownlee, *The Dead Sea Scrolls of St Mark's Monastery* I (American Schools of Oriental Research, New Haven, 1950): Isaiah*ᵃ*, Habakkuk Commentary; II/2 (1951): Manual of Discipline. II/1 never appeared.

E. L. Sukenik, *The Dead Sea Scrolls of the Hebrew University* (Bialik, Jerusalem, 1955): Isaiah*ᵇ*, War Scroll, Thanksgiving Hymns. The same work with Hebrew title and introduction was published in 1954.

D. Barthélemy, J. T. Milik, *Discoveries in the Judaean Desert* I: *Qumran Cave I* (Clarendon, Oxford, 1955): all the fragments found in Cave 1.

N. Avigad, Y. Yadin, *A Genesis Apocryphon* (Bialik, Jerusalem, 1956).

Caves 2–3, 5–10

M. Baillet, J. T. Milik, R. de Vaux, *Discoveries in the Judaean Desert of Jordan* III: *Les petites grottes de Qumrân* (Clarendon, Oxford, 1962): fragments and the Copper Scroll.

Cave 4

J. M. Allegro, A. A. Anderson, *Discoveries in the Judaean Desert of Jordan* V: *I (4Q158–4Q186)* (Clarendon, Oxford, 1968): mostly exegetical fragments. For suggested improvements see J. Strugnell, 'Notes en marge du volume V des *"Discoveries in the Judaean Desert of Jordan"'*, RQ 7 (1970), 163–276.

J. T. Milik, *The Books of Enoch: Aramaic Fragments of Qumran Cave 4* (Clarendon, Oxford, 1976).

R. de Vaux, J. T. Milik, *Discoveries in the Judaean Desert* VI; *Qumran Grotte 4* II (4Q 128–4Q 157) (Clarendon Press. Oxford, 1977).

Cave 11
J. A. Sanders, *Discoveries in the Judaean Desert of Jordan* IV. *The Psalms Scroll of Qumran Cave 11 (11QPs^a)* (Clarendon, Oxford, 1965).

J. P. M. van der Ploeg, A. S. van der Woude, B. Jongeling, *Le Targum de Job de la grotte XI de Qumrân* (Brill, Leiden, 1971).

Y. Yadin, *M^{e}gillat ha-Miqdash [The Temple Scroll]* I–III (Israel Exploration Society, Jerusalem, 1977).

Unidentified Cave
Y. Yadin, *Tefillin from Qumran (XQPhyl 1–4)* (Israel Exploration Society, Jerusalem, 1969).

Preliminary editions are listed by J. A. Sanders, 'Palestinian Manuscripts 1947–1972', JJS 24 (1973), 74–83; Schürer–Vermes–Millar I, 120; J. A. Fitzmyer, *The Dead Sea Scrolls. Major Publications and Tools for Study* (Scholars Press, Missoula, 1975), 11–52.

CHAPTER 2

Authenticity and Dating of the Scrolls

Nowadays the authenticity and antiquity of the Dead Sea Scrolls are no longer in dispute, indeed they are taken for granted. But such was not the case in the late 1940s when the world of learning still remembered an earlier claim of the same kind concerning another biblical manuscript. Not only had that 'discovery' turned out to be a fraud; some specialists had almost been deceived by it. Moses William Shapira, a Jerusalem antique dealer, acquired notoriety in 1883 when he produced fifteen leather strips inscribed with archaic Hebrew characters which he said he had bought from Arabs who had found them in Transjordan. He took his fragments (from the Book of Deuteronomy) to Germany and tried unsuccessfully to find a buyer there. Raising his price to a million pounds (which was worth rather more at that time than it is now), he travelled undeterred to London, where he had the satisfaction of getting his manuscript exhibited in the British Museum. But his hopes were short-lived. A cursory inspection persuaded the French epigraphist, C. Clermont-Ganneau, that the text was a forgery. It had been written on pieces of leather cut from the margins of synagogue scrolls, and the letters had been copied from the mid-ninth century BC inscription of Mesha, king of Moab, discovered in Trans-jordan a few years earlier in 1868.

Clermont-Ganneau's evaluation was most unwelcome to the British public, who had looked forward to possessing a Penta-teuch text almost as old as the Exodus from Egypt. Among other things, it would have discomfited once and for all those ungodly people who would not accept that Deuteronomy was composed by Moses himself. Nevertheless, though not without much hesitation, the officially appointed expert Hebraist C. D. Ginsburg was obliged to concur with the judgement of his foreign colleague and declare the document fraudulent. In the following year Shapira committed suicide, but understandably his ghost has continued to haunt later scholars faced with alleged manuscript finds.

Is it in any case wise to be so sure that the Dead Sea Scrolls are authentic? More explicitly, is it reasonable to accept the story of the Taamire tribesmen that their texts came from the Dead Sea caves? If so, were they actually deposited there in antiquity, or did the Arabs plant them there to make them look genuine?

That the Scrolls came from the caves can now be demonstrated fairly easily: the undisturbed sites of Caves 3, 5, 7, 8, 9 and 10, all of which yielded manuscript fragments, were discovered, not by the Bedouin, but by Father de Vaux and his team of searchers. Furthermore, an exploration of the hiding-places first found by the Taamires uncovered yet more scraps overlooked by them, some of which were part of the very manuscripts already removed by the Bedouin.

As for the theory that the Scrolls were planted to deceive the archaeologists, this cannot stand up to serious scrutiny. It is not impossible to imagine that experienced forgers – which the Taamire Bedouin were not – might have introduced a few fragments into the caves which they would afterwards name as the source of their texts. But to organize six (out of eleven) hiding-places, to provide each of them with fragments and one of them with the valuable Copper Scroll, to block the entrances so that they would appear as if abandoned for centuries, to arrange the interiors so that they looked genuinely antique, finally to hope that credulous archaeologists would find the caves and be persuaded by the fragments to accept all the manuscripts offered to them for sale as authentic – the very idea is absurd.

The scientific technique of radio-carbon analysis also helped to establish the authenticity and age of the discovery. The cloths in which the Scrolls were wrapped were subjected to a carbon-14 test and the date obtained was AD 33. Unfortunately, in the early 1950s an inevitable margin of error could add or deduct about two hundred years to or from this figure, but even so the cloths were shown to be not more recent than AD 230, and possibly as old as 170 BC.

The sceptic may suggest that the date of the wrappings need not necessarily be that of the manuscripts (which cannot be tested short of burning them!). But the fact that a Scroll fragment in an advanced state of decomposition was found adhering to one of these cloths is evidence that the manuscripts and wrappings genuinely belong together. Roland de Vaux's judgement is in other words acceptable: until the contrary is proved true, the wrappings found at the same time and in the same place as the manuscripts must be considered contemporaneous with the concealment of the documents in the caves.

Having settled these points, three separate questions still remain to be answered. First, when were the Scrolls placed in hiding? Second, when were they written? Third, when were the original documents, of which the Scrolls are copies, themselves composed?

Archaeology provides an answer to the first enquiry. It also reveals the chronological framework of the sect's history. The second, the problem of the age of the different handwritings on Scrolls and fragments is determined by the scientific study of ancient Hebrew scripts or palaeography. And finally, the literary content, especially the historical allusions, supplies pointers to the respective periods of Jewish history to which the various works belong.

It should be noted that none of the Qumran documents are dated. Nor do the biblical manuscripts have colophons, i.e. a statement appended to the text, revealing when the copyist completed his work. If they did, or if they referred to identifiable contemporaneous events, there would be no problem. The Bar Kokhba documents, by contrast, give precise dates. For example, document 42, published by Y. Yadin, opens with the words, 'On the first day of Iyyar in the first year of the redemption of Israel b[y Simeo]n bar Kosiba, Prince of Israel' (IEJ 12, 1962, 249). There is therefore no doubt that this text was drawn up in April AD 132. No such direct historical indications are included in the Qumran texts, however, and we have to rely solely on their indirect and cryptic hints, deciphering them and associating them as best we can with otherwise known persons or happenings.

1 ARCHAEOLOGY AND THE SCROLLS

Archaeology is not an exact science, as the dogmatic and erroneous assertions made by the explorers of Cave 1 plainly demonstrate. The interpretation of data revealed during an excavation depends not only on the correct identification of the material objects uncovered, but also on the solidity of the working hypothesis into which individual facts are inserted.

In 1949, Father de Vaux, whilst admitting that the shape of the jars found in the cave was unparallelled, assumed initially that almost all the potsherds were Hellenistic, i.e. from the end of the second or the beginning of the first century BC, and that the few specimens of Roman pottery belonged to the third century AD and were irrelevant to the dating of the Scrolls. 'No manuscript', he felt entitled to write in the 1949 volume of *Revue Biblique* (p. 236), 'is posterior to the first century BC, while some of them may be older.' He then concluded (ibid., p. 429) that all the Scrolls were hidden during the reign of the Jewish priest-king Alexander Jannaeus (103–76 BC). Fellow-archaeologist W. F. Albright disagreed. He preferred the second half of the first century BC, and even allowed for the possibility of a date as late as the destruction of Jerusalem in AD 70. Other literary and historical critics, chief among them A. Dupont-Sommer, argued in the same vein.

The following general account of the archaeological work at Qumran will show how the five seasons of excavation between 1951 and 1956 helped to correct this initial bias in the matter of dating.

It was established first of all that an eighth century BC settlement had been destroyed and abandoned at the end of the seventh century BC, and that a modest fresh occupation had begun in the second half of the second century (150–140) BC. Some of the older remains had been restored and new rooms added at that time. This early phase, thought to have been of relatively short duration and known as Period Ia, apparently came to an end some time during the rule of John Hyrcanus I (134–104 BC).

Period Ib is distinguished by an increase in building activity in the form of a substantial enlargement of the occupied area. The complex now included a two-storey tower, a large assembly hall, a refectory, workshops and extensive water installations. Roland de Vaux could consequently write in *Archaeology and the Dead Sea Scrolls* (p. 10): 'Khirbet Qumran is not a village or a group of houses; it is the establishment of a community.' Coins discovered in this layer of the ruins indicate that Period Ib corresponded to that of the Hasmonaean government of Palestine from the time of John Hyrcanus I (134–104 BC) to Antigonus Mattathias (40–37 BC) and on to the beginning of the reign of Herod the Great (37–4 BC). Its end was marked by an earthquake and, in view of de Vaux's theory, based on traces of burning, that Khirbet Qumran was destroyed by fire and earthquake, it is tempting to identify the latter with the catastrophe described by the first century AD Jewish historian Flavius Josephus as having occurred in 31 BC: 'Meanwhile the battle of Actium took place between Caesar and Antony, in the seventh year of Herod's reign, and there was an earthquake in Judaea, such as had not been seen before' (*Antiquities* xv, 121).

Father de Vaux's archaeological reconstruction of the history of the site includes at this point an interval during which the settlement was unoccupied, though to defend this hypothesis he had to explain the presence of ten coins of Herod, probably dating to later than 31 BC, by suggesting that they were brought to the site at the time of its re-occupation after Herod's death. But in fact it is quite possible that the place was continuously inhabited, however sparsely, until the beginning of the Christian era.

Period II opens with the rebuilding of Qumran after its devastation. One of the most suggestive finds connected with this era, the remains of a table made of mud brick and covered with plaster, with near by two ink wells, one of them still containing traces of ink, led de Vaux to maintain that they were part of a *scriptorium*, i.e. a room used for copying manuscripts.

Apart from the ten Herodian coins already mentioned, the numismatic evidence relating to Period II points firmly to the first century AD. The coins begin with Herod Archelaus (4 BC–AD 6) and finish with the first revolution of AD 66–70. Ninety-four bronze pieces struck by the rebels have survived, eighty-three dating to the 'second year' (AD 68–9): the dates of the rest are illegible. Now in the summer of AD 68, the Roman armies led by the future emperor Vespasian captured Jericho, only eight miles north of Qumran. Father de Vaux therefore concluded that the Qumran establishment must also have fallen to the Romans at the same time in June AD 68.

Roman coins found in the layer known as Period III indicate that the site was held by a Roman garrison, probably the Tenth or *Fretensis* Legion, until the end of hostilities; for it should be borne in mind that the Zealots continued to resist in the Judaean desert until the fall of Masada in AD 74, four years after the conquest of Jerusalem.

Assuming that this historical reconstruction is correct, and that the Romans assaulted Qumran in AD 68 and expelled its occupants, who were either members of the Dead Sea sect or some other group of militant Jewish revolutionaries in possession of the site because of its strategic importance, it is highly probable that the Dead Sea Scrolls were concealed at that time in face of the expected danger. The establishment in any case of the summer of AD 68 as the *terminus ad quem* of the Qumran settlement has a number of important consequences, both in regard to the dating of the Scrolls, but also, as will be seen, for our knowledge of the history of the Dead

Sea Community.

1. All the manuscripts, and consequently all the events to which they allude, are to be considered as prior to AD 68.

2. The period of occupation of the Qumran site – *c.* 150–140 BC to AD 68 – provides the most likely chronological framework into which the literary works attributable to the sect are to be inserted.

3. These time-limits do not exclude the possibility that the Community owned further manuscripts written earlier.

4. The persons and events associated with the origins of the sect should probably be placed in the middle of the second century BC and are unlikely to have belonged to the second half of the first century AD.

2 PALAEOGRAPHY AND THE SCROLLS

As has been said, the dating of the concealment of the manuscripts has merely determined that all the Scrolls and fragments preceded AD 68. It remained now for palaeography to define their age more closely.

At its best, this branch of science offers no more than an approximation to the truth, and Hebrew palaeography in particular, when first called on to aid with the dating of the Scrolls, was still very much in embryo. Furthermore, it had in those years to rely on only a limited amount of comparative material assembled from Egyptian Aramaic papyri, Palestinian Jewish inscriptions (mostly on ossuaries), and a single biblical document, the Nash papyrus, none of which, apart from the latter, were specially well suited *a priori* for the task in hand. Letters engraved or scratched on stone or plaster are usually shaped differently from those traced with pen and ink, and papyri are often composed in a hastily scribbled cursive script bearing little resemblance to the calligraphy expected of scribes of literary works. Before Qumran, however, there were simply no Hebrew literary manuscripts in existence pre-dating the Middle Ages. As for the closest parallel to the Scrolls, the Nash papyrus with its extract from Deuteronomy 5:6–6:5 (the Ten Commandments and the *Shema'* or 'Hear O Israel'), the dates proposed for it before the Dead Sea discoveries varied from the second century BC to the second century AD.

In such circumstances, the palaeographers invited to pronounce on the date of the Scrolls were confronted, one would have thought, with serious difficulties. Yet not only did they not shrink from advancing firm opinions – in my view, often far too firm – but they arrived at datings, independently of each other, which were roughly the same and which soon appeared compatible with the time-scale suggested by archaeology. They noted that the script of the Scrolls antedated that of the early third century AD Jewish inscriptional material from Dura Europos on the Euphrates. The slight fluctuation in the use of the five final letters peculiar to the square Hebrew alphabet indicated the end of the Second Temple era namely from the second century BC to AD 70, and the letters of the Qumran manuscripts displayed definite similarities to ossuary inscriptions dating to the first century BC and AD. Their verdict therefore was that the Scrolls were to be ascribed to between 200 BC and the first century AD.

Since those heroic days, the discovery of the Bar Kokhba documents and the Masada manuscripts and ostraca or inscribed potsherds has transformed Hebrew palaeography. The papyri and other texts found at Murabbaat and Nahal Hever, many of them dated to the early second century AD, prompt the palaeographer to estimate that the Qumran script is older than theirs. The Masada texts, on the other hand, show a script similar to that of the Scrolls. But as the fortress fell in AD 74, they were demonstrably contemporaneous with the Qumran library.

One of the consequences of this improvement in palaeographical knowledge, an advance that has enabled scholars to elaborate systematically the history of the square Hebrew alphabet, has been that several experts have felt confident that some of the Qumran biblical fragments go back to the third century BC, the century preceding the foundation of the Qumran establishment. They find the earliest manuscripts to be those from Cave 4; a fragment of 1 Samuel, another of Exodus and another of Jeremiah are dated by them to *c.* 225–200 BC, while a fragment of Ecclesiastes is placed to 175–150 BC.

From this same palaeographical point of view the Dead Sea Scrolls fall into three categories: pre-Hasmonaean, Hasmonaean and Herodian. The biblical fragments from between 225 and 150 BC belong to the first of these groups. The Hasmonaean category (150–30 BC) is represented by the large Isaiah manuscript, the Community Rule from Cave 1, and the oldest copy of another sectarian document, the Damascus Rule from Cave 4. The bulk of the extant texts however is Herodian (30 BC–AD 70), e.g., most of the biblical commentaries, the second Isaiah Scroll, the Hymns, the War Rule, the Genesis Apocryphon from Cave 1, the Psalms Scroll and the Job Targum from Cave 11.

Some of the biblical manuscripts from Qumran employ in the narrative, or in the writing of the Tetragram YHWH and other divine names, the ancient Hebrew or Phoenician script, an alphabet in general use among Jews until the Babylonian exile but eventually replaced by the square Hebrew or Aramaic lettering. This archaizing phenomenon in the text of the Scrolls is comparable to the revival of the ancient characters in the legends on Hasmonaean coins and was no doubt inspired by nationalistic sentiments. The choice, on the other hand, of a different script for the divine names reflects Jewish usage of the time. A Greek papyrus fragment of Deuteronomy dated to the second century BC gives the Tetragram in square Hebrew letters, a custom considered by Origen in the third century AD to be old and characteristic of the best codices of the Greek Bible.

Thus palaeography and archaeology have confirmed each other's findings in such a way that it can be asserted with a high degree of verisimilitude that the Scrolls are to be dated to a period extending from the second century BC to the first century AD.

3 HISTORICAL ALLUSIONS IN THE SCROLLS
The final aspect of the problem of dating concerns internal

criteria such as the mention of persons and events which fix the historical perspective of the writer of a document, but since a special chapter is to be devoted to the reconstruction of the sect's history, the present enquiry will be restricted to a few telling data.

The Qumran texts are notoriously poor in chronologically identifiable facts. No historical documents proper figure among them, and they recount the story of their own movement cryptically in the form of Bible interpretation. Nevertheless, a few indications do exist that are immediately meaningful. There is, for example, the negative pointer that no mention is made of the destruction of the Second Temple. The inauguration of the eschatological worship described in the second column of the War Rule is envisaged as taking place in the existing Temple of Jerusalem. Positively, on the other hand, the few historical characters referred to by name belong either to the second or first century BC. The Nahum Commentary speaks of a Greek king called Antiochus who captured Jerusalem, and of another, Demetrius, who tried without success to perform the same feat. The first personage was Antiochus IV Epiphanes, the Seleucid ruler of Syria (175–164 BC), and the second was no doubt Demetrius III Eucaerus (92–89 BC). Again, an as yet unpublished calendar from Cave 4 is said to contain the names of Shelamzion, the Hebrew for the queen Alexandra-Salome (76–67 BC), and Hyrcanus, probably John Hyrcanus II (63–40 BC). It alludes also to an Aemilius who was responsible for a massacre, i.e. M. Aemilius Scaurus, the first Roman governor of Syria (65–62 BC).

Less specific but still significant is the information contained in the Scrolls that during the initial phase of the Community's history Jerusalem was governed by priestly rulers, men identifiable within our chronological context as members of the Maccabaean-Hasmonaean dynasty (153–37 BC). These Jewish rulers were to be defeated by a foreign enemy, the Kittim, led, according to the Commentaries on Habakkuk and Nahum, by commanders, a terminology suggestive of republican Rome. By contrast, the War Rule places at their head a king, an allusion applicable to Rome after 27 BC when Augustus became emperor.

In sum, the clearest of the historical allusions confirm the principal conclusions reached independently by archaeology and palaeography: namely, that the period in question covers at least the second and first centuries BC, but possibly also the first century AD.

The evidence is thus broadly based and perfectly convergent. The Scrolls and fragments found in the eleven Qumran caves were deposited there during the first war of the Jews against Rome, probably in AD 68. The large majority of them were copied or composed during the occupation of the Qumran settlement by the Dead Sea Community which first took up residence there in about 150–140 BC. Palaeographical evidence suggests, however, that a few of the biblical manuscripts can be traced back further, some of them to the beginning of the third century BC. Qumran, in other words, has provided the world with the oldest Hebrew writings preserved on leather or papyrus in existence, a priceless library of biblical and post-biblical Jewish literature whose effect has been totally to transform our knowledge of inter-Testamental Judaism.

A brief account of the vicissitudes of the Shapira Deuteronomy may be found in Enc. Jud. 14 (1971), 1301–2 (F. F. Bruce, 'Shapira Fragments'). For a contemporary presentation read C. Clermont-Ganneau's fascinating book, *Les fraudes archéologiques en Palestine* (1885).

After the discovery of Qumran fragments written in archaic Hebrew characters, M. Mansoor endeavoured to re-open the old Shapira story with a view to setting the record straight. See his article, 'The Case of Shapira's Dead Sea (Deuteronomy) Scroll of 1883' in *Transactions of the Wisconsin Academy of Sciences, Arts and Letters* 47 (1959), 183–229. The spuriousness of the Shapira scroll is re-confirmed by M. H. Goshen-Gottstein in 'The Shapira Forgery and the Qumran Scrolls', JJS 7 (1956), 187–93. Cf. also A. D. Crown, 'The Fate of the Shapira Scroll', RQ 7 (1970), 421–3.

The preliminary issues relating to the authenticity of the Scrolls and their relationship with the Qumran caves are treated authoritatively by R. de Vaux, *Archaeology and the Dead Sea Scrolls* (1973), 95–102. The result of the carbon-14 test was originally described by O. R. Sellers in 'Radiocarbon Dating of the Cloth from the 'Ain Feshkha Cave', BASOR 123 (1951), 24–6. For a subsequent analysis of charred wood from the Qumran building, see F. E. Zeuner, 'Notes on Qumrân', PEQ 92 (1960), 27–8 (AD 16 plus or minus eighty years).

1 ARCHAEOLOGY AND THE SCROLLS

R. de Vaux's initial views are contained in 'La cachette des manuscrits hébreux', RB 56 (1949), 234–6; 'La grotte des manuscrits hébreux', ibid., 586–609. A more satisfactory archaeological dating was proposed by W. F. Albright in his Postscript to *BASOR Supplementary Studies* 10–12 (1951), 58. On the basis of literary data, A. Dupont-Sommer argued that the Scrolls must have been concealed during the first Jewish war: *Aperçus préliminaires sur les manuscrits de la Mer Morte* (Maisonneuve, Paris, 1950), 105, E.T. *The Dead Sea Scrolls* (Blackwell, Oxford, 1952), 85.

The most influential interpretation of the Qumran excavations is given in the revised English translation of R. de Vaux's 1959 Schweich Lectures, *Archaeology and the Dead Sea Scrolls* (O.U.P., London, 1973). See also E.-M. Laperrousaz, *Qumrân: L'Établissement essénien des bords de la Mer Morte. Histoire et archéologie du site* (Picard, Paris, 1976).

The view of de Vaux that the mud brick table came from a *scriptorium* is rejected by G. R. Driver in 'Myths of Qumran', *Dead Sea Scroll Studies 1969*, ALUOS 6 (1969), 23–7. Driver's arguments in favour of an upper storey dining-room table are answered by de Vaux, op. cit., 29, n.1.

The Qumran numismatic finds are as follows (cf. de Vaux, op. cit., 18–44; Laperrousaz, op. cit., 149–54):

The earliest group consists of twelve Seleucid coins, six bronze and six silver, Three of the latter are dated to the reign of Antiochus VII Sidetes, viz. to 132–131, 131–130 and 130–129 BC. The oldest Jewish pieces, according to de Vaux, are a coin of John Hyrcanus I (134–104 BC) and one of Judah Aristobulus (104–103 BC). This identification is founded on the theory, held generally, that Hasmonaean coinage began under John Hyrcanus (cf. B. Kanael, 'The Beginning of Maccabean Coinage', IEJ 1 (1951), 170–5). It would clash, however, with the rival thesis advanced by Y. Meshorer, *The Jewish Coins of the Second Temple Period* (Jerusalem, 1967), 41–55, according to which Alexander Jannaeus (103–76 BC) was the first ruler to strike his own coins, with the consequence that the pieces marked John and Judah are to be attributed to John Hyrcanus II (63–40 BC) and Judah Aristobulus II (67–63 BC).

One hundred and forty-three coins derive from the rule of Alexander Jannaeus. For the rest of the Hasmonaeans, we have one coin minted by Alexandra Salome with her son Hyrcanus II (76–67 BC); five by Hyrcanus II and four by Antigonus Mattathias (40–37 BC).

The reign of Herod the Great (37–4 BC) is represented by

ten coins; the ethnarchy of Archelaus (4 BC–AD 6) by sixteen; the reign of Agrippa I (AD 41–4) by seventy-eight; the period of Roman prefects (AD 6–41) and procurators (AD 44–66) by ninety-one; and the first Jewish war against Rome by ninety-four bronze coins, most of them struck in AD 67 and 68.

The Roman occupation of Qumran is attested by nine coins from Caesarea and four from Dora dated to AD 67–8; two undated coins from Nero's reign; one silver coin of Vespasian and Titus (AD 69–70); another, undated, of Vespasian; two coins from Ashkelon (AD 72–3); and four undated, but clearly post-70, coins celebrating the Roman conquest of the Jewish state with the legend, *Iudaea capta*. To the same era belongs a single coin of the last Herodian ruler, Agrippa II (AD 50–?92–3), dated to AD 87, but since it was found outside the building area, it may not be relevant to the chronology of Qumran.

In addition to these coins, the archaeologists also discovered three pots containing a hoard of five hundred and sixty-one silver pieces. They are almost exclusively Tyrian and the most recent of them dates to 9–8 BC.

A short survey of Hebrew coins is given in Schürer–Vermes–Millar I, 602–6.

2 PALAEOGRAPHY AND THE SCROLLS

The most comprehensive tractate on Hebrew palaeography is that by S. A. Birnbaum, *The Hebrew Script. Part One: The Text* (Brill, Leiden, 1971) – *Part Two: The Plates* (Palaeographia, London, 1954–7).

For the study of Qumran palaeography consult S. A. Birnbaum, 'The Qumrân (Dead Sea) Scrolls and Palaeography', *BASOR Supplementary Studies* 13–14 (1952); F. M. Cross, 'The Oldest Manuscript from Qumran', JBL 74 (1955), 147–72 [= F. M. Cross, S. Talmon, eds, *Qumran and the History of the Biblical Text* (Harvard U.P., Cambridge, Mass. and London, 1975), 147–76]; N. Avigad, 'The Palaeography of the Dead Sea Scrolls and Related Documents', *Aspects of the Dead Sea Scrolls, Scripta Hierosolymitana* IV (1958), 56–87.

A pioneering study of palaeography in the light of the new discoveries is F. M. Cross, 'The Development of Jewish Script', *The Bible and the Ancient Near East: Essays in Honor of William Foxwell Albright,* ed. E. G. Wright (Doubleday, New York, 1961), 133–202.

The Nash papyrus was originally published by S. A. Cook, 'A Pre-Massoretic Biblical Papyrus', *Proceedings of the Society of Biblical Archaeology* 25 (1903), 34–56. The photograph is reproduced in E. Würthwein, *The Text of the Old Testament* (Blackwell, Oxford, 1957), plate 5. For the most thorough study, see W. F. Albright, 'A Biblical Fragment from the Maccabaean Age: the Nash Papyrus', JBL 56 (1937), 145–76, and 'On the Date of the Scrolls from Ain Feshkha and the Nash Papyrus', BASOR 115 (1949), 10–19.

For the third century AD epigraphical material from Dura Europos, see C. Kraeling, *The Excavations at Dura Europos* VIII, 1. *The Synagogue* (New Haven, 1956).

The sources of the Masada and Bar Kokhba texts are listed on p. 26 above.

The oldest Qumran manuscripts are discussed by F. M. Cross, art. cit., JBL 74 (1955), 147–72, and J. Muilenburg, 'A Qoheleth Scroll from Qumran', BASOR 135 (1954), 20–8.

The revival of the archaic Hebrew script is discussed by F. M. Cross, 'The Development . . .', 189, n.4.

The divine Name is written with square Hebrew characters in the Greek Papyrus Fouad 266 published by W. G. Waddell, 'The Tetragrammaton in the LXX', JTS 45 (1944), 157–61. In fragments discovered in the Cairo Geniza, the name YHWH is reproduced with archaic Hebrew letters in the Greek translation of the Bible by Aquila. See F. C. Burkitt, *Fragments of the Books of Kings according to the Translation of Aquila* (Cambridge, 1897), and C. Taylor, *Hebrew-Greek Cairo Genizah Palimpsests* (Cambridge, 1900). The custom of spelling the name of God in Hebrew in Greek biblical manuscripts is mentioned by Origen in his commentary on Psalm 2:2 (*Patrologia Graeca* XII, 1104).

3 HISTORICAL ALLUSIONS IN THE SCROLLS

The issue will be discussed fully in Chapter 6; for a brief outline see DSSE, 58–65.

The unpublished calendar from Cave 4 containing historical names is referred to by J. T. Milik, *Ten Years of Discovery in the Wilderness of Judaea* (S.C.M., London, 1959), 73.

CHAPTER 3

The Qumran Library

The non-biblical Dead Sea Scrolls have been reliably rendered into almost every European tongue and there is no better approach to them than by reading the texts themselves. A list of complete translations appears in the General Bibliography, though for excerpts quoted in this book I use, and occasionally emend, the second edition of my own volume, *The Dead Sea Scrolls in English* (1975), this being the most comprehensive and up-to-date collection. The introductory comments to the individual Scrolls forming the present chapter are intended for those who wish to familiarize themselves with these sectarian writings. For the benefit of readers aiming at a more advanced study, I have also added an essential bibliography to the discussion of each of the forty-three documents which follow.

The works are classed under the four headings: rules; poetic, liturgical and wisdom texts; Bible interpretation; miscellaneous compositions. Only material substantial enough to be defined properly, and intelligible enough, is included, but a register of the entire library (Bible, Apocrypha, Pseudepigrapha, sectarian writings) is extant in J. A. Fitzmyer, *The Dead Sea Scrolls. Major Publications and Tools for Study* (Scholars Press, Missoula, 1975), 11–39.

I THE RULES

1 The Community Rule (1QS)
Known also as Manual of Discipline (and in Hebrew as *Serekh ha-Yahad*), this Scroll from Cave 1 has been assigned, according to the evidence of the writing used, to the first half

of the first century BC. Fragments of the same document were also found in Caves 4 and 5. Eleven columns long, it bears the marks of editorial alterations, particularly in columns 8 and 9, introduced in the course of its transmission. It is reasonable to suppose therefore that the actual composition may date back to the second half of the second century BC.

The work, which appears to have served as a handbook of instruction for the Master or Guardian of the community, opens with a general outline of the sect's aims and purpose (1:1–18), followed by an account of the ceremony of entry into the Covenant. Priests and Levites (1:18–3:12) invoke blessings on those who have joined the sect and elected to live a holy life, and curses on those others who have decided to cast in their lot with Satan.

> May He bless you with all good and preserve you from all evil. May He lighten your heart with life-giving wisdom and grant you eternal knowledge! May He raise His merciful face towards you for everlasting bliss! (2:2–4 – DSSE 73).

> May He deliver you up for torture at the hands of vengeful Avengers! May He visit you with destruction by the hands of the Wreakers of Revenge! Be cursed without mercy because of the darkness of your deeds! (2:5–7 – DSSE 73).

Another section advises the Master how to assess the spiritual condition of the people in his charge, how to distinguish the 'kind of spirit which they possess', the spirit of truth or falsehood, or the spirit of light or darkness (3:13–4:26 – DSSE 75–8).

The principal substance of the Rule, however (5:1–9:11 – DSSE 78–87), is concerned with statutes relating to the common life, the various stages of progress within the sect, and a detailed penal code intended to remain in force until the Messianic age.

The Scroll ends with directives addressed to the Master, the sect's teaching on the times for worship (9:12–10:8 – DSSE

78–9), and finally with the Master's own hymn of thanksgiving (10:9–11:22 – DSSE 89–94).

The Community Rule is one of several Qumran legislative codes, but apart from these, has no parallel in inter-Testamental Jewish literature. It may on the other hand be seen as a forerunner of the so-called 'Church orders', such as the *Didache* or Teaching of the Twelve Apostles, the *Apostolic Constitutions*, and the earliest rules of Christian monasticism, all of which are to be placed between the second and the fourth century.

Edition
  M. Burrows *et al.*, *The Dead Sea Scrolls of St Mark's Monastery* I (1950). For variants from Cave 4, see J. T. Milik, RB 67 (1960), 411–16.
English Translation
  DSSE 71–94.
Literature
  W. H. Brownlee, 'The Dead Sea Manual of Discipline', *BASOR Suppl. Studies* 10–12 (1951).
  P. Wernberg-Møller, *The Manual of Discipline* (Brill, Leiden, 1957).
  M. Weise, *Kultzeiten und kultischer Bundesschluss in der 'Ordensregel' vom Toten Meer* (Brill, Leiden, 1961).
  J. Licht, *Megillat he-Serakhim: The Rule Scroll* (Bialik, Jerusalem, 1965), in Hebrew.
  A. R. C. Leaney, *The Rule of Qumran and its Meaning* (S.C.M., London, 1966).
  J. Murphy-O'Connor, 'La genèse littéraire de la Règle de la Communauté', RB 76 (1969), 528–49.
  P. Wernberg-Møller, 'The Nature of YAHAD according to the Manual of Discipline and related Documents', ALUOS 6 (1969), 53–81.
  J. Pouilly, *La Règle de la Communauté de Qumrân* (Gabalda, Paris, 1976).

2 *The Messianic Rule* (1QSa)
Sometimes designated as the Rule of the Congregation, this

short two-columned appendix to the Community Rule pre-scribes for the Last Days when the sect's affairs would be in the hands of the two Messiahs of Israel and Aaron. Addressed to the whole congregation of Israel, including women and children, under the authority of the priests the sons of Zadok, it decrees a programme for the individual reaching from childhood education, to marriage, and to adult participation in matters of litigation and in the sect's militia.

The document further outlines how sectaries were to move upward towards higher positions of authority, and gives various causes for disqualification from doing so.

The function of the Levites is defined as that of an executive body, and a list is provided of the 'men of renown' called to council meetings. The closing lines are devoted to a description of the Messianic assembly and meal.

When the common table shall be set for eating and the new wine [poured] for drinking, let no man extend his hand over the first-fruit of bread and wine before the Priest; for (it is he) who shall bless the first-fruits of bread and wine, and shall be the first [to extend] his hand over the bread. There-after, the Messiah of Israel shall extend his hand over the bread (2:17–21 – DSSE 121).

Edition
   D. Barthélemy, J. T. Milik, DJD I (1955), 107–30.
English translation
   DSSE 118–21.
Literature
   J. M. Baumgarten, '1QSa I, 11 – Age of Testimony or Responsibility', JQR 49 (1958–9), 157–60.
   Y. Yadin, 'A Crucial Passage in the Dead Sea Scrolls (1QSa II, 11–17)', JBL 78 (1959), 238–41.
   G. Vermes, *Jesus the Jew* (Collins, London, 1973 and Fortress, Philadelphia, 1981), 198–9, 262–3.

3 The Damascus Rule (CD)

The Damascus Rule or Zadokite Document had been preserved

in two incomplete medieval manuscripts of the tenth (MS A) and twelfth centuries (MS B) and were first discovered in the Cairo Geniza at the end of the last century by Solomon Schechter, who published them in 1910. Now, however, we have fragments of the same work from Caves 4, 5 and 6 of Qumran, and these are dated by J. T. Milik to the first half of the first century BC and are said to correspond to the recension contained in MS A.

The Damascus Rule opens with an exhortation (A1:1-8:21; B1:1-2:34 [= 19:1-20:34] - DSSE 97-108) to the followers of the sons of Zadok to remain faithful to the Covenant made by those who retreated from Judaea to the Land of Damascus. They are assured by means of a theological interpretation of the history of Israel that God always rewards fidelity and punishes apostasy. Valuable historical allusions to the origins of the Community also emerge from this sermon and these will be discussed in chapter 6.

For when they were unfaithful and forsook Him, He hid His face from Israel and His Sanctuary and delivered them up to the sword. But remembering the Covenant of the forefathers, He left a remnant to Israel and did not deliver it up to be destroyed. And in the age of wrath, three hundred and ninety years after He had given them into the hand of king Nabuchadnezzar of Babylon, He visited them, and caused a plant-root to spring from Israel and Aaron to inherit His land and to prosper on the good things of His earth. And they perceived their iniquity and recognized that they were guilty men, yet for twenty years they were like blind men groping for the way. And God observed their deeds, that they sought Him with a whole heart, and He raised for them a Teacher of Righteousness to guide them in the way of His heart (1:3-11 - DSSE 97).

The second section, the Statutes (9:1-16:19 - DSSE 108-17), consists of laws arranged according to their subject matter: on vows and oaths, on the tribunal, on witnesses and judges, on purification by water, on sabbath observances, on ritual cleanness and uncleanness. To a large extent they are sectarian re-interpretations of biblical precepts, but rules relating to the organization and institutions of the Community are also included. A fragmentarily preserved penal code is appended, similar to that contained in the Community Rule.

The Qumran fragments have revealed that the Geniza manuscripts do not represent the whole original composition or always follow the authentic order of contents; in particular, the beginning and the end are missing. But in addition, several sections have been omitted from the first part of the statutes concerned with priestly purity, diseases, marriage, agriculture and tithes, Gentiles and magic. Moreover, it should also be noted that pages 15 and 16 of the Cairo MS A should precede page 9.

The Exhortation which opens the work corresponds to a literary *genre* well known in both Jewish and Christian writings (e.g. Testaments of the Twelve Patriarchs, 4 Maccabees – Hebrews, 1 Peter). The Statutes, on the other hand, with their systematic grouping of laws, prefigure the Mishnah, the Tosefta and the Talmud, i.e. the rabbinic codes compiled between AD 200 and 500.

Editions

>   S. Schechter, *Documents of Jewish Sectaries: Fragments of a Zadokite Work* (C.U.P., Cambridge, 1910). A reprint with a Prolegomenon and bibliography (pp. 25–34) has been issued by J. A. Fitzmyer (Ktav, New York, 1970).
>
>   L. Rost, *Die Damaskusschrift neu bearbeitet* (de Gruyter, Berlin, 1933).
>
>   S. Zeitlin, *The Zadokite Fragments* (Dropsie College, Philadelphia, 1952). A not particularly good photographic reproduction of the Cambridge manuscripts with an introduction.
>
>   C. Rabin, *The Zadokite Documents* (Clarendon, Oxford, 1954). Text, translation and full commentary.

For the Qumran fragments see DJD III, 128 (M. Baillet); 181 (J. T. Milik). See also Milik, 'Fragment d'une source',

RB 73 (1966), 105 and *Ten Years of Discovery* (1959), 151–2 (a description of the Qumran sequence).

English translation
DSSE 95–117.

Important pre-Qumran studies

I. Lévi, 'Un écrit sadducéen antérieur à la destruction du Temple', REJ 61 (1911), 161–205; 63 (1912), 1–19.

M.-J. Lagrange, 'La secte juive de la Nouvelle Alliance au pays de Damas', RB 9 (1912), 213–40, 321–60.

A. Büchler, 'Schechter's "Jewish Sectaries"', JQR 3 (1912–13), 429–85.

R. H. Charles, *The Apocrypha and Pseudepigrapha of the Old Testament* II (Clarendon, Oxford, 1913), 785–834.

L. Ginzberg, *An Unknown Jewish Sect* (Jewish Theological Seminary, New York, 1976 – English translation of a book published in German in 1922).

Recent special studies

A.-M. Denis, *Les Thèmes de connaissance dans le Document de Damas* (Studia hellenistica 15, Louvain, 1967).

J. Murphy-O'Connor, 'An Essene Missionary Document? CD II, 15 – VI, 1', RB 77 (1970), 101–29.
'A Literary Analysis of Damascus Document VI, 2 – VIII, 3', RB 78 (1971), 210–32.
'The Critique of the Princes of Juda (CD VIII, 3–19)', RB 79 (1972), 200–16.
'A Literary Analysis of Damascus Document XIX, 33 – XX, 34', RB 79 (1972), 544–64.

L. Rossi-Ubigli, 'Il Documento di Damasco e la Halakah Settaria (Rassegna di Studi)', RQ 9 (1978), 357–99.

4 The War Rule (1QM)

The nineteen incomplete columns of this manuscript are concerned with the eschatological war which the sectaries believed would be waged during the last forty years of their epoch. The work is nevertheless not a military manual, but a theological consideration of a perpetual struggle between good and evil in which the opposing forces are of equal strength and to which only God's intervention can bring an end. The author places the spiritual battle within an imaginary historical context and provides the armies of angels and demons with earthly allies: the Sons of Light are represented by the children of Levi, Judah and Benjamin; the Sons of Darkness, by the Gentiles headed by the final enemy, the Kittim. Jerusalem is foreseen as reconquered after six years of the war, and the Temple worship restored, and plans for a defeat of all the foreign nations are elaborated in the seventh year. Another thirty-three years of combat would however remain.

> During the remaining thirty-three years of the war, the men of renown, those summoned to the Assembly, together with the heads of family of the congregation, shall choose for themselves fighting-men for all the lands of the nations. They shall arm for themselves warriors from all the tribes of Israel to enter the army year by year when they are summoned to war (2:6–8 – DSSE 126).

Columns 3 and 4 describe in stirring language the trumpets and standards and their inscriptions (e.g. on the trumpets of ambush, 'The hidden powers of God can destroy wickedness'); column 5, the disposition of the lines of battle and the weapons; column 6, the movements of infantry and cavalry.

The weapons and tactics portrayed seem to reflect the Roman art of warfare, and reference to the 'king' of the Kittim would suggest the Roman imperial era. The most likely date for the composition of this work is consequently the end of the first century BC, or more probably, the first half of the first century AD. But in spite of the writer's familiarity with real Roman warfare, the unreality of his story is obvious if only for the fact that the fighters are elderly or middle-aged, and the auxiliaries young and strong.

> The men of the army shall be from forty to fifty years old. The inspectors of the camps shall be from fifty to sixty years old. The officers shall be from forty to fifty years old. The despoilers of the slain, the plunderers of booty, the cleansers of the land, the keepers of the baggage, and those who

furnish the provisions shall be from twenty-five to thirty years old (7:1–3 – DSSE 132).

Ritual purity was to be strictly maintained in the camps. Women and young boys were to be forbidden access to them and the physically unfit and ritually unclean were not to be permitted to take part in the fighting.

A further eight columns enlarge on a battle liturgy, with priests and Levites blowing the trumpets and the rams' horns and reciting prayers; and the final five (15–19) project in vigorous language the vision of the closing phase of the war and the victory of the Sons of Light.

The Priests shall sound to marshal them into the divisions of the formation; and at the sound of the trumpets the columns shall deploy until [every man is] in his place. Then the Priests shall sound a second signal on the trumpets for them to advance, and when the [foot]-soldiers approach throwing distance of the formation of the Kittim, every man shall seize his weapon of war. The Priests shall blow the trumpets of Massacre, [and the Levites and all] the blowers of rams' horns shall sound a battle alarm, and the foot-soldiers shall stretch out their hands against the host of the Kittim; [and at the sound of the alarm] they shall begin to bring down the slain. All the people shall cease their clamour, but the Priests shall continue to blow [the trumpets of Massacre and the battle shall be fought against the Kittim.] (17:10–15 – DSSE 146).

Compared to the first fourteen columns, these last five are repetitious because they apply to the battle against the Kittim the rules and ordinances laid down earlier in general terms. But this does not necessarily imply that the document is not a literary unity. It may be understood as entailing an introduction (col. 1), general rules (cols 2–14) and a sketch of the ultimate battle (cols 15–19). A better explanation distinguishes a primitive composition (cols 1, 15–19) inspired by Daniel 11:40–12:3 of a battle against the Kittim, from an account of a series of wars against all the different Gentile nations conducted according to highly developed religious rules.

An interesting parallel to the military symbolism of the War Scroll may be found in the New Testament, in Ephesians 6:10–17.

Edition
   E. L. Sukenik, *The Dead Sea Scrolls of the Hebrew University* (1954–5) – C. H. Hunzinger, 'Fragmente einer älteren Fassung des Buches Milḥamā aus Höhle 4 von Qumran', ZAW 68 (1957), 131–51.

English translation
   DSSE 122–48.

Literature
   Y. Yadin, *The Scroll of the War of the Sons of Light against the Sons of Darkness* (O.U.P., Oxford, 1962). [The fullest study of the Scroll based on a Hebrew book published in 1955.]
   J. Carmignac, *La Règle de la guerre des fils de lumière contre les fils de ténèbres* (Letouzey & Ané, Paris, 1958).
   J. van der Ploeg, *Le Rouleau de la guerre* (Brill, Leiden, 1959).
   B. Jongeling, *Le Rouleau de la guerre des manuscrits de Qumrân* (Van Gorcum, Assen, 1962).
   P. R. Davies, IQM, *the War Scroll from Qumran* (Biblical Institute Press, Rome, 1977).

5 The Temple Scroll (11Q Temple)
The Temple Scroll, which is still unpublished, covers sixty-six columns. According to its editor, Y. Yadin, the script is Herodian (*c.* 30 BC–AD 70), but the compositon itself dates either to the end of the second or to the first century BC.

The work falls into four parts: rules governing purity and impurity; the celebration of festivals; the building of the Temple; and a section on the Israelite king and his army. The laws are often phrased as though issuing from the mouth of God in the form of a revelation.

Only two brief passages, both from the section on the King and his army, have so far appeared in print. The first determines that even a monarch is subject to the law of monogamy, but that he is permitted to remarry if his wife dies.

He shall not take another wife in addition to her (the first wife), for she alone shall be with him all the days of her life. But if she dies, he shall marry another (57:17–19 – DSSE 250).

The second passage (64:6–13) condemns the calumniator and traitor of the nation to die by hanging on a tree, which as may be deduced from the Nahum Commentary and other parallel sources, probably meant death by crucifixion.

If a man slanders his people and delivers his people to a foreign nation and does evil to his people, you shall hang him on a tree and he shall die (64:6–7 – DSSE 251).

Preliminary edition
> Y. Yadin, 'Pesher Nahum (4QNahum) reconsidered', IEJ 21 (1971), 1–12.
> 'L'attitude essénienne envers la polygamie et le divorce', RB 79 (1972), 98–9.

Edition
> Y. Yadin, *Mᵉgillat ha-Miqdash* I-III (1977).

Translations
> A. Caquot, 'Le Rouleau du Temple de Qoumrân', *Études théologiques et religieuses* 53 (1978), 443-500.
> J. Maier, *Die Tempelrolle vom Toten Meer* (Reinhardt, Munich, 1978).

Literature
> Y. Yadin, 'The Temple Scroll', BA 30 (1967), 135–9 [= *New Directions in Biblical Archaeology*, ed. D. N. Freedman and J. C. Greenfield (Doubleday, Garden City, 1971), 139–48].

G. Vermes, 'Sectarian Matrimonial Halakhah in the Damascus Rule', JJS 25 (1974), 197–202 [= PBJS, 50–56].

J. A. Fitzmyer, 'The Matthean Divorce Texts and some new Palestinian Evidence', *Theol. Studies* 37 (1976), 197–226.

J. M. Baumgarten, 'Does *TLH* in the Temple Scroll refer to Crucifixion?', JBL 91 (1972), 472–81 [an argument against crucifixion and in favour of hanging in the modern sense].

A. Dupont-Sommer, 'Observations nouvelles sur l'expression "Suspendu vivant sur le bois"', CRAI 1972, 709–20.

II POETIC, LITURGICAL AND WISDOM TEXTS

6 The Hymns (1QH)

The Hymns or *Hodayoth* Scroll consists of eighteen columns, none of them complete, and a number of fragments. Its bad state of preservation has prevented scholars from determining exactly how many poems are included and estimates vary from between twenty-five to forty. The script proves it to belong to the first century AD.

The compositions, which resemble biblical Psalms, are individual prayers of thanksgiving normally beginning with, 'I thank Thee, O Lord'. The two central religious ideas conspicuous throughout the whole collection are salvation, and knowledge. The following two examples are characteristic.

I thank Thee, O Lord,
    for Thou hast [fastened] Thine eye upon me.
Thou hast saved me from the zeal
    of lying interpreters,
and from the congregation of those
    who seek smooth things.
Thou hast redeemed the soul of the poor one
    whom they planned to destroy
    by spilling his blood because he served Thee.
                    (2:31–33 – DSSE 156)

I [thank Thee, O Lord],
   for Thou hast enlightened me through Thy truth.
In Thy marvellous mysteries,
and in Thy loving kindness to a man [of vanity,
and] in the greatness of Thy mercy to a perverse heart,
   Thou hast granted me knowledge.

(7:26–27 – DSSE 175)

The subject matter of most of the Hymns is of a general
sort, but a few appear to reflect the experiences of a religious
teacher persecuted by his enemies and abandoned by his disciples. These may be references to the Teacher of Righteousness.
One passage seems to allude to a revolt within the sect against
his authority.

[All who have ea]ten my bread
   have lifted their heel against me,
and all those joined to my Council
   have mocked me with wicked lips.
The members of my [Covenant] have rebelled
   and have murmured round about me;
they have gone as talebearers
   before the children of mischief
concerning the mystery which Thou hast hidden in me.

(5:23–25 – DSSE 167)

We can only speculate on the purpose of a collection of
individual Hymns, but assuming that they were recited by the
Guardian and the new members of the Community during the
Feast of the Renewal of the Covenant on the Feast of Weeks,
it is worth recalling that the Therapeutae, or Egyptian 'contemplative Essenes', each chanted hymns, one after the other,
during their Pentecostal vigil (cf. below, p. 178).

Edition
   E. L. Sukenik, *The Dead Sea Scrolls of the Hebrew University*
   (1954–5). Cf. DJD I, 136–8.
English translation
   DSSE 149–201.

Literature

A. Dupont-Sommer, *Le Livre des Hymnes découvert près de la Mer Morte* (Semitica 7, Paris, 1957).

J. Licht, *The Thanksgiving Scroll* (Bialik, Jerusalem, 1957), in Hebrew.

S. Holm-Nielsen, *Hodayot, Psalms from Qumran* (Universitetsforlaget, Aarhus, 1961).

M. Mansoor, *The Thanksgiving Hymns* (Brill, Leiden, 1961).

G. Morawe, *Aufbau und Abgrenzung der Loblieder von Qumran* (Berlin, 1961).

M. Delcor, *Les Hymnes de Qumrân* (*Hodayot*) (Paris, 1962).

P. Wernberg-Møller, 'Contribution of the Hodayot to Biblical Textual Criticism', *Textus* 4 (1964), 133–75.

7 A Lamentation (4Q179)

In Cave 4, the remains were found of a poem resembling the biblical Book of Lamentations.

[How] solitary [lies] the city,

. . .

the princess of all the peoples is desolate
like a forsaken woman . . . (Frag. 2:4–5 – DSSE 254)

Edition

J. M. Allegro, DJD V, 75–7. Cf. J. Strugnell, 'Notes en marge du volume V des "Discoveries in the Judaean Desert of Jordan"', RQ 7 (1970), 250–52.

English translation

DSSE 254–5.

Literature

M. P. Horgan, 'A Lament over Jerusalem', JSS 18 (1973), 222–34.

H. Pabst, 'Eine Sammlung von Klagen in den Qumranfunden (4Q179)', *Qumrân* (ed. M. Delcor, 1978), 137-49.

8 Apocryphal Psalms (11QPs)

In the substantial vestiges of this manuscript, dated on palaeographical grounds to the second century BC, are preserved forty-one canonical Psalms, a poem identical with 2 Samuel 23:1–7, four apocryphal Psalms previously known from Greek,

Latin and Syriac translations, and in addition three new compositions and a prose supplement.

The known apocryphal Psalms are Psalm 151 (11QPs^a 28:3–14), a variant recension of the corresponding poem in the Psalter of the Greek Bible on the election of David; Psalm 154 (11QPs^a 18:1–16), extant also in Syriac, a hymn praising God's wisdom; and Psalm 155 (11QPs^a 24:3–17) a supplication also attested in Syriac. The fourth composition (11QPs^a 21:11–17; 22:1) glorifies divine Wisdom and is related to a song appearing in the Greek Bible as Ecclesiasticus 51:13–19, 30.

Of the previously unknown Psalms, the first is entitled by the editor, 'A Plea for Deliverance' (11QPs^a 19:1–18).

> I was destined to death because of my sins,
>   and my iniquities sold me to the underworld.
> But YHWH, Thou hast saved me
>   according to Thy great mercies,
> and according to the multitude
>   of Thy deeds of justification.

The second new Psalm (11QPs^a 22:1–18) celebrates Zion and is an acrostic poem, i.e. one in which the first character of each line represents the successive letters of the Hebrew alphabet (aleph, beth, gimel, etc.).

> I remember thee, O Zion, as a blessing,
> By all my might, I love thee:
>   may thy memory be blessed for ever.
> Great is Zion's hope:
>   may peace and thine awaited salvation come.

The third Psalm in this category is addressed to the Creator (11QPs^a 26:9–15).

> Great and holy is YHWH,
>   the holiest for all generations.
> Majesty goes before Him,
>   and behind Him the roar of many waters.

Grace and truth surround His face,
truth, judgement and justice support His throne.

The prose supplement (11QPs*a* 27:2–11) is a record of David's poetic achievements crediting him not with the traditional figure of 150 Psalms but with 3600, together with 364 Songs for the daily Sacrifice, 52 Songs for the Sabbath offering, 30 Songs for festivals, and 4 Songs for exorcism.

In all, they were 4050. All these he uttered through prophecy which was given him from before the Most High (27:10–11 – DSSE 265).

Editions

J. A. Sanders, DJD IV. *The Psalms Scroll of Qumran Cave 11* (1965).
The Dead Sea Psalms Scroll (Cornell, Ithaca, 1967).
J. van der Ploeg, 'Fragments d'un manuscrit de psaumes de Qumrân (11QPs*b*)', RB 74 (1967), 408–12.
'Un petit rouleau de psaumes apocryphes (11QPsAp*a*)', *Tradition und Glaube . . . Festgabe für K. G. Kuhn*, ed. G. Jeremias *et al.* (Vandenhoeck & Ruprecht, Göttingen, 1971), 128–39. Cf. also J. Starcky, 'Psaumes apocryphes de la grotte 4 de Qumrân', RB 73 (1966), 353–71.

English translation

Sanders, op. cit. – DSSE 264–5.

Literature

(a) *The Syriac Psalms*

W. Wright, 'Some Apocryphal Psalms in Syriac', *Proceedings of the Soc. of Bibl. Archaeol.* 9 (1887), 257-66.
M. Noth, 'Die fünf syrischen überlieferten apocryphen Psalmen', ZAW 48 (1930), 1–23.
M. Delcor, 'Cinq nouveaux psaumes esséniens?', RQ 1 (1958), 85–102.

(b) *Studies*

P. W. Skehan, 'The Apocryphal Psalm 151', CBQ 25 (1963), 407–9.
H. W. Brownlee, 'The 11Q Counterpart to Psalm 151, 1–5', RQ 4 (1963), 379 87.

J. Carmignac, 'La forme poétique de Psaume 151 de la grotte 11', RQ 4 (1963), 371–8.

A. Dupont-Sommer, 'Explication des textes hébreux découverts à Qoumrân: Le psaume hébreu extra-canonique', *Annuaire du Collège de France 64* (1964), 317–20; 'The Psalms Scroll of Qumran Cave 11', ibid. 66 (1966), 357–68; 67 (1967), 364–8.

M. Delcor, 'L'Hymne à Sion du rouleau des Psaumes de la grotte 11 de Qumrân', RQ 6 (1967), 71–88.

A. S. van der Woude, *Die fünf syrischen Psalmen – Jüdische Schriften aus hellenistisch-römischer Zeit* IV/1 (Mohn, Gütersloh, 1974), 29–47.

9 The Blessings (1QSb)

A series of liturgical blessings forms a second appendix to the Community Rule (the first being the Messianic Rule, cf. above, pp. 47–8). They were to be recited by the Master, who was to bless, first, all the members of the Covenant, then the High Priest (or possibly the Priestly Messiah), then the priests, and finally the Prince of the Congregation (the Messiah of Israel?).

Words of blessing. The Mas[ter shall bless] the sons of Zadok the Priests, whom God has chosen to confirm His Covenant for [ever, and to inquire] into all His precepts in the midst of His people, and to instruct them as He commanded . . .
May the Lord bless you from His holy [Abode]; may He set you as a splendid jewel in the midst of the congregation of the saints (3:22–6 – DSSE 207–8).

Edition
J. T. Milik, DJD I, 118–29.
English translation
DSSE 206–9.
Literature
S. Talmon, 'The "Manual of Benedictions" of the Sect of the Judaean Desert', RQ 2 (1960), 475–500.
J. Carmignac, 'Quelques détails de lecture dans . . . le "Recuil de Bénédictions"', RQ 4 (1963), 83–96.

10 *The Words of the Heavenly Lights* (4QDib Ham)

These liturgical prayers for recitation on the various days of the week are preserved in two long fragments, palaeographically dated to the mid-second century BC.

> Hymns for the Sabbath Day . . .
> Give thanks . . .
> [Bless] His holy Name unceasingly
> . . . all the angels of the holy firmament
> (7:4–6 – DSSE 205).

Preliminary edition
   M. Baillet, 'Un recuil liturgique de Qumrân, grotte 4: "Les Paroles de Luminaires"', RB 68 (1961), 195–250.
English translation
   DSSE 202–5.
Literature
   M. R. Lehmann, 'A Re-Interpretation of 4Q *Dibrē ham-me'-oroth*', RQ 5 (1964), 106–10.

11 *A Liturgical Prayer* (1Q34^{bis})

This badly damaged text is probably part of the liturgy of the Renewal of the Covenant.

> And Thou didst renew for them Thy Covenant (founded) on a glorious vision and on the words of Thy Holy [Spirit], on the works of Thy hands and the writing of Thy right hand, that they might know the foundations of glory and the steps towards eternity (2:6–7 – DSSE 206).

Edition
   J. T. Milik, DJD I, 152–5.
English translation
   DSSE 205–6.

12 *The Triumph of Righteousness* (1Q27)

These fragments, which may derive from a sermon, expound the theme of the battle between good and evil.

And this shall be the sign for you that these things shall come to pass. When the breed of iniquity is shut up, wickedness shall then be banished by righteousness as darkness is banished by the light (1:5–6 – DSSE 209–10).

Edition
J. T. Milik, DJD I, 102–5.
English translation
DSSE 209–10.

13 The Angelic Liturgy (4QShirShab)
Known as the Song of the Sabbath Sacrifice, the two fragments of this work describe divine worship in heaven. Another piece of the same document was found at Masada (cf. above, p. 20).

In the first fragment, the seven principal angels bless the saints, both celestial and earthly.

In the name [of the might of the God] of gods,
the sixth sovereign Prince shall bless
with seven words of His marvellous mighty deeds
all who are mighty in wisdom.
He shall bless all the perfect of way
with seven marvellous words
that they may stand with them that live for [ever].
(1:21–22 – DSSE 212).

The second fragment describes the divine Throne-Chariot, the *Merkabah* drawn by the Cherubim (cf. Ezek. 1 and Rev. 4). Meditation on this theme was central to early Jewish mysticism.

Preliminary edition
J. Strugnell, 'The Angelic Liturgy. 4Q Serek Širôt 'olat Hašabbât', *Congress Volume, Oxford 1959* (*Suppl. to VT* VII, Leiden, 1960), 318–45.
English translation
DSSE 210–13.

Literature
G. Scholem, *Major Trends of Jewish Mysticism* (Thames & Hudson, London, 1955), 40–79.
Jewish Gnosticism, Merkabah Mysticism and Talmudic Tradition (Jewish Theological Seminary, New York, 1965). 'Merkabah Mysticism', Enc. Jud. 11, 1386–9.

14 The Wicked and the Holy (4Q181)
This appears to be a fragment of a liturgical text concerned with the destinies of the damned and the elect.

In conformity with their congregation of uncleanness, (they are to be separated) as a community of wickedness until (wickedness) ends.

In accordance with the mercies of God, according to His goodness and wonderful glory, He caused some of the sons of the world to draw near (Him) . . . to be counted with Him in the com[munity of the g]ods as a congregation of holiness (1:2–4 – DSSE 251).

Edition
J. M. Allegro, DJD V, 79–80. Cf. J. Strugnell, RQ 7 (1970), 254–5.
English translation
DSSE 251–2.
Literature
J. T. Milik, '*Milkî-ṣedeq* et *Milkî-resha*' dans les anciens écrits juifs et chrétiens', JJS 23 (1972), 114–18.

15 Liturgical Curses (4Q280–282; 286–287)
The first of these two fragments is a parallel to Community Rule 2 and contains the name Melkiresha, one of Satan's titles (cf. pp. 46, 70).

[Be cur]sed, Melkiresha, in all the thou[ghts of your guilty inclination! May] God [deliver you up] for torture at the hands of the vengeful Avengers! (2:2–3 – DSSE 254).

The second fragment corresponds to Community Rule 2 and War Rule 13. The curses are preceded by blessings of the party of God.

Afterwards [they] shall damn Satan and all his guilty lot. They will answer and say, Cursed be [S]atan in his hostile design, and damned in his guilty dominion! (10 II, 2-3 – DSSE 253).

Preliminary edition
> J. T. Milik, '*Milkî-ṣedeq* et *Milkî-resha*' . . .', JJS 23 (1972), 126–35.

English translation
> DSSE 252–4.

16 *The Seductress* (4Q184)

In this Wisdom poem the dangers and temptations of error and false doctrine are symbolized by the harlot.

She will never re[st] from wh[orin]g,
her eyes glance hither and thither,
She lifts her eyelids naughtily
to stare at the virtuous man and join him,
and at an important man to trip him up,
at upright men to pervert their way (1:13–14 – DSSE 256).

Edition
> J. M. Allegro, DJD V, 82–5. Cf. J. Strugnell, RQ 7 (1970), 263–8.

English translation
> DSSE 255–7.

Literature
> A. Dupont-Sommer, 'Explication des textes hébreux et araméens découverts à Qoumrân: (1) The Wiles of the Wicked Woman', *Annuaire du Collège de France* 65 (1965), 353–5.

A. M. Gazov-Ginsberg, 'Double Meaning in a Qumran Work', RQ 6 (1967-69), 322-37.

17 Exhortation to seek Wisdom (4Q185)
A teacher encourages his 'people' and 'sons' to meditate on the power of God revealed in the history of Israel.

Now pray hearken to me, my people,
heed me, O you simple;
become wise through the might of God.
Remember his miracles which he did in Egypt
and his marvels in the land of Ham.
(1:13-15 – DSSE 257).

Edition
J. M. Allegro, DJD V, 85-7. Cf. J. Strugnell, RQ 7 (1970), 269-73.
English translation
DSSE 257-9.

III BIBLE INTERPRETATION

A first group of exegetical writings (nos 18-34) comment on single scriptural books. They are followed by another collection in which the exposition is based on bringing diverse texts together with a view to explaining one by another (nos 35-40).

18 The Genesis Apocryphon (1QapGen)
The Genesis Apocryphon, called the Lamech Scroll before it was unrolled, is a fragmentary paraphrase in Aramaic of the Genesis story. The writing of the Scroll is dated to the first half of the first century BC, and the composition itself to the early first, or possibly second, century BC. From the literary point of view, it is the Bible re-written, i.e. made colourful by supplementary stories and interpretations.

The first section (col. 2) recounts the miraculous birth of Noah to Bathenosh. Lamech, her husband, suspects that the child may be the result of Bathenosh's intercourse with an angel, and although she denies this, Lamech sends Methuselah, his father, to visit Enoch, Lamech's grandfather in Paradise, to learn the truth from him.

My heart was then greatly troubled within me, and when Bathenosh, my wife, saw that my countenance had changed ... Then she mastered her anger and spoke to me saying, 'O my lord, O my [brother, remember] my pleasure! I swear to you by the Holy Great One, the King of [the heavens] ... that this seed is yours and that [this] conception is from you ... and by no stranger, or Watcher or Son of Heaven (2:11–16 – DSSE 216).

After several damaged columns (cols 3–18) telling the story of various episodes in Noah's life and also the beginning of the history of Abraham, the main part of the Scroll, corresponding to Genesis 12:8 to 15:4, gives an account of the Patriarch's stay in Canaan, and of a journey to Egypt that ended with Sarah's abduction by Pharaoh and a visitation of plagues and afflictions on the Egyptian king by God until Pharaoh returned Sarah safely to her husband, (cols 19–20).

When Harkenosh (an Egyptian prince) heard the words of Lot, he went to the king and said, 'All these scourges and afflictions with which my lord the king is scourged and afflicted are because of Sarai, the wife of Abram. Let Sarai be restored to Abram her husband, and this scourge and the spirit of festering shall vanish from you.' (20:24–26 – DSSE 219).

On leaving Egypt, Abraham is described as worshipping God at Bethel and being shown from a mountain top the land his seed is to inherit. He is then ordered to take symbolical possession of it by walking its boundaries. This promised land includes the entire Near East, from the Mediterranean to the Euphrates, and from the Taurus-Amanus range of mountains in Southern Turkey to the Persian Gulf and the Arabian peninsula. At the close of his journey, Abraham settles in Hebron until the invasion of the land of Canaan by the five Mesopotamian kings; the account here closely follows Gen. 14. The narrative ends with the patriarch complaining that because of his childlessness his wealth will be inherited by a servant. God however promises him a natural heir (cols 21–2).

Editions
> N. Avigad, Y. Yadin, *A Genesis Apocryphon* (Magnes, Jerusalem, 1956). Cf. J. T. Milik, DJD I, 86–7.
> J. A. Fitzmyer, *The Genesis Apocryphon of Qumran Cave I: A Commentary* (Biblica et Orientalia 18, Rome, 1966, ²1971). This work contains a detailed bibliography.
> B. Jongeling, C. J. Labuschagne, A. S. van der Woude, *Aramaic Texts from Qumran* I (Brill, Leiden, 1976), 77–119.

English translation
> DSSE 215–24.

Literature
> E. Y. Kutscher, 'The Language of the Genesis Apocryphon. A Preliminary Study', *Scripta Hierosolymitana* IV (1958, ²1965), 1–35.
> H. Lignée, 'Concordance de 1Q Genesis Apocryphon', RQ 1 (1958–9), 163–86.
> G. Vermes, *Scripture and Tradition in Judaism* (Brill, Leiden, 1961, ²1973), 96–126.
> T. Muraoka, 'Notes on the Aramaic of the Genesis Apocryphon', RQ 8 (1972), 7–51.

19 The Ages of the Creation (4Q180)
This badly worn document includes a reference to the myth of the fallen angels (Gen. 6:1–4).

And the interpretation concerns Azazel and the angels who [came to the daughters of men; and] they bore to them giants (1:7–8 – DSSE 259).

Edition
J. M. Allegro, DJD V, 77–9. Cf. J. Strugnell, RQ 7 (1970), 252–4.
English translation
DSSE 259.
Literature
J. T. Milik, '*Milkî-ṣedeq* et *Milkî-reshaʿ* . . .' JJS 23 (1972), 110–24.

20 The Blessings of Jacob (4QPBless)
The only extract so far published of the Blessings of Jacob expounds the messianic passage (Gen. 49:10), 'The sceptre shall not depart from Judah, nor the ruler's staff from between his feet, until he comes to whom it belongs', to mean that the descendants of David possess an inalienable right to the throne of Israel.

Whenever Israel rules there shall [not] fail to be a descendant of David upon the throne. For the *ruler's staff* is the Covenant of kingship, [and the clans] of Israel are the *feet*, until the Messiah of Righteousness comes, the Branch of David (1–4 – DSSE 224).

Preliminary edition
J. M. Allegro, 'Further Messianic References in Qumran Literature', JBL 75 (1956), 174–6.
English translation
DSSE 224.
Literature
N. Wieder, 'Notes on the New Documents from the Fourth Cave of Qumran', JJS 7 (1956), 72–4.
Y. Yadin, 'Some Notes on Commentaries on Genesis XLIX and Isaiah from Qumran Cave 4', IEJ 7 (1957), 66–8.
G. Vermes, *Scripture and Tradition in Judaism* (Brill, Leiden, 1961, ²1973), 52–3.
H. Stegemann, 'Weitere Stücke von 4QpPs37, von 4Q Patriarchal Blessings . . .', RQ 6 (1967–9), 193–227.

21 The Testament of Amram (4Q Amram)

Five incomplete copies are extant of this Aramaic composition
purporting to be the deathbed admonition made by Amram,
the father of Moses, to his children. The context is that of
Exodus. Amram speaks of a dream in which he sees Melkiresha
(i.e. Satan, cf. p. 64 above) and addresses the chief of the Sons
of Light, probably Melkizedek (cf. p. 82 below).

Copy of the words of the vision of Amram, son of Kehat,
son of Levi, al[l that] he explained to his sons and enjoined
on them on the day of [his] death, in his one hundred and
thirty-seventh year, which was the year of his death, [in]
the one hundred and fifty-second year of Israel's exile in
Egypt (4Q Amram – DSSE 260).

Preliminary edition
> J. T. Milik, '4Q visions d'"Amram et une citation d'Origène',
> RB 79 (1972), 77–97.

English translation
> DSSE 260–1.

Literature
> J. Heinemann, '210 Years of Egyptian Exile', JJS 22 (1971),
> 19–30 (on a special chronology implied in this text).
> K. Berger, 'Der Streit des guten und des bösen Engels um
> Seele. Beobachtungen zu 4QAmr^b und Judas 9', JSJ 4
> (1973), 11–18.

For *21a*, see page 86.

22 The Words of Moses (1Q22)

This composition, inspired by Deuteronomy, takes the form
of a farewell speech by Moses and is characterized by the stress
laid on the choice of Levites and priests as teachers of the Law.

[God spoke] to Moses in the [fortieth] year after [the children
of] Israel had come [out of the land of] Egypt, in the eleventh
month, on the first day of the month, saying: '[Gather
together] all the congregation and go up to [Mount Nebo]
and stand [there], you and Eleazar son of Aaron. Inter[pret

to the heads] of family of the Levites, and to all the [priests], and proclaim to the children of Israel, the words of the Law which I proclaimed [to you] on Mount Sinai (1:1–4 – DSSE 225).

Edition
J. T. Milik, DJD I, 91–7.
English translation
DSSE 225–6.

23 The Vision of Samuel (4Q160)
Seven badly mutilated fragments seem to describe a vision of Samuel in the house of Eli (cf. 1 Sam. 3).

Samuel lay in front of Eli. And he arose and opened the d[oors . . .] to announce the oracle to Eli. Eli answered and [said, . . .] Let me know the vision of God (1:3–5).

Edition
J. M. Allegro, DJD V, 9–11.

24 Commentaries on Isaiah (4Q161–165)
These are four fragments, each representing a Qumran *pesher*, or fulfilment interpretation of prophecy. Fragment A comments on the Messianic passage Isa. 11 ('And there shall come forth a rod from the stem of Jesse', etc.). Fragments B and C allude to the enemies of the sect, described as 'scoffers' and the 'seekers after smooth things'.

Referring to the last days, this saying concerns the congregation of those who seek smooth things in Jerusalem (Frag. C, 2:10–11 – DSSE, 228).

Fragment D identifies the Community with the heavenly city of Jerusalem.

Edition
J. M. Allegro, DJD V, 11–28.

English translation
DSSE 226–9.

Literature

Y. Yadin, 'Some Notes on the newly published Pesharim of Isaiah', IEJ 9 (1959), 39–42.

J. Carmignac, 'Notes sur les Pesharim', RQ 3 (1962), 505–38.

D. Flusser, 'The Pesher of Isaiah and the Twelve Apostles', *Eretz Israel* 8 (*E. L. Sukenik Memorial Volume*, 1967), 52–62 in Hebrew.

25 The New Jerusalem

Fragments of a visionary Aramaic writing inspired by Ezekiel 40–48 have been found in Cave 1 (1Q32), 2 (2Q24), 4, 5 (5Q15) and 11 (11QJN ar). They portray the Jerusalem of the end of time, with its measurements, avenues, street, houses, rooms, etc.

[And the] mid[dle street passing through the mid]dle of the city, its [width measures] thirt[een] ree[ds] and one cubit = 92 cubits. And all t[he streets of the city] are paved with white stone . . . marble and jasper (1:5–7 – DSSE 263).

Edition

J. T. Milik, DJD III, 184–93 (5Q fragments supplemented by an unpublished text from 4Q). For other fragments see Milik, DJD I, 134–5; M. Baillet, DJD III, 84–90; B. Jongeling, 'Publication provisoire d'un fragment de la grotte 11 de Qumrân', JSJ 1 (1970), 58–64.

26 The Prayer of Nabonidus (4QPsDan ar^{a-c})

The Prayer is an important fragment of an Aramaic work related to the Book of Daniel with its story of the miraculous recovery of the Babylonian king Nebuchadnezzar (605–562 BC) in Dan. 4. The Qumran document describes the healing of the last ruler of Babylon, Nabonidus (555–539 BC) by a Jewish exorcist.

I was afflicted [with an evil ulcer] for seven years . . . and an exorcist pardoned my sins. He was a Jew from among the [children of the exile of Judah, and said,] 'Recount this in writing to [glorify and exalt] the Name of the [Most High God'] (1:3-5 - DSSE, 229).

Preliminary edition

J. T. Milik, '"Prière de Nabonide" et autres écrits d'un cycle de Daniel, fragments de Qumrân 4', RB 63 (1956), 407-15.

B. Jongeling et al., *Aramaic Texts from Qumran* I (Brill, Leiden, 1976), 123-31.

English translation

DSSE 229.

Literature

A. Dupont-Sommer, 'Exorcismes et guérisons dans les écrits de Qoumrân', *Congress Volume Oxford, 1959* (*Suppl. to VT* VII, 1960), 246-61.

R. Mayer, *Das Gebet Nabonidus* (Berlin, 1962).

G. Vermes, *Jesus the Jew* (Collins, London, 1973 and Fortress, Philadelphia, 1981), 67-8, 240-1.

P. Grelot, 'La prière de Nabonide (4Q Pr Nab)', *RQ* 9 (1978), 483-95.

27 Pseudo-Daniel (4Q243)

The contents of this Aramaic fragment (4QpsDan Aᵃ), sometimes referred to as the 'Son of God' text, were disclosed by J. T. Milik in a lecture given at Harvard University in 1972 and have been published on the basis of that lecture by J. A. Fitzmyer. The work appears to be historico-eschatological and, like the War Rule (1:2-4), contains allusions to the king of 'Assyria' and to 'Egypt'. One of the characters is designated as 'son of God' but is represented as being distinct from the triumphant 'people of God'.

(7) . . . he shall be great on earth

(8) . . . will make . . . and all will serve

(9) [him] . . . great . . . he shall be called and by his name he shall be designated.

(1) He shall be proclaimed son of God and they shall call him son of the Most High. Like a shooting star
(2) of a vision, so shall be their kingdom. They shall reign for some years on
(3) the earth and trample everything. One nation shall trample on another nation and one province on another province
(4) until the people of God shall rise and all will cease from the sword.

Milik is said to have identified the 'son of God' as the Seleucid ruler Alexander Balas (150–145 BC). Fitzmyer prefers to see in him the son of a Jewish king. Neither considers the titles 'son of God' and 'son of the Most High' to be messianic.

Preliminary edition
> J. A. Fitzmyer, 'The Contribution of Qumran Aramaic to the Study of the New Testament', NTS 20 (1974), 391–4.

28 Commentary on Hosea (4Q166–167)
The prophet's metaphor of the unfaithful wife is interpreted as referring to Israel and her Gentile lovers.

> Interpreted, this means that He smote them with hunger and nakedness that they might be shamed and disgraced in the sight of the nations on which they relied. They will not deliver them from their miseries (2:12–14 – DSSE 230).

Another fragment mentions the 'furious young lion' (cf. below, p. 75), described also as 'the last Priest' who attacked 'Ephraim'.

Edition
> J. M. Allegro, DJD V, 31–2.

English translation
> DSSE 230.

29 Commentary on Micah (1Q14)
In this very badly preserved document the commentator reads

into Micah allusions to the sect, to the Teacher of Righteousness, and to the 'Spouter of Lies', an enemy of the movement.

[Interpreted, this concerns] the Teacher of Righteousness who [expounded the Law to] his [Council] and to all who freely pledged themselves to join the elect of [God to keep the Law] in the Council of the Community (Frag. 8; 10, 6–8 – DSSE 231).

Edition
J. T. Milik, DJD I, 78. Cf. J. M. Allegro, DJD V, 36.
English translation
DSSE 230.

30 Commentary on Nahum (4Q169)
The four fragmentary columns of the Nahum Pesher constitute one of the most important sources for the reconstruction of the sect's history. The commentary mentions by name the Seleucid kings Antiochus and Demetrius, accuses a Jewish ruler of crucifying his opponents, and also records a split among the enemies of the Community, Ephraim and Manasseh. The allusions are discussed fully in Chapter 6.

Interpreted, this concerns the furious young lion [who executes revenge] on those who seek smooth things and hangs men alive, [a thing never done] formerly in Israel (1:5–8 – DSSE 232).

Edition
J. M. Allegro, DJD V, 37–42.
English translation
DSSE 231–5.
Literature
A. Dupont-Sommer, 'Observations sur le commentaire de Nahum découvert près de la Mer Morte', *Journal des Savants* (1963), 201–27.
J. D. Asmusin, 'Ephraïm et Manassé dans le Péshèr de

Nahum', RQ 4 (1964), 389–96.

S. B. Hoenig, 'Dorshé Halakot in the Pesher Nahum Scroll', JBL 83 (1964), 119–38.

'Pesher Nahum "Talmud"', JBL 86 (1967), 441–5.

Y. Yadin, 'The Pesher Nahum Reconsidered', IEJ 21 (1971), 1–12.

A. Dupont-Sommer, 'Observations nouvelles sur l'expression "Suspendu vivant sur le bois"', CRAI 1972, 709–20.

I. Rabinowitz, 'The Meaning of the Key ("Demetrius") Passage of the Qumran Nahum Pesher', *Journal of the American Oriental Society* 98 (1978), 394–9.

31 Commentary on Habakkuk (1QpHab)

Application of the first two chapters of Habakkuk to the sect's history makes of this commentary a principal historical source of information. In it, the Chaldean enemy becomes the Kittim (Romans) sent by God to punish the 'last (Hasmonaean) priests of Jerusalem' for the injustice done to the Teacher of Righteousness by the ruling Wicked Priest. For a further discussion, see Chapter 6. It is worth noting that the Tetragram is written in the archaic script (cf. above, p. 37).

Interpreted, this concerns the Wicked Priest who pursued the Teacher of Righteousness to the house of his exile that he might confuse him with his venomous fury. And at the time appointed for rest for the Day of Atonement, he appeared before them to confuse them, and to cause them to stumble on the Day of Fasting, their Sabbath of repose (11:4–8 – DSSE 241–2).

Edition

M. Burrows, *et al.*, *The Dead Sea Scrolls of St Mark's Monastery* 1 (1950).

English translation

DSSE 235–43.

Literature

K. Elliger, *Studien zum Habakuk-Kommentar vom Toten Meer* (Mohr, Tübingen, 1953).

F. F. Bruce, 'The Dead Sea Habakkuk Scroll', ALUOS 1 (1958–9), 5–24.

L. H. Silberman, 'Unriddling the Riddle. A Study in the Structure and Language of the Habakkuk Pesher', RQ 3 (1961–2), 323–64.

W. H. Brownlee, *The Midrash Pesher of Habakkuk* (Scholars Press, Missoula, 1979).

32 Commentary on Zephaniah (1Q15; 4Q170)

Minute fragments of Zephaniah Commentaries have been found in Caves 1 and 4 but the interpretative sections are never long enough for translation. As in the Habakkuk Commentary, the Tetragram appears here too in archaic Hebrew letters.

Edition
J. T. Milik, DJD I, 80.
J. M. Allegro, DJD V, 42.

33 Commentary on Psalm 37 (4Q171)

In the four mutilated columns of this work the fate is described of the good and the evil as reflected in the history of the Community and its opponents, Ephraim and Manasseh. The conflict between the Teacher of Righteousness and the Wicked Priest occupies a central place. The Tetragram is again written in archaic letters.

Interpreted, this concerns the wicked of Ephraim and Manasseh, who shall seek to lay hands on the Priest and the men of his Council at the time of trial which shall come upon them. But God will redeem them from out of their hand. And afterwards they shall be delivered into the hand of the violent among the nations for judgement (2:17–19 – DSSE 244).

Edition
J. M. Allegro, DJD V, 42–50.

English translation
DSSE 243–5.

Literature
J. Carmignac, 'Notes sur les Pesharim', RQ 3 (1961–2), 505–38.

A. Dupont-Sommer, 'Explication des textes hébreux . . .: Commentaire du Psaume XXXVII', *Annuaire du Collège de France 64* (1964), 320–3.

'4QpPs37', ibid. 69 (1969–70), 395–404.

H. Stegemann, 'Der Pešer Psalm 37', RQ 4 (1963–4), 235–70.

'Weitere Stücke von 4QPsalm 37 . . .', RQ 6 (1967–9), 193–227.

D. Pardee, 'A Restudy of the Commentary on Psalm 37 from Qumran Cave IV', RQ 8 (1973), 163–94.

For further badly mutilated Psalms commentaries see DJD V, 49 (Ps. 60:8–9); 51–3 (Pss 127:2–3, 5; 129:7–8; 118:26).

34 The Targum of Job (11QtgJob)

This is an Aramaic rendering neither fully literal nor properly paraphrastic of substantial sections of Job between 17:14 and 42:11. The editors date the writing of the Scroll to the first century AD and its composition to *c.* 100 BC. They judge it to be Palestinian, and its language to represent the Aramaic spoken by Jesus. It is further suggested that the work is identical with the Targum of Job condemned by Rabban Gamaliel I in the first half of the first century AD (yShabbath 15c; bShabbath 115a). A detailed linguistic analysis of the Scroll carried out by another scholar, T. Muraoka, has however led him to conclude that the Targum was composed in Mesopotamia between 250 and 150 BC, in which case any direct connection between the language of this document and Galilean Aramaic used by Jesus and his followers would be excluded.

Edition

J. P. M. van der Ploeg, A. S. van der Woude, *Le Targum de Job de la grotte 11 de Qumrân* (Brill, Leiden, 1971).

Aramaic text and English translation

M. Sokoloff, *The Targum to Job from Qumran Cave XI* (Bar Ilan University, Ramat Gan, 1974).

B. Jongeling *et al.*, *Aramaic Texts from Qumran* I (Brill, Leiden, 1976), 3–73.

Literature

J. A. Fitzmyer, 'Some Observations on the Targum of Job from Qumran Cave 11', CBQ 36 (1974), 503–24.

T. Muraoka, 'The Aramaic of the Old Targum of Job from

Qumran Cave XI', JJS 25 (1974), 425–43; 'Notes on the Old Targum of Job from Qumran Cave XI', RQ 9 (1977), 117–25.

35 Commentary on Biblical Laws (4Q159)

Known also as 'Ordinances', this document re-interprets a variety of biblical precepts. For example, Deut. 23:25–26 ('When you go into your neighbour's standing grain, you may pluck the ears with your hand') is understood to mean that a poor Jew may eat corn plucked in a field but not take it home. He may however do so with grain collected from a threshing floor. Exod. 30:11–16 (38:26–28) is interpreted as imposing the duty of a single payment of ransom money; nothing is said here of the annual Temple tax traditionally associated with this passage. Lev. 25:39–46, prohibiting the buying of compatriots as slaves, forbids in this commentary their sale to Gentiles. Deut. 22:5 enlarges on the unlawfulness of wearing clothes of the opposite sex, and 22:13–14 legislates on the case of a husband claiming that his wife was not a virgin at the time of their wedding.

And they shall examine her [concerning her] worthiness, and if he has not lied concerning her she shall be put to death. But if he has humiliated her [false]ly, he shall be fined two minas, and shall not divorce her all his life (2:8–10 – DSSE 252).

Edition
J. M. Allegro, DJD V, 6–9. Cf. J. Strugnell, RQ 7 (1970), 175–9.
English translation
DSSE 249, 252.
Literature
J. Liver, 'The Half-Shekel Offering in Biblical and Post-Biblical Literature', HTR 56 (1963), 173–98.

Y. Yadin, 'A Note on 4Q159 (Ordinances)', IEJ 18 (1968), 250–2.

F. D. Weinert, '4Q159: Legislation for an Essene Community
Outside of Qumran', JSJ 5 (1974), 179–207.
G. Vermes, PBJS, 41–2.

36 Midrash (or Commentary) on the Last Days (4Q174)
Two fragmentary columns have survived of 4Q Florilegium.
In it, excerpts from Exodus 15, Amos 9, Psalm 1, Isaiah 8,
Ezekiel 44 and Psalm 2, are combined so that they re-interpret
the story of the building of the Temple by Solomon (2 Sam.
7:10–14) in such a way as to introduce the establishment of
the Community and the coming of the Davidic Messiah.

I [shall be] his father and he shall be my son. He is the Branch
of David who shall arise with the Interpreter of the Law [to
rule] in Zion [at the end] of time (1:11–12 – DSSE 246).

Further tiny but identifiable fragments comment on Deuteronomy 33:8–11, 12, 19–21.

Edition
J. M. Allegro, DJD V, 53-7. Cf. J. Strugnell, RQ 7 (1970),
220–5.
English translation
DSSE 245–7.
Literature
Y. Yadin, 'A Midrash on 2 Sam. VII (4Q Florilegium)',
IEJ 9 (1959), 95–9.
D. Flusser, 'Two Notes on the Midrash on 2 Sam. VII
(4Q Florilegium)', IEJ 9 (1959), 99–109.

37 A Messianic Anthology (4Q175)
The Testimonia or scriptural texts considered as the foundation
of the messianic teachings of the Community, consist of five
Bible quotations arranged in four groups. The biblical text in
the last group is accompanied by a citation from a sectarian
writing.
   The first group combines Deuteronomy 5:28–29 with Deut.
18:18–19 ('I will raise up a prophet like you from among their

brethren', etc.). The second gives the oracle of Balaam from
Numbers 24:15-17 (which includes 'A star shall come out of
Jacob and a sceptre shall rise out of Israel', etc.). The third
repeats the blessing of the Levites by Moses and, implicitly, of
the priestly Messiah in Deuteronomy 33:8-11 ('Bless his power,
O Lord, and delight in the work of his hands', etc.). The fourth
unit opens with Joshua 6:26, then expounds this text with the
help of the sectarian Psalms of Joshua as applying to the
principal opponents of the Community.

When Joshua had finished offering praise and thanksgiving,
he said: *Cursed be the man who rebuilds this city! May he
lay its foundation on his first-born, and set its gate upon his
youngest son!* Behold, an accursed man, a man of Satan, has
risen to become a fowler's net to his people and a cause of
destruction to all his neighbours. And [his brother] arose
[and ruled], both being instruments of violence. They have
rebuilt [Jerusalem and have set up] a wall and towers to
make of it a stronghold of ungodliness . . . (1:21-26 – DSSE
248).

Edition
J. M. Allegro, DJD V, 57-60. Cf. J. Strugnell, RQ 7 (1970),
225-9.
English translation
DSSE 247-9.
Literature
J. Asmusin, '4Q Testimonia, 15-17', *Hommages à André
Dupont-Sommer* (Adrienne-Maisonneuve, Paris, 1971),
357-61.

38 Words of Consolation (4Q176)
This collection designated *Tanhumim* (Consolations) contains
excerpts from Psalm 79:2-3, Isaiah 40:1-5, 41:8-9, 43:1-2,
4-6, 49:7, 13-17, 51:22-23, 52:1-3, 54:4-10, 52:1-2 and
Zechariah 13:9. The biblical texts are followed by comments
but they are so fragmentary as to be untranslatable.

Edition
   J. M. Allegro, DJD V, 60–7. Cf. J. Strugnell, RQ 7 (1970),
   229–36.

39 Catenae (4Q177, 182, 183)
These Catenae or 'chains' of quotations and interpretations are
too damaged for any continuous sense to be made of them
but the following biblical passages can be identified: Deutero-
nomy 7:15; Ezekiel 20:32; Hosea 5:8; Isaiah 37:30, 32:7;
Psalms 11:1, 12:1; Isaiah 22:13. Psalms 12:7, 13:2–3, 5;
Ezekiel 25:8; Jeremiah 4:4. Jeremiah 18:18; Psalm 6:2–3;
Joel 2:30. Psalm 16:3; Nahum 2:11; Psalm 17:1.

Edition
   J. M. Allegro, DJD V, 80–2. Cf. J. Strugnell, RQ 7 (1970),
   236–7.

40 The Melkizedek Document (11Q Melch)
These thirteen fragments are the remains of an eschatological
midrash, i.e. a commentary on diverse scriptural themes
relating to the end of time. They are based on Leviticus 25:13,
Deuteronomy 15:2 and Isaiah 61:1 and were found in Cave 11.
The deliverance proclaimed is seen as part of the general restoration of property in every fiftieth or Jubilee year, a restoration
regarded in the Bible as a remission of debts. The deliverer,
the chief of the heavenly beings (literally 'gods', *elohim*), is
Melchizedek, identical with the archangel Michael. He will
judge and condemn Belial, the Prince of Darkness. The final
liberation will come on the Day of Atonement when all the
sins of the Sons of Light will be pardoned.

[*To proclaim liberty to the captives* (Isa. 61:1). Its interpretation is that He] will assign them to the Sons of Heaven and
to the inheritance of Melchizedek; f[or He will cast] their
[lot] amid the po[rtions of Melchize]dek, who will return
them there and will proclaim to them liberty, forgiving them
[the wrongdoings] of all their iniquities (2:4–6 – DSSE 266).

Edition
A. S. van der Woude, 'Melchisedek als himmlischer Erlöser-
gestalt in den neugefundenen eschatologischen Midraschim
aus Qumran Höhle XI', *Oudtestamentische Studien* 14
(1965), 354–73.

English translation
DSSE 265–8.

Literature
Y. Yadin, 'A Note on Melchizedek and Qumran', IEJ 15
(1965), 152–4.

M. de Jonge, A. S. van der Woude, '11Q Melchizedek and
the New Testament', NTS 12 (1966), 301–26.

A. Dupont-Sommer, 'Explication des textes hébreux découverts à Qoumrân . . . 11QMelch', *Annuaire du Collège de
France 68* (1968–9), 426–30.

J. A. Fitzmyer, *Essays on the Semitic Background of the New
Testament* (Chapman, London, 1971), 245–67.

M. Delcor, 'Melchizedek from Genesis to the Qumran Texts
and the Epistle to the Hebrews', JSJ 2 (1971), 115–35.

J. T. Milik, '*Milkî-ṣedeq* et *Milkî-resha'* . . .', JJS 23 (1972),
96–109.

F. du T. Laubscher, 'God's Angel of Truth and Melchizedek.
A Note on 11QMelch 13b', JSJ 3 (1972), 46–51.

F. L. Horton, *The Melchizedek Tradition* (C.U.P., Cambridge,
1976), 64–82.

IV MISCELLANEOUS COMPOSITIONS

41 The Copper Scroll (3Q15)
This list of real or imaginary treasures was found in two parts
in Cave 3. As neither section could be unrolled because of the
advanced state of oxidization of the material, they were cut
into longitudinal strips by H. W. Baker and deciphered by
J. T. Milik and J. M. Allegro. Written in the post-biblical
(Mishnaic) Hebrew dialect, the Scroll records sixty-four caches
of gold, silver, aromatics and manuscripts. The total is so
enormous that Milik suggests it is fictional; but another theory

is that these riches either belonged to the Essene sect, or that they were removed from the Jerusalem Temple by the Zealot defenders of the capital and hidden by them in the Judaean desert.

At Horebbeh which is in the Vale of Akhor, under the steps that go eastwards, (at) forty cubits: a box of silver totalling 17 talents (1:1-4).

Edition
J. T. Milik, DJD III, 211-302.
Literature
J. M. Allegro, *The Treasure of the Copper Scroll* (Doubleday, Garden City, 1960).
J. Jeremias, J. T. Milik, 'Remarques sur les rouleaux de cuivre de Qumrân', RB 67 (1960), 220-3.
E. Ullendorff, 'The Greek Letters of the Copper Scroll', VT 11 (1961), 227-8.
E.-M. Laperrousaz, 'Remarques sur l'origine des rouleaux de cuivre découverts dans la grotte 3 de Qumrân', RHR 159 (1961), 157-72.
B. Z. Lurie, *The Copper Scroll from the Wilderness of Jerusalem* (Kiryath Sepher, Jerusalem, 1963) in Hebrew.
M. R. Lehmann, 'Identification of the Copper Scroll based on its Technical Terms', RQ 5 (1964), 97-105.

42 Horoscopes (4Q186)
This is a curious document written in Hebrew, but from left to right instead of from right to left, incorporating a mixture of archaic and square Hebrew lettering and also Greek letters. It appears to associate physical characteristics with specific spiritual qualities, and to relate both to the position of the planets at the moment of a person's birth. Of the three people mentioned here, one is very bad, with a proportion of Light to Darkness of 1:8; his physique is fat, with thick short toes, hairy fat thighs and uneven teeth. One is middling good, with a ratio of Light to Darkness 6:3; physically he is lean, with long thin toes; his disposition is meek. The third is very good. His

Light to Darkness ratio is the reverse of the first man, i.e.
8:1.

> His eyes are black and glowing . . . His voice is gentle. His
> teeth are fine and well aligned. He is neither tall or short . . .
> And his fingers are thin and long. And his thighs are smooth
> . . . [And his toes] are well aligned (4Q186[2] 2:1–6).

Edition
J. M. Allegro, DJD V, 88–91. Cf. J. Strugnell, RQ 7 (1970),
274–6.
English translation
DSSE 268–70.
Literature
J. Carmignac, 'Les horoscopes de Qumrân', RQ 5 (1965),
199–217.
A. Dupont-Sommer, 'Deux documents horoscopiques es-
séniens découverts à Qumrân près de la Mer Morte', CRAI
(1965), 239–53.
R. Gordis, 'A Document in Code from Qumran', JSS 11
(1966), 37–9.
M. Delcor, 'Recherches sur un horoscope en langue hébraïque
provenant de Qumrân', RQ 5 (1966), 521–42.

43 A Messianic Horoscope (4QMess ar)
This Aramaic horoscope appears to foretell the physical
appearance and the character of the future Prince of the
Congregation or royal Messiah. It prophesies that he will have
red hair and a birthmark on his thigh, and will have reached
the age of discretion by the time he is two years old.

> Counsel and prudence will be with him, and he will know
> the secrets of man. His wisdom will reach all the peoples,
> and he will know the secrets of all the living. And all their
> designs against him will come to nothing, and (his) rule
> over all the living will be great. His designs [will succeed]
> for he is the Elect of God (1:7–10 – DSSE 270).

Preliminary edition

J. Starcky, 'Un texte messianique araméen de la grotte 4 de Qumrân', *Mémorial du Cinquantenaire 1914–1964 de l'École des langues orientales anciennes de l'Institut Catholique de Paris* (Bloud et Gay, Paris, 1964), 51–66.

English translation

DSSE 270.

Literature

J. A. Fitzmyer, *Essays on the Semitic Background of the New Testament* (Chapman, London, 1971), 127–60.

P.S. To the section of Bible interpretation may now be added: *21a Targum of Leviticus* (4Q156) covering parts of Lev. 16:12–15, 18–21; *34a* Targum of Job (4Q157) relating to Job 3:5–9; 4:16–5:4. J. T. Milik, DJD VI 86–90.

CHAPTER 4

Life and Institutions of the Sect

Piece by piece, the scraps of information garnered from the Scrolls and other ancient sources, as well as from archaeological remains, have been combined by experts in the course of the last three decades to form a reasonable and persuasive portrait of the people and events to which they allude. On the basis of the evidence collected, dates and personalities have been proposed, and religious expectations and moods delineated. Aspects of an ascetic life led at Qumran have come into view, with men attempting to find in the solitude of the desert 'perfection of way'. But also, another sort of sectarian existence has made itself known, of men and women living as an exclusive brotherhood within the larger confines of Palestinian society, subject nevertheless to the same stern discipline *vis-à-vis* the Law of Moses as that embraced by their desert companions.

Yet for all the advances made in knowledge and understanding, the enigma of the Dead Sea sect is by no means definitely solved. After all this time, we are still not certain that we have interpreted the whole evidence correctly or collated it properly. Questions continue to arise in the mind and there is still no way to be sure of the answers.

Our perplexity is mainly due to an absence in the documents, singly or together, of any systematic exposition of the sect's constitution and laws. The Community Rule legislates for a kind of monastic society, the statutes of the Damascus Rule for an ordinary lay existence; and the War Rule and Messianic Rule in their turn, while associated with the other two, and no doubt reflecting to some extent a contemporary state of affairs, plan for a future age.

Taken together, however, it is clear from this literature that the sectaries regarded themselves as the true Israel, the repository of the authentic traditions of the religious body from which they had seceded. Accordingly, they organized their movement so that it corresponded faithfully to that of Israel itself, dividing it into priests and laity, the priests being described as the 'sons of Zadok' – Zadok was High Priest in David's time – and the laity grouped after the biblical model into twelve tribes. This structure is described in the War Rule's account of Temple worship as it was expected to be at the end of time:

> The twelve chief priests shall minister at the daily sacrifice before God . . . Below them shall be the chiefs of the Levites to the number of twelve, one for each tribe . . . Below them shall be the chiefs of the tribes (1QM 2:1-3 – DSSE 125).

Still following the biblical pattern, sectarian society (apart from the tribe of Levi) was further distinguished into units of Thousands, Hundreds, Fifties and Tens (1QS 2:21; CD 13:1-2 – DSSE 74, 115). To what extent these figures are symbolical, we do not know, but it is improbable that 'Thousands' amounted to anything more than a figure of speech. It is not irrelevant, in this connection, to note that the archaeologists have deduced from the fact that the cemetery contained eleven hundred graves, dug over the course of roughly two hundred years, that the population of Qumran, an establishment of undoubted importance, can never have numbered more than 150 to 200 souls at a time (R. de Vaux, *Archaeology*, p. 86). Also, as will be shown in chapter 5, the total membership of the Essene sect in the first century AD only slightly exceeded 'four thousand' (cf. p. 125).

To consider now the two types separately, the monastic brotherhood at Qumran alludes to itself in the Community Rule as 'the men of holiness' and 'the men of perfect holiness', and to the sect as 'the Community', and 'Council of the Community'. The establishment was devoted exclusively to religion. Work must have formed a necessary part of their existence;

it is obvious from the remains discovered at Qumran that they farmed, made pots, cured hides and reproduced manuscripts. But no indication of this appears in the documents. It is said only that they were to 'eat in common, pray in common and deliberate in common' (1QS 6:2–3 – DSSE 81), living in such a way as to 'seek God with a whole heart and soul' (1QS 1:1–2 – DSSE 72). Perfectly obedient to each and every one of the laws of Moses and to all that was commanded by the prophets, they were to love one another and to share with one another their 'knowledge, powers and possessions' (1QS 1:11 – DSSE 72). They were to be scrupulous in their observance of the times appointed for prayer, and for every other event of a liturgical existence conducted apart from the Temple of Jerusalem and its official cult. 'Separate from the habitation of ungodly men' (1QS 8:13 – DSSE 85–6), they were to study the Torah in the wilderness and thereby 'atone for the Land' (1QS 8:6, 10 – DSSE 85) and its wicked men, for whom they were to nourish an 'everlasting hatred' (1QS 9:21 – DSSE 88), though this went together with a firm conviction that their fate was in God's hands alone. As the poet proclaims in the Hymn with which the Community Rule ends:

> I will pay to no man the reward of evil;
> I will pursue him with goodness.
> For judgement of all the living is with God
> And it is He who will render to man his reward.
> (1QS 10:17–18 – DSSE 90–1)

They were to be truthful, humble, just, upright, charitable and modest. They were to

> watch in community for a third of every night of the year, to read the Book and study the law and to pray together (1QS 6:7–8 – DSSE 81).

These are, as may be seen, mostly the sort of recommendations to be expected of men devoting themselves to contemplation. A point to bear in mind, however, is that the contemplative life is not a regular feature of Judaism. An additional distinctive trait of these sectaries is that another qualification was required of them besides holiness: they were expected to become proficient in the knowledge of the 'two spirits' in which all men 'walk', the spirits of truth and falsehood, and to learn how to discriminate between them. They were taught, in other words, how to recognize a 'son of Light' or potential 'son of Light', and how to distinguish a 'son of Darkness' belonging to the 'lot of Belial' (1QS 3:13 – 4:25 – DSSE 75–8; cf. below pp. 171–2).

The hierarchy at Qumran was strict and formal, from the highest level to the lowest. Every sectary was inscribed in 'the order of his rank' (1QS 6:22 – DSSE 82) – the term 'order' recurs constantly – and was obliged to keep to it in all the community meetings and at table. But the 'sons of Zadok, the priests' came first in the order of precedence. Although nothing to this effect is mentioned specifically in the Community Rule, the superior, the so-called *mebaqqer* or Guardian, was undoubtedly one of their number, as was the Bursar of the Congregation entrusted with handling the material affairs of the Community. In their hands lay the ultimate responsibility for decisions on matters of doctrine, discipline, purity and impurity, and in particular matters pertaining to 'justice and property' (1QS 9:7 – DSSE 87). It was also a basic rule of the order that a priest was required to be present at any gathering of ten or more meeting for debate, Bible study or prayer. A priest was to recite the grace before the common meals and to pronounce blessings (1QS 6:3–8 – DSSE 81). He was no doubt the man whose duty it was to study the Law continually (1QS 6:7; 8:11–12 – DSSE 81, 85). One interesting feature of the priesthood at Qumran is that their precedence was absolute. In Judaism as represented by the Mishnah, the priest is superior to the Levite, the Levite to the Israelite, and the Israelite to the 'bastard' (mHorayoth 3:8). But the priestly precedence is conditional. If the 'bastard' is a man of learning, we are told, and the High Priest a 'boor', 'the bastard . . . precedes the High Priest'.

The highest office was vested in the person of the Guardian, known also as the 'Master' (*maskil*). The Community was to be taught by him how to live in conformity with the 'Book of the Community Rule' (1QS 1:1 – DSSE 72), and to be instructed by him in the doctrine of the 'two spirits'. He was to preside over assemblies, giving leave to speak to those wishing to do so (1QS 6:11–13 – DSSE 81). He was to assess, in concert with the brethren, the spiritual progress of the men in his charge and rank them accordingly (1QS 6:21–2 – DSSE 82). And negatively, he was not to dispute with 'the men of the Pit' and not to transmit to them the sect's teachings (1QS 9:16–17 – DSSE 88).

Of the sect's institutions, the most significant appears to have been the Council of the Community, or assembly of the Congregation. From a passage ordering all the members to sit in their correct places – 'The priests shall sit first, and the elders second, and all the rest of the people according to their rank' (1QS 6:8–9 – DSSE 81) – it would seem to have been a gathering of the whole community, under the priests and men of importance, with the Guardian at the head. But in another text the rule is that

In the Council of the Community there shall be twelve men and three Priests, perfectly versed in all that is revealed of the Law, whose works shall be truth, righteousness, justice, loving-kindness and humility. They shall preserve the faith in the Land with steadfastness and meekness and shall atone for sin by the practice of justice and by suffering the sorrows of affliction. They shall walk with all men according to the standard of truth and the rule of the time (1QS 8:1–4 – DSSE 85).

These three priests and twelve men are referred to nowhere else, so we cannot be sure of their place in the Qumran order. Their presence was obviously essential: the Rule states that when 'these are in Israel, the Council of the Community shall be established in truth' (1QS 8:4–5 – DSSE 85). But whether they formed the nucleus of the sect as a whole, or the minimum quorum of the sect's leadership symbolizing the twelve tribes and the three Levitical clans, or a special elite within the Council designated elsewhere 'the Foundations of the Community', must be left open to question. The purpose of the meetings is in any case clear. It was to debate the Law, to discuss their current business, to select or reject newcomers under the guidance of the Guardian, to hear charges against offenders, and to conduct a yearly enquiry into the progress of every sectary, promoting or demoting them in rank, again under the Guardian's supervision (1QS 5:23–4; 6:13–23 – DSSE 80–2). During their sessions, order and quiet was to prevail: a person wishing to offer his opinion or ask a question was to crave permission in a prescribed way. He was to rise and tell the Guardian and the Congregation, 'I have something to say to the Congregation' and then wait for their consent before going ahead (1QS 6:8–13 – DSSE 81).

The procedure followed in enquiries into infringements of the Law and the sect's rule has been preserved, and the list of faults with their corresponding sentences tells us more about the mentality of the Dead Sea ascetics than any isolated exposition of their doctrine and principles can do.

Beginning with the blackest sins: any transgression, by commission or omission, of 'one word of the Law of Moses, on any point whatever' earned outright expulsion. No former companion might from then on associate with the sinner in any way at all (1QS 8:21–24 – DSSE 86).

Expulsion followed, secondly, the pronouncement for any reason whatever of the divine Name:

If any man has uttered the [Most] Venerable Name, even though frivolously, or as a result of shock, or for any other reason whatever, while reading the Book or praying, he shall be dismissed and shall return no more (1QS 6:27 – 7:2 – DSSE 84).

Thirdly, a sectary was expelled for slandering the Congregation

(1QS 7:16 – DSSE 84). Fourthly, he was sent away for rebelling against the 'Foundations' of the Community:

> Whoever has murmured against the Foundations of the Community shall be expelled and shall not return (1QS 7:17 – DSSE 84).

Lastly, where a man had been a member of the Council for at least ten years and had then defected to 'walk in the stubbornness of his heart', not only was he to be expelled, but the same judgement was extended to any of his former colleagues who might take pity on him and share with him their food or money (1QS 7:22–23 – DSSE 84–5).

The remaining offences are of a kind that might be confessed and censured in any Christian monastic chapter of today, though one cannot perhaps say the same of the penances imposed for them.

In a descending order of gravity: a man who 'betrayed the truth and walked in the stubbornness of his heart' (1QS 7:18–21 – DSSE 84), or transgressed the Mosaic Law inadvertently (1QS 8:24–9:1 – DSSE 86), was visited with two years of penance. He was to lose his rank and during the first year be separated from the 'purity' of the Congregation, and during the second year, from its 'drink'. Both notions will be developed presently. He was then to be re-examined by the Congregation and subsequently returned to his place in the order.

Lying in matters of property, in all probability, the partial concealment of personal possessions, earned exclusion from 'purity' for a year and a cut by one quarter in the food ration (1QS 6:25–27 – DSSE 82–3). Disrespect to a companion of higher rank, rudeness and anger towards a priest, slander and deliberate insult, all earned one year of penance and exclusion from 'purity' (1QS 6:25–27; 7:2–5 – DSSE 82–4). After this, the sentences decrease to six months, three months, thirty days and ten days of penance.

For lying deliberately and similarly deceiving by word or deed, for bearing malice unjustly, for taking revenge, for murmuring against a companion unjustly, and also for going 'naked before his companion without having been obliged to do so' – a curious proviso – the sectary was to atone for six months. For failing to care for a companion and for speaking foolishly: three months. For falling asleep during a meeting of the Council, for leaving the Council while members were standing (in prayer?), for spitting in Council, for 'guffawing foolishly', for being 'so poorly dressed that when drawing his hand' – 'hand' being a euphemism – 'from beneath his garment his nakedness was seen': thirty days. And for leaving an assembly three times without reason, for interrupting another while speaking, for gesticulating with the left hand: ten days (1QS 7 – DSSE 83–4).

That the common table was of high importance to Qumran daily life is evident from the fact that only the fully professed and the faultless, that is to say those who were 'inscribed . . . for purity' and not subsequently disqualified, were allowed to sit at it. There is no explicit mention of a ritual bath preceding the meals, but from various references to purification by water, as well as the presence of at least two bathing installations at Qumran, it is likely that the sectaries immersed themselves before eating. But little more is learnt of the meal itself from the Community Rule than that when the table had been 'prepared for eating and the new wine for drinking', the priest was to be the first to bless the food and drink (1QS 6:4–5– DSSE 81). The implication would be that after him the others did the same, an inference supported by the Messianic Rule, where a similar meal is described attended by two Messiahs (1QSa 2:17–21 – DSSE 121). Some uncertainty surrounds the meaning of 'new wine', but it would seem from the use in the Scrolls of the alternative Hebrew words for wine – *tirosh* and *yayin* – that the latter has pejorative connotations. More likely than not, the 'wine' drunk by the sectaries, 'the drink of the Congregation', was unfermented grape-juice.

Another topic to be considered under the heading of the sect's life and institutions is the crucial one of induction into the sect. And if it should seem strange to place it towards the end rather than at the beginning, the explanation is that with an idea, however sketchy, of what was entailed by adherence to the movement, the process by which it admitted a Jew into its company becomes easier to follow.

According to the regime followed at Qumran, a person desiring to join the sect remained on probation, certainly for two years and possibly for three or more. His first move was to appear before the Guardian 'at the head of the Congregation', meaning no doubt during a session of the Congregation, who enquired into his principles to discover if he was a suitable postulant. If they were satisfied, he 'entered the Covenant' (1QS 6:13-15 - DSSE 81-2). That is to say, he solemnly swore there and then to adhere to the Torah as the sect interpreted it, vowing

> by a binding oath to return with all his heart and soul to every commandment of the Law of Moses in accordance with all that has been revealed of it to the sons of Zadok, the Keepers of the Covenant (1QS 5:7-11 - DSSE 79).

After a further period of unspecified length, during which he received instruction from the Guardian 'in all the rules of the Community', he appeared once more before the Congregation, who confirmed him as a novice or dismissed him. But although he was now accepted into the Council of the Community, he was nevertheless still not admitted to 'purity' for another full year.

This concept of pure things (*ṭohorah, ṭaharah* or *ṭohoroth,* literally 'purity' or 'purities') needs some comment. In rabbinic literature, *ṭohoroth* signifies in general ritually pure food as well as the vessels and utensils in which it is contained or cooked. It includes also garments. The *ṭohoroth,* moreover, are distinguished by the rabbis from *mashqin,* liquids, the latter being considered much more susceptible to contract impurity than solid comestibles. Hence, in ordering the novice not to touch the pure things of the Congregation, the Community forbade him all contact with its pots, plates, bowls, and necessarily the food that they held. He was not, in effect, to attend the common table.

During this first year of the novitiate, the newcomer to the sect could not share the sect's property. At a third community enquiry, he was examined for 'his understanding and observance of the Law' and, if his progress was judged to be acceptable, he handed over his money and belongings to the 'Bursar of the Congregation', but they were set aside and not yet absorbed into community ownership. During this second year, furthermore, the ban on touching the pure things was relaxed, but he could still not touch liquids, the 'drink of the Congregation'. Finally, the second year over, the novice had once more to undergo an examination, after which, 'in accordance with the judgement of the Congregation', he was at last inscribed among the brethren in the order of his rank 'for the Law and for justice and for purity'. Also, his property was amalgamated with theirs and he possessed the right from then on to speak his mind in the Council of the Community (1QS 6:13–23 – DSSE 81–2).

In sum, this strict and extended curriculum falls into two stages. The postulant is first brought into the Covenant, swearing total fidelity to the Mosaic Law as interpreted by the sect's priesthood, and to 'separate from all the men of falsehood who walk in the way of wickedness' (1QS 5:10–11 – DSSE 79.) He then secondly embarks on a course of training as a preliminary to joining the 'holy Congregation' (1QS 5:20 – DSSE 80). In other words, entering the Covenant and entering the Community was not one act, but two.

It has long been debated whether the Qumran sectaries were married or celibate. From the image of their life projected so far, few will probably disagree that the idea of the presence of women among them appears incongruous. The impression received is that of a wholly masculine society: indeed, they were actually enjoined 'not to follow a sinful heart and lustful eyes, committing all manner of evil' (1QS 1:6 – DSSE 72). Moreover, in support of the argument for celibacy, the word *ishah*, woman, occurs nowhere in the Community Rule. Or rather, to be more exact, it is encountered once in the final Hymn, in the cliché, 'one born of woman' (1QS 11:21 – DSSE 94). Yet the fact cannot be overlooked that although in the grave-yard itself the twenty-six tombs so far opened at random (out of eleven hundred) have all contained adult male skeletons, the archaeologists have uncovered on the peripheries of the cemetery the bones of a few women and children.

The Damascus Rule, as well as the Messianic Rule and occasionally the War Rule, is concerned with a style of religious existence quite at variance from that at Qumran. In the 'towns' or 'camps', as the Damascus Rule terms them (CD 12:19, 23 – DSSE 114), adherents of the sect lived an urban or village life side by side, yet apart from, their fellow-Jews and Gentile neighbours. Rearing children, employing servants, engaging in commerce and trade (even with Gentiles), tending cattle, growing vines and corn in the surrounding fields, discharging their duties to the Temple by way of offerings and sacrifice, they were obliged like their brothers in the desert to show absolute obedience to the Law and to observe the sect's 'appointed times'. There is no indication, however, that the intensive study of the Torah played any part in their lives. Nor is there any mention in their regard of instruction in the doctrine of the two spirits.

How many of these people, if any, lived in Jerusalem is not known, but they must at least have visited the city from time to time, since a statute forbids them to enter the 'house of worship' in a state of ritual uncleanness, or to 'lie with a woman in the city of the Sanctuary to defile the city of the Sanctuary with their uncleanness' (CD 1:22; 12:1 – DSSE 113).

Little is revealed in the Damascus Rule of how the life-span of the individual progressed in the 'towns', and for this we have to turn to the Messianic Rule in the hope that it reflects contemporary actuality as well as the ideal life of an age to come.

According to the latter Rule, members of the Covenant were permitted to marry at the age of twenty, when they were estimated to have reached adulthood and to 'know [good] and evil' (1QSa 1:9–11 – DSSE 119). For the subsequent five years they were then allowed to 'assist' (as opposed to taking an active part) at hearings and judgements. At twenty-five, they advanced one grade further and qualified to 'work in the service of the Congregation' (1QSa 1:12–13 – DSSE 119). At thirty, they were regarded as at last fully mature and could 'participate' in the affairs of the tribunals and assemblies, taking their place among the higher ranks of the sect, the 'chiefs of the Thousands of Israel, the Hundreds, the chiefs of the Fifties and Tens, the judges and the officers of their tribes, in all their families [under the authority] of the sons of [Aar]on the Priests' (1QSa 1:8–16 – DSSE 119). As office-holders, they were expected to perform their duties to the best of their ability and were accorded more honour or less in conformity with their 'understanding' and the 'perfection' of their 'way'. As they grew older, so their burdens became lighter (1QSa 1:19 – DSSE 119).

As at Qumran, supreme authority rested in the hands of the priests, and every group of ten or more was to include a priest 'learned in the Book of Meditation' and to be 'ruled by him' (CD 13:2 – DSSE 115). His precedence, on the other hand, is not represented as absolute in the 'towns'. It is explicitly stated that in the absence of a properly qualified priest, he was to be replaced by a Levite who would perform all the functions of a superior except those specially reserved in the Bible to the priesthood such as applying the laws of leprosy (CD 13:3–7 – DSSE 115).

As in the Community Rule, the head of the 'camp' is given in the Damascus Rule as the *mebaqqer*, Guardian. He appears, however, not to be supported by a council. In fact, the words 'Council of the Community' are absent from this document. There is reference to the 'company of Israel', on the advice of which it would be licit to attack Gentiles (CD 12:8 – DSSE 114), but this type of war council, mentioned also in the Messianic Rule (1QSa 1:26 – DSSE 120), can surely have had nothing to do with the assemblies described in the Community Rule. The Guardian of the 'camps', in any case, stands on his own as teacher and helper of his people. He shall love them, writes the author,

> as a father loves his children, and shall carry them in all their distress like a shepherd his sheep. He shall loosen all the fetters that bind them so that in his Congregation there may be none that are oppressed and broken (CD 13:9–10 – DSSE 115).

The Guardian was to examine newcomers to his congregation, though not, it should be noted, to determine their 'spirit', and was to serve as the deciding authority on the question of their admission. These offices are of course already familiar to us from the Community Rule. But an additional task of the *mebaqqer* in the towns was to ensure that no friendly contact occurred between his congregation and the 'men of the Pit', i.e. everyone outside the sect. Whatever exchanges took place had to be paid for; and even these transactions were to be subject to his consent (CD 13:14–16 – DSSE 115).

Instead of dealing with offenders in Community courts of inquiry the towns had their tribunals for hearing cases, equipped moreover with 'judges'. These were to be ten in number, elected for a specific term and drawn from the tribes of Levi, Aaron and Israel; four priests and Levites, and six laymen (CD 10:4–7 – DSSE 111). They were to be not younger than twenty-five and not older than sixty – in the Messianic Rule, which also speaks of judges, the age-limits are thirty and sixty years (1QSa 1:13–15 – DSSE 119) – and were to be expert in biblical law and the 'constitutions of the Covenant'. The arrangement would seem, in fact, to be fairly straightforward. Yet it is not entirely so. For example, it is evident that the Guardian was also implicated in legal matters; he had to determine whether a proper case had been made out against a sectary and whether it should be brought before the court (CD 9:16–20 – DSSE 111) and in certain cases he appears to have imposed penalties on his own (CD 15:13–14 – DSSE 109). We are not told whether these ten judges sat together, whether they were all drawn from the locality in which they lived, or whether they travelled on circuit as in the present day. The code of law they were expected to administer, as laid down in the Damascus Rule, is in any case totally different in both content and tone from that of the Community Rule: the offences envisaged bear no relation to existence in a quasi-monastic community. Furthermore, although, unlike the Qumran code, a sentence is prescribed but rarely, sometimes it is the death penalty. Thus, instead of recommendations not to spit or guffaw at a meeting of the Council, we have here a sectarian reformulation of scriptural laws regulating Jewish life as such.

The first group of statutes, concerned with vows, opens with the injunction that in order to avoid being put to death for the capital sin of uttering the names of God, the sectary must swear by the Covenant alone. Such an oath would be fully obligatory and might not be cancelled (CD 16:7–8 – DSSE 109). If he subsequently violated his oath, he would then have only to confess to the priest and make restitution (CD 15:1–5 – DSSE 108). The sectary is also ordered not to vow to the altar articles acquired unlawfully, or the food of his own house (CD 16:13–15 – DSSE 109–10), and not to make any vow 'in the fields' but always before the judges (CD 9:9–10 – DSSE 110). He is threatened with death if he 'vow another to destruction by the laws of the Gentiles' (CD 9:1 – DSSE 110). As for the right conferred by the Bible on fathers and husbands to annul vows made by their daughters or wives, the Damascus Rule limits it to the cancellation of oaths which should have never been made (CD 16:10–12 – DSSE 109).

A few ordinances follow concerned with witnesses. No one under the age of twenty was to testify before the judges in a capital charge (CD 9:23 – 10:2 – DSSE 111). Also, whereas the normal biblical custom is that two or three witnesses are needed before any sentence can be pronounced (Deut. 19:15), a single witness being quite unacceptable, *unus testis nullus testis*, sectarian law allowed the indictment of a man guilty of repeating the same capital offence on the testimony of single witnesses to the separate occasions on which it was committed, providing they reported it to the Guardian at once and that the Guardian recorded it at once in writing (CD 9:17-20 – DSSE 111). In regard to the capital cases, to which should be added apostasy in a state of demonic possession (CD 12:2-3 – DSSE 113), the adultery of a betrothed girl (4Q186, 2-4: 10-11 – DSSE 252), slandering the people of Israel and treason (11Q Temple 64:6-13 – DSSE 251), it is highly unlikely that either the Jewish or the Roman authorities would have granted any rights of execution to the sect. So this is probably part of the sect's vision of the future age, when it as Israel *de jure* would constitute *de facto* the government of the chosen people.

A section devoted to Sabbath laws displays a marked bias towards severity. In time, rabbinic law developed the Sabbath rules in still greater detail than appears here, but the tendency is already apparent.

The sectary was not only to abstain from labour 'on the sixth day from the moment when the sun's orb is distant by its own fullness from the gate (wherein it sinks)' (CD 10:15-16 – DSSE 112), he was not even to speak about work. Nothing associated with money or gain was to interrupt his Sabbath of rest (CD 10:18-19 – DSSE 112). No member of the Covenant of God was to go out of his house on business on the Sabbath. In fact, he was not to go out, for any reason, further than one thousand cubits (about 500 yards), though he could pasture his beast at a distance of two thousand cubits from his town (CD 10:21; 11:5-6 – DSSE 112). He could not cook. He could not pick and eat fruit and other edible things 'lying in the fields'. He could not draw water and carry it away, but must drink where he found it (CD 10:22-23 – DSSE 112). He could not strike his beast or reprimand his servant (CD 11:6, 12 – DSSE 112-13). He could not carry a child, wear perfume or sweep up the dust in his house (CD 11:10-11 – DSSE 112-13). He could not assist his animals to give birth or help them if they fell into a pit; he could, however, pull a man out of water or fire with the help of a ladder or rope (CD 11:13-14, 16-17 – DSSE 113). Interpreting the Bible restrictively (Lev. 23:38), the sect's lawmaker (or makers) commanded him to offer nothing on the

Sabbath save the Sabbath burnt-offering, and never to send a gift to the Temple by the hand of one 'smitten with any un-cleanness permitting him thus to defile the altar' (CD 11:19–20 – DSSE 113). And as has been said earlier (p. 97), he was also never to have intercourse while in the 'city of the Sanctuary' (CD 12:1–2 – DSSE 113).

The punishment imposed for profaning the Sabbath and the feasts in any of these ways was not death as in the Bible (Num. 15:35), and not even expulsion as in the Community Rule. It was seven years of imprisonment.

> It shall fall to men to keep him in custody. And if he is healed of his error, they shall keep him in custody for seven years and he shall afterwards approach the assembly (CD 12:4–6 – DSSE 114).

In the last group, the ordinances appear to be only loosely connected, though some of them involve relation with the larger Jewish-Gentile world. One such forbids killing or stealing a non-Jew, 'unless so advised by the company of Israel' (CD 12: 6–8 – DSSE 114). Another proscribes the sale to Gentiles of ritually pure beasts and birds, and the produce of granary and wine-press, in case they should blaspheme by offering them in heathen sacrifice. A ban is similarly laid on selling to Gentiles foreign servants converted to the Jewish faith (CD 12:11 – DSSE 114). But in addition to these regulations affecting contacts with non-Jews, a few are concerned with dietary restrictions. Thus:

> No man shall defile himself by eating any live creature or creeping thing, from the larvae of bees to all creatures which creep in water (CD 12:12–13 – DSSE 114).

Others deal with the laws of purity (CD 12:16–18 – DSSE 111) and purification (CD 10:10–13 – DSSE 111–12).

Two types of meeting are provided for, with equal laconism;

the 'assembly of the camp' presided over by a priest or a Levite (cf. above, p. 98) and the 'assembly of all the camps' (CD 14:3–6 – DSSE 116). Presumably the latter was the general convention of the whole sect held on the Feast of the Renewal of the Covenant, the annual great festival when both the 'men of holiness' and the 'men of the Covenant' confessed their former errors and committed themselves once more to perfect obedience to the Law and the sect's teachings. In the circumstances it would be remarkable, therefore, that so little space is given to it were we not told that a whole section dealing with the feast has disappeared from the Cairo manuscript but is attested in unpublished fragments from Cave 4. According to the available texts, the sectaries were to be mustered and inscribed in their rank by name, the priests first, the Levites second, the Israelites third. A fourth group of proselytes is unique to the 'towns', but as has been observed, these were Gentile slaves converted to Judaism. A further remark that they were in this order to 'be questioned on all matters' leads one to suppose that the allusion must be to the yearly enquiry into the members' spiritual progress mentioned in the Community Rule (CD 14:3–6 – DSSE 116).

Apart from these familiar directions, we learn only that the priest who mustered the gathering was to be between thirty and sixty years old and, needless to say, 'learned in the Book of Meditation'. The 'Guardian of all the camps', in his turn, was to be between thirty and fifty, and to have 'mastered all the secrets of men and the language of all their clans'. He was to decide who was to be admitted, and anything connected with a 'suit or judgement' was to be brought to him (CD 14:7–12 – DSSE 116).

As for the initiation of new members, the Statutes appear to legislate for young men reaching their majority within the brotherhood and for recruits from outside. This is not entirely clear, but the instruction that an aspirant was not to be informed of the sect's rules until he had stood before the Guardian can hardly have applied to a person brought up within its close circle (CD 15:5–6, 10–11 – DSSE 108).

Of the sect's own young men the Damascus Rule writes merely:

> And when the children of all those who have entered the Covenant granted to all Israel for ever reach the age of enrolment, they shall swear with an oath of the Covenant (CD 15:5-6 – DSSE 108).

The Messianic Rule is more discursive. There, enrolment into the sect is represented as the climax of a childhood and youth spent in study. Teaching in the Bible and in the 'precepts of the Covenant' began long before the age of ten, at which age a boy embarked on a further ten years of instruction in the statutes. It was not until after all this that he was finally ready.

> From [his] youth they shall instruct him in the Book of Meditation and shall teach him, according to his age, the precepts of the Covenant. He [shall be edu]cated in their statutes for ten years . . . At the age of twenty [he shall be] enrolled, that he may enter upon his allotted duties in the midst of his family [and] be joined to the holy congregation (1QSa 1:6-9 – DSSE 119).

The newcomer from outside who repented of his 'corrupted way' was to be enrolled 'with the oath of the Covenant' on the day that he spoke to the Guardian, but no sectarian statute was to be divulged to him 'lest when examining him the Guardian be deceived by him' (CD 15:7-11 – DSSE 108). Nevertheless, if he broke that oath, 'retribution' would be exacted of him. The text subsequently becomes fragmentary and unreliable, but he is told where to find the liturgical calendar which his oath obliges him to follow.

> As for the exact determination of their times to which Israel turns a blind eye, behold it is strictly defined in the Book of the Divisions of the Times into their Jubilees and Weeks (CD 16:2-4 – DSSE 109).

It should be added here that one big difference between the organization of the brethren in the towns and those of the monastic settlement is that new members were not required to surrender their property. There was none of the voluntary communism found at Qumran. On the other hand, where the desert sectaries practised common ownership, those of the towns contributed to the assistance of their fellows in need. Every man able to do so was ordered to hand over a minimum of two days' wages a month to a charitable fund, and from it the Guardian and the judges distributed help to the orphans, the poor, the old and sick, to unmarried women without support and to prisoners held in foreign hands and in need of redemption (CD 14:12–16 – DSSE 116).

When the two varieties of sectarian life are compared, the differences seem at first to outnumber the similarities. In the desert of Qumran men lived together in seclusion; in the towns they were grouped in families, surrounded by non-members with whom they were in inevitable though exiguous contact. The desert brotherhood kept apart from the Temple in Jerusalem; that of the towns participated in worship there. The 'Foundations' of the Qumran community had no counterparts in the towns; the judges of the towns had no counterparts at Qumran. The Qumran Guardian was supported by a Council; the town Guardians acted independently. Unfaithful desert sectaries were sentenced to irrevocable excommunication, or to temporary exclusion from the common life, or to suffer lighter penances; offenders from the towns were condemned to death (whether or not the verdict was carried out) or committed to corrective custody. The common table and the 'purity' associated with it played an essential role at Qumran; in connection with the towns the table goes unmentioned and 'purity' in that sense receives attention only once. Furthermore, at Qumran all the new recruits came from outside; in the towns, some were converts but others were the sons of sectaries. The desert novices underwent two years of training and were instructed in the doctrine of the 'two spirits'; the towns' converts were subjected to neither experience. In the desert, property was owned in common; in the towns, it was not. And last but not least, the desert community appears to have practised celibacy, whereas the town sectaries patently did not.

Yet despite these many dissimilarities, at the basic level of doctrine, aims and principles, a perceptible bond links the brethren of the desert with those of the towns. They both claim to represent the true Israel. They both follow the Zadokite priesthood, both form units of Thousands, Hundreds, Fifties and Tens, both insist on a whole-hearted return to the Mosaic Law in accordance with their own particular interpretation of it. They are both governed by priests (or Levites). The principal, superior, teacher and administrator of both is known by the unusual title of *mebaqqer*. In both cases, initiation into the sect is preceded by entry into the Covenant, sworn by oath. Both groups convene yearly to review the order of precedence of their members after an enquiry into the conduct of each man during the previous twelve months. Above all, both embrace the same 'unorthodox' liturgical calendar that sets them apart from the rest of Jewry.

There can be only one logical conclusion: this was a single religious movement with two branches. It does not, however, answer all our questions. It does not tell us in particular whether the sectaries of desert and towns maintained regular contact among themselves. After all, the history of religions furnishes scores of examples of sister sects which turned into mortal enemies. Did the Qumran and towns fellowships profess and practise unity? A few vital clues suggest that they did.

One indication of a living relationship between the two groups derives from the Qumran library itself. In it were discovered no less than ten copies of the Damascus Rule. It seems hardly likely that it would have been represented in such numbers if it had been the manual of some rival institution, or have figured so prominently among the Qumran literary treasures. Besides, there was no trace of any other book in the caves relating to an opposing religious faction. Another pointer towards unity appears in the passage of the Damascus

Rule outlining the procedure for the 'assembly of all the camps' and prescribing that the members were to be 'inscribed by name' in hierarchical rank. This clause corresponds exactly to the statute in the Community Rule ordaining a yearly ranking of the sectaries (1QS 2:19-23 – DSSE 74, 80), with a solemn ritual for the Renewal of the Covenant (for an analysis of the rite see pp. 178-9). This leads us to suppose that the Feast of the Covenant, when the desert brethren held their annual spiritual survey, was also the occasion for that of the towns. Can we go further still and establish that the two ceremonies took place, not only at the same time, but at the same place? In effect, the literary and archaeological evidence tends to support the theory that the 'assembly of all the camps', identical with the yearly assembly of the Qumran branch, forgathered at Qumran.

The first clue turns on the qualifications of the *mebaqqer* of the Community Rule and the Damascus Rule respectively. As may be remembered, the superior at Qumran was required to be expert in recognizing 'the nature of all the children of men according to the kind of spirit which they possess' (1QS 3:13-14 – DSSE 35), while the *mebaqqer* of the towns was to be concerned rather more with a man's 'deeds', 'possessions', 'ability' etc., than with his inner spirit. When, however, the Damascus Rule describes the attributes needed of the 'Guardian of all the camps', what do we find but a reformulation of those accredited to the superior of the desert community, that he should know 'all the secrets of men and all the languages of their clans'? It would emerge from this, therefore, that the Guardian of all the camps and the Guardian at Qumran were one and the same person.

The next hint comes from the fact that the Damascus Rule is directed to both desert and town sectaries. As an example, the passage from the Exhortation advising men to choose whatever is pleasing to God and to reject whatever he hates, 'that you may walk perfectly in all his ways and not follow after thoughts of the guilty inclination and after eyes of lust' (CD 2:14-16 – DSSE 98-9), is plainly meant for celibates.

Yet in this very same document we later come upon injunctions addressed explicitly to non-celibates:

> And if they live in camps according to the rule of the earth, marrying and begetting children, they shall walk according to the Law and according to the statute concerning binding vows, according to the rule of the Law which says, 'Between a man and his wife and between a father and his son' (Num. 30:17) (CD 7:6–9 – DSSE 103–4).

The Exhortation would seem in short to be a sermon intended for delivery on a certain occasion to married and unmarried members of the sect; and as its theme is perseverance in the Covenant, the appropriate setting would be the Feast of the Renewal of the Covenant, and the venue, Qumran.

These literary pointers are supported by two archaeological finds. Firstly, the twenty-six deposits of animal bones buried on the Qumran site – goats, sheep, lambs, calves, cows or oxen – have for long intrigued scholars. Can J. T. Milik be correct in identifying them as the remains of meals served to large groups of pilgrims in the Qumran mother-house of the sect (*Ten Years of Discovery*, 117)? Naturally, he too connects the gathering with the Covenant festival.

The second archaeological clue also is concerned with bones. The skeletons, as may be recalled, of four women and one child, and possibly of two further female bodies and those of two children, were found in the extension of the Qumran cemetery. Now, if the Renewal of the Covenant was attended by sectaries from the towns and their families, might not this account for the presence of dead women and children among the otherwise male skeletons of the graveyard proper?

Drawing the threads of these various arguments together, there would seem to be little doubt that not only were the desert and town sectaries united in doctrine and organization, but that they remained in actual and regular touch with each other, under the ultimate administrative and spiritual authority of the shadowy figure of the Priest, of whom we hear so little, and his dominant partner, the Qumran Guardian, Guardian of all the camps. Qumran, it seems, was the seat of the sect's hierarchy and also the centre to which all those turned who professed allegiance to the sons of Zadok the Priests, the Keepers of the Covenant.

As was said at the beginning of this chapter, there is still a great deal we do not know or fully understand about the Dead Sea sect. But although this reconsideration may not have obviated all the difficulties of interpretation or illuminated all the obscurities, perhaps it is not too much to hope that a few of the uncertainties have been dispelled. More positively, enough distinctive traits of Community customs and organization have come to light to allow us at least to place the Qumran movement within the larger context of inter-Testamental Judaism with a view to discovering where, if at all, they meet.

A full account of the priestly government of the Jews during the Persian and Hellenistic eras may be found in Schürer–Vermes–Millar–Black II, §23 IV, §24 I. The question of the Zadokite priesthood is discussed ibid. §24 I, n.56. For the Zadokite genealogy of Ezra, see Ezr. 7:1–5. The Qumran use of the phrase, 'sons of Zadok' is examined by J. Liver, 'The "Sons of Zadok the Priests" in the Dead Sea Sect', RQ 6 (1967), 3–30. The following general works may also be consulted: J. Jeremias, *Jerusalem in the Time of Jesus* (S.C.M., London and Fortress, Philadelphia, 1969), 147–221; A. Cody, *A History of the Old Testament Priesthood* (Biblical Institute Press, Rome, 1969).

For the various offices, see J. F. Priest, 'Mebaqqer, Paqid, and the Messiah', JBL 81 (1962), 55–61; A. S. Kapelrud, 'Die aktuellen und die eschatologischen Behörden der Qumrangemeinde', *Qumran-Probleme*, ed. by H. Bardtke (Akademie Verlag, Berlin, 1963) 259–67; P. Osten-Sacken, 'Bemerkungen zur Stellung des Mebaqqer in der Sektenschrift', ZNW 55 (1964), 18–26. There are two schools of thought concerning the function of the Law interpreter (1QS 6:6; 8:12 – DSSE 81, 85). According to one, no special person was entrusted with this task; all the sectaries had their study periods in rotation. The other view is that a particular individual, no doubt a priest, was chosen to meditate on Scripture 'day and night', thus foreshadowing the work of the priestly Messiah known also as the 'Interpreter of the Law' (CD 7:18; 4QFlor 1:11 – DSSE 104, 246). For a comparison with Essene and Christian leadership, see chapters 5 and 8.

On the terminology, 'Community', 'Congregation', etc., consult A. Dupont-Sommer, *Essene Writings*, 44; P. Wernberg-Møller, 'The Nature of YAHAD . . .', ALUOS 6 (1969), 56–81.

The latest monograph on the problem of excommunication is G. Forkman, *The Limits of the Religious Community. Expulsion from the Religious Community within the Qumran Sect, within Rabbinic Judaism and within Primitive Christianity*

(Gleerup, Lund, 1972). For a general survey see Enc. Jud. 8, 344–55, and Schürer–Vermes–Millar–Black II, §27 II.

In regard to the *tirosh* drunk at the common table, the rabbis explain that in the 'language of men', i.e. in ordinary spoken Hebrew, *tirosh* is a sweet, unfermented drink distinct from wine. If a person vowed to abstain from *tirosh*, he might not touch any kind of fruit-juice, but was free to drink as much wine as he liked. If, on the other hand, he formulated his vow in the 'language of the Torah', i.e. biblical Hebrew, where *tirosh* is synonymous with wine, he must take no alcohol (tNedarim 4:3; yNedarim 40b; Sifre to Deut. 42 on Deut. 11:14).

It should also be noted in support of our hypothesis that the Qumran sectaries drank grape-juice, that priests participating in Temple worship were to abstain from wine according to Lev. 10:8–11, and the 'sons of Zadok' in particular, in Ezek. 44:21.

For 'purity' and 'the drink of the Congregation', see S. Lieberman, 'The Discipline in the so-called Dead Sea Manual of Discipline', JBL 71 (1951), 199–206 [*Texts and Studies* (Ktav, New York, 1974), 200–7]. Cf. also J. Licht, 'Ḥumrat mashqeh harabbim miṭohorat harabbim beSerekh hayyaḥad', *Sefer Segal*, ed. J. M. Grintz (Kirjath Sepher, Jerusalem, 1964), 300–9.

The terminology relating to the training and admission of candidates is analysed by M. Delcor, 'Le vocabulaire juridique, cultuel et mystique de l'initiation dans la secte de Qumrân', *Qumran-Probleme*, ed. H. Bardtke (Akademie Verlag, Berlin, 1963), 109–34.

Apropos of initiation, the view has been advanced that the Feast of the Renewal of the Covenant was the occasion for new members to make their sworn pledge (cf. Milik *Ten Years*, 114). This, however, is not borne out by the evidence published so far. The Covenant ritual mentions no oaths and the Damascus Rule expressly states that the oath was to be taken on the very day the candidate was accepted by the Guardian (CD 15:7–8 – DSSE 108). It would be reasonable to suppose that the noviciate began on that particular feast-day and ended exactly two years later, but this too is purely speculative.

Essene 'communism' will be examined in chapter 5 and the

use of the common purse in the Jerusalem Church in chapter 8. For the Qumran evidence see L. M. Pákozdy, 'Der wirtschaftliche Hintergrund der Gemeinschaft von Qumran', *Qumran-Probleme*, 269–91; W. Tyloch, 'Quelques remarques sur le caractère social du mouvement de Qumran'; ibid., 341–51; J. G. Greehy, 'Community of Goods – Qumran and Acts', *Irish Theol. Quart.* 32 (1965), 230–40; J. A. Fitzmyer, 'Jewish Christianity in Acts in the Light of the Qumran Scrolls', *Essays on the Semitic Background of the New Testament* (Chapman, London, 1971), 271–303.

For a discussion of Essene celibacy, see chapter 5, p. 126 and chapter 7, pp. 181–2.

On the similarities and differences between the Qumran Community and the rabbinic *haburoth* or guilds devoted to the strict observance of purity and tithe-laws, cf. S. Lieberman, art. cit. (on p. 111 above); G. Vermes, *Discovery*, 48–52; C. Rabin, 'Yaḥad, Ḥaburah and Essenes', *Studies in the Dead Sea Scrolls . . . in Memory of E. L. Sukenik* (Kirjath Sepher, Jerusalem, 1957), 104–22 in Hebrew. On the *haburoth* in general, see Schürer–Vermes–Millar–Black II, §26 I. See also below, pp. 120–1.

On Qumran halakhah, see L. H. Schiffman, *The Halakhah at Qumran* (Brill, Leiden, 1975); J. M. Baumgarten, *Studies in Qumran Law* (Brill, Leiden, 1977).

The ban on sexual intercourse 'in the city of the Sanctuary' has been interpreted as referring to fornication (R. H. Charles, *Apocrypha and Pseudepigrapha* II, 828), but as has been suggested it more probably alludes to intercourse between married pilgrims in the holy city (C. Rabin, *Zadokite Documents*, 59).

On the age of twenty as marking a youth's majority, see S. B. Hoenig, 'On the Age of Mature Responsibility in 1QSa', JQR 48 (1957), 371–5; 'The Age of Twenty in Rabbinic Tradition and 1QSa', JQR 49 (1958), 209–14. The recommended age for marriage for a man is eighteen years in rabbinic tradition (mAboth 5:21).

The problem of divorce is treated nowhere explicitly in the Scrolls. A number of scholars see in the prohibition on taking two wives 'in their lifetime' (CD 4:20–5:2) an outlawing of both

polygamy and divorce, but a careful analysis of the passage
makes it plain that the author is arguing against polygamy
alone, and was not concerned with the question of a divorce
followed by remarriage. For the most recent literature on the
subject, see Y. Yadin, 'L'attitude essénienne envers la polygamie
et le divorce', RB 79 (1972), 98–9; G. Vermes, 'Sectarian
Matrimonial Halakhah in the Damascus Rule', JJS 25 (1974),
197–202 [= PBJS, 50–56]; J. A. Fitzmyer, 'The Matthean
Divorce Texts and some new Palestinian Evidence', *Theol.
Studies* 37 (1976), 197–226.

The nature and identity of the 'Book of Meditation (*Hagu*)'
are still debated. It has been suggested that this is an alternative
title for the Community Rule (A. Dupont-Sommer, *Essene
Writings*, 70) or a 'written corpus of Torah exegesis' (P.
Wernberg-Møller, ALUOS 6 (1969), 79–80, n.32). However,
the fact that it is represented as the basic text-book studied
at the one extreme by the Guardian and the Judges, and at
the other by young children, points to the Bible, and more
particularly the Pentateuch. Note also that Moses instructed
Joshua, and the Psalmist the just man in general, to *meditate*
on the Law day and night (Jos. 1:8; Ps. 1:2). In fact, a rabbinic
dictum goes so far as to restrict all 'meditation' (*hege*) to 'the
words of the Law' (Gen. R. 49:17). Cf. L. H. Schiffman, *The
Halakhah at Qumran* (Brill, Leiden, 1975), 44, n.144.

Rabbinic legislation for the composition of Jewish tribunals
is contained in the tractate Sanhedrin (Mishnah, Tosefta and
Talmud). The special court of ten judges is mentioned in
mMegillah 4:3; mSanhedrin 1:3. The Ordinances of Cave 4
know also of a tribunal of twelve, two priests and ten laymen,
endowed apparently with capital jurisdiction (4Q 159 – DSSE
252).

For a comparison of Qumran with the primitive Church,
see M. Delcor, 'Les tribunaux de l'église de Corinthe et les
tribunaux de Qumrân', *Studiorum Paulinorum Congressus
Catholicus 1961* (Rome, 1963), 535–48 [= *Paul and Qumran*,
ed. J. Murphy-O'Connor (Chapman, London, 1968), 69–84)];
J. M. Baumgarten, 'The Duodecimal Courts of Qumran, Revelation and the Sanhedrin', JBL 95 (1976), 57–78. See further,

J. Pouilly, 'L'évolution de la législation pénale dans la Communauté de Qumrân', RB 82 (1975), 522–51.

Apropos of the death penalty, the interpretation of CD 9:1 is controversial. C. Rabin (*Zadokite Fragments, in loc.*) understands it to mean that criminals condemned to death by the sect were to be handed over to the Gentiles for execution. But the exegesis advanced by P. Winter makes better sense: the mere laying of a capital charge against a sectary (or perhaps simply against another Jew) before a Gentile court constituted a crime punishable by death: cf. 'Ṣadoqite Fragment IX.1', RQ 6 (1967), 131–6. See also Z. W. Falk, '*Beḥuqei hagoyim* in Damascus Document IX.1', ibid. (1969), 569.

In connection with Qumran allusions to crucifixion, the following points are to be borne in mind. Josephus twice records that Alexander Jannaeus crucified eight hundred of his political opponents (Pharisees) in *c.* 88 BC. (*Antiquities* xiii, 380; *War* i, 97). 4QpNah 1:7–8 (DSSE 232) appears to echo this event if the phrase 'to hang man alive (on the tree)' is interpreted in the light of Sifre to Deut. 221, where this form of death penalty is represented as characteristic of the Roman authorities. If, as is likely, the legislation recorded in the Temple Scroll (64:6–13 – DSSE 251) concerns the future age, its choice of 'hanging/crucifixion' for the execution of persons guilty of crimes against the Jewish State may be seen as inspired by Roman law. On crucifixion in general, see P. Winter, *On the Trial of Jesus* (de Gruyter, Berlin, [2]1974), 90–6. For the Qumran texts, cf. N. Wieder, 'Notes on the New Documents from the Fourth Cave of Qumran', JJS 7 (1956), 71–2; Y. Yadin, 'Pesher Nahum Reconsidered', IEJ 21 (1971), 1–12; Schürer–Vermes–Millar I, 224–5. J. M. Baumgarten takes the Hebrew verb 'to hang' in the sense of an execution by hanging because he finds crucifixion repugnant to Jewish law: cf. 'Does *tlh* in the Temple Scroll refer to Crucifixion?', JBL 91 (1972), 472–81.

The problem of single witnesses has been considered recently by several scholars: B. Levine, 'Damascus Document IX, 17–22: A New Translation and Comments', RQ 8 (1973), 195–6; J. Neusner, '"By the Testimony of Two Witnesses" in the Damascus Document IX, 17–22 and in Pharisaic-Rabbinic Law', ibid., 197–217; L. H. Schiffman, 'The Qumran Law of Testimony', ibid., 603–12; N. L. Rabinovitch, 'Damascus Document IX, 17–22 and Rabbinic Parallels', RQ 9 (1977), 113–16; B. S. Jackson *Testes singulares* in Early Jewish Law and the New Testament', *Essays in Jewish and Comparative Legal History* (Brill, Leiden, 1975), 172–201. Both Neusner and Jackson explain the text as demanding three separate single witnesses reporting the commission on three separate occasions of the same capital crime by the same sectary. If the witnesses were trustworthy, the Guardian could start proceedings against the accused.

For the liturgical calendar of the sect and its connection with the Book of Jubilees, see chapter 7, pp. 176–7, 191–2.

The stipulation that the Guardian of all the camps should be versed in all the languages of mankind may be compared to the statement in the Babylonian Talmud (bSanhedrin 17a) that only men acquainted with the seventy languages of the creation were eligible to sit on the Jerusalem Sanhedrin.

For the female skeletons in the Qumran cemetery, see in addition to de Vaux (*Archaeology*, 47–8), S. H. Steckoll, 'Preliminary Excavation Report in the Qumran Cemetery', RQ 6 (1968), 323–44; N. Haas, H. Nathan, 'Anthropological Survey of the Human Skeletal Remains from Qumran', ibid., 345–52. Steckoll claims to have excavated in 1966 and 1967 nine further tombs at Qumran which yielded the bones of six men, two women, one of them buried with a baby, and a little girl. R. de Vaux expressed serious doubts about the researches of 'this Sherlock Holmes of archaeology' (*Archaeology*, 48).

It is worth noting that lay heads of the sect appear only in the Messianic Rule and the War Rule – the chiefs of tribes, Thousands, Hundreds, Fifties and Tens. The eschatological lay leader, the Messiah of Israel, is interestingly never called 'King'. His title is 'Prince' (*nasi*, 1QSb 5:20; 1QM 5:1; CD 7:20), following the model of Ezek. 34:24. The same style was used by the commander of the second Jewish revolution, Simeon ben Kosiba, as witnessed by his coins and the Murabbaat and Nahal Hever papyri. Cf. above p. 17 and Schürer-Vermes-Millar I, 544, 606.

CHAPTER 5

Identification of the Community

During the period with which this study is concerned (140 BC–
AD 70), Palestinian society did not consist of a majority of
'orthodox' Jews interspersed with small minorities of heretics
and sectaries. The 'one-party system' which was to prevail in
the second century AD did not come into being until after
years of hard thinking and argument by the rabbis who survived
the unsuccessful revolution of AD 66–70. Assembled during
the final decades of the first century in the little town of Jamnia
(Yavneh), about fifteen miles south of Tel Aviv, they set out to
re-think and re-shape a Judaism deprived of Temple and
sacrifice, and by the end of the first century, had reached
agreement on all the essentials. The bulk of the Jewish inhabitants of the Holy Land adhered from then on to their teaching,
and the minority distinguishable by their lack of 'orthodoxy'
were excommunicated and cursed daily in the famous prayer
of the synagogue, the Eighteen Benedictions: 'May . . . the
heretics perish quickly and may they be erased from the Book
of Life!'

Prior to this unification, the situation was very different in
that cohesion within Judaism was the outcome, not of conformity in matters of belief and practice, but of the concrete
presence in Israel of legislative and administrative State institutions – supreme among them the Great Sanhedrin – and above
all of the universally acknowledged cultic centre, the Temple
of Jerusalem. These tangible criteria of unity allowed for a
much greater elasticity as long as the central core of Judaism
– Bible interpretation, teaching and religious observance –
remained intact.

Thus as two first-century AD Jewish writers, Philo and Josephus, and indirectly the New Testament, make abundantly
clear, the Jewish population of Palestine was at that period
influenced by four parties or sects (in Greek designated as
haireseis, 'heresies', i.e. divisions, with no pejorative meaning
attached to the term). Three of these, the Sadducees, the
Pharisees and the Zealots, competed for the leadership of the
nation; a fourth, the Essenes, withdrew from the political scene
and made their moral and doctrinal impact from outside it.
A more recent foundation was that of the Judaeo-Christians,
who formed themselves into an autonomous community in the
thirties of the first century. These were the major religious
movements of Palestine and, as might be expected since they
display more or less striking similarities with the Qumran
Community, each has been suggested as a likely candidate in
the search for an identification.

Judaeo-Christianity can be eliminated first; for despite the
arguments, more specious than real, of two scholars, J. L.
Teicher of Cambridge and Y. Baer of Jerusalem, equating the
Dead Sea sect with the primitive Church, and despite parallels
which undoubtedly exist between the Scrolls and the New
Testament as will be shown in chapter 8, it will be obvious to
most readers, whether experts or not, that the Qumran writings
cannot be mistaken for Christian literature. Neither can the
persons of Jesus and other New Testament characters be found
in the leading figures alluded to in the Dead Sea manuscripts.
But if this were not enough, proponents of the Christian
hypothesis must further explain away the archaeological data,
all of which point to a pre-Christian (second century BC)
origin of the Qumran sect. The conclusion must be that the
theory is untenable, and we are left in consequence with four
serious alternatives: Sadducees, Pharisees, Zealots and Essenes.
In examining them, we will look for a correspondence of aims
and organization rather than of doctrines and beliefs, which
could easily have been shared.

1 The Sadducees

The Sadducees, so called by Josephus and the New Testament, formed the upper tier of Jewish society. They were the select few of highest standing, the party of the wealthy, allied to the high priests and leading sacerdotal families (*Antiquities* xiii, 296, 298; xviii, 4; xx, 199; Acts 5:17, etc.). It is this association with the Zadokite priesthood that is no doubt responsible for their name *zadduqim*, or Sadducees. As true aristocrats, they were conservative. Standing firm by the written law, they tended to apply it in its original strictness and severity, resisting the innovations attempted by their opponents in the guise of Bible exegesis (*Antiquities* xiii. 294, 296; xviii. 16; xx. 199). Apart from the short rule of Queen Alexandra-Salome or Shelamzion (76–67 BC), who surrounded herself with Pharisees, the political and religious influence of the Sadducees predominated in the high court and senate of Judaea, the Jerusalem Sanhedrin, from the time when John Hyrcanus I (134–104 BC) joined their ranks to the outbreak of the first revolution against Rome in AD 66.

A scholarly endeavour to identify the Qumran Community with this group does not seem *a priori* impossible. Both parties flourished during the same period. Both had, or claimed to possess, close bonds with the priesthood, the Sadducees appearing as regular supporters and champions of the pontifical leadership in Jerusalem and the Qumran sectaries subjecting themselves to the supreme authority of the priests, the sons of Zadok, assisted by the lay members of their Covenant.

These resemblances, however, are heavily outweighed by dissimilarities between the two groups. Thus the Sadducees are described in Greek as a *hairesis*, a sect (*Antiquities* xiii. 171; Acts 5:17), but there is no indication whatever of their having had any sectarian organization like that of the Qumran Community. Again, the Qumran Community knew itself as 'the Poor' (1QpHab 12:3, 6), the very opposite of the condition of the Sadducee movement. Also, the Sadducees were nearly always the governing party in Judaea, whereas the Qumran brotherhood considered their existence as spent in exile.

Finally, whilst Sadducee High Priests and their associates were the principal figures in the Temple of Jerusalem, one branch of the Dead Sea sect, the Zadokites of the desert, looked on the Sanctuary as contaminated, and on worship offered there as an abomination, and refused to have anything to do with it. Their dream was of the day, in the seventh year of the eschatological war, when all that wicked priesthood would be swept away and replaced by holy priests and a pure divine office. It is safe enough therefore to assert that the Qumran sectaries were emphatically not Sadducees.

2 The Pharisees

According to the popular Jewish view, traceable to an uncritical acceptance of the information contained in rabbinic literature, the Pharisees from the second century BC onwards were the doctrinal leaders of the nation, occupied as a rule both the presidency and vice-presidency of the Jerusalem Sanhedrin, and exercised absolute and effective control over Palestinian Jewry. The Pharisee, moreover, was a man whose strict observance of the entire Mosaic Law, of the written Bible as well as of the revelation received on Sinai and transmitted by oral tradition, was inspired by deep learning and piety. The Christian popular concept, derived from the polemical exaggerations of Matthew 23, is very different: Pharisaism was an amalgam of hypocrisy, ambition and narrow-mindedness, an overwhelming concern with the minutiae of religion and a consequent neglect of its essence. 'Woe to you, scribes and Pharisees, hypocrites! for you tithe mint and dill and cummin, and have neglected the weightier matters of the law, justice and mercy and faith' (Mt. 23:23). Needless to say, both these portraits, Jewish and Christian, distort historical reality.

Josephus, who himself decided to embrace Pharisaism despite his priestly descent (*Life* 1, 12), asserts that at the beginning of the reign of Herod, the Pharisees were a sect, a *hairesis*, numbering hardly more than six thousand members. They were therefore slightly more numerous than the Essene brotherhood with its four thousand adherents. By no stretch of the imagination can they be represented as a large body within the Jewish nation. Their nickname may also point to their sectarian nature. For although rabbinic sources very seldom employ it, preferring to allude to them as scribes or sages, Josephus and the New Testament regularly use the title Pharisee. This word, *parish* in Aramaic and *parush* in Hebrew, signifies a separated person, and is in all probability intended to convey the meaning of one who keeps himself apart from the common people, from the peasants or *am ha-arez*. The Pharisees, in short, were a fairly small pious enclave within Jewish society.

Yet though their numbers were restricted, their influence was unquestionably great, above all in the towns and cities (*Antiquities* xviii. 15). In particular, they enjoyed high renown for their expertise in the interpretation of the Bible, and especially of biblical law; when the ancient sources take the trouble to reveal the party allegiance of great teachers such as Pollion and his pupil Samaias, Gamaliel and his son Simeon, each of them turns out to be a Pharisee (*Antiquities* xv. 3, 370; *Life* 191; Act. 5:34).

Josephus also discloses that the Pharisees were popular (*Antiquities* xii. 294) and that they were liked by devout women (xvii. 41). In matters of worship their teaching was regularly followed (xviii. 15), and in public functions even the Sadducees adopted their rulings 'since otherwise the masses would not tolerate them' (xviii. 17). But Pharisee piety was extra zealous in matters pertaining to dietary laws, tithing and ritual purity, all of which necessitated continuous attention to petty details. It had nevertheless not been the intention of the creators of Pharisaism, noble characters such as Antigonus of Sokho, Hillel, or Gamaliel the Elder, to lose sight of the essence of religion. Rather was it the reverse; the status of every Pharisee was to be raised to the dignity of a Temple priest, and his table to the holiness of God's table in Jerusalem.

To pursue these aims, the Pharisees formed themselves into closed fellowships or *haburoth* to which new members were admitted after a trial period varying from thirty days to a year, though where candidates were familiar with the rules of the

ḥaburah and accustomed to practising them, they could be
admitted immediately. Once accepted, a man could be either
a *neeman*, a 'trustworthy man', or a *ḥaber*, a fellow. A *neeman*
was obliged merely to tithe everything bought, sold and eaten
by him, and to refrain from staying in the house of a non-
initiate. A *ḥaber* was required to submit in his daily life to the
stringent rules of levitical purity to which the priests were
subject when partaking of their sacred meals.

Membership of the *ḥaburah* was thought to be incompatible
with certain professions considered dishonourable. If a *ḥaber*
became a tax-collector, he was expelled. If on the other hand,
he resigned from this detested calling, he could re-enter as a
'trustworthy man', though not as a fellow.

These fragments of information provide no more than an
outline of the complex reality of Pharisaism but they show
parallels with the Qumran sect. The Pharisees and the people
at Qumran were devout, consecrated to the study and practice
of biblical religion; both parties aimed at purity and holiness
and kept themselves apart in order to attain to it. In connection
with the initiation of new members and the rejection of the
unworthy, other similarities are evident, more general than
distinctive. Yet, although these coincidences reveal common
aspirations and possibly a common origin, the most important
Qumran features are lacking in documents relating to the
Pharisees.

One of these is the placing of ultimate authority at Qumran
in the hands of the priests: the Pharisees were essentially a lay
organization. Some Pharisees belonged to priestly families –
Josephus was one of them – but this appears to have been the
exception rather than the rule. Another difference is that
whereas the Qumran sectaries and the Pharisees set themselves
apart from the common people, the Pharisees continued to be
involved with them and to teach them, while the Dead Sea
brotherhood reserved the treasures of their doctrine for initiates
alone. Also, although admission to the Pharisee *ḥaburah*
proceeded by stages, they were more elastic than their Qumran
counterparts; the Pharisee could for instance enter without

undergoing a 'noviciate'. And again, there is no hint in accounts of the Pharisees of the common ownership of property so emphatically stressed in the Scrolls as a precondition to membership of the Council of the Community.

Last but not least, celibacy at Qumran cannot be ruled out and remains indeed highly probable. Among the Pharisees such a custom not only did not exist but was disapproved of in principle, if that is to say we are allowed to see in them the source of the firmly established and strongly held view of their rabbinic successors that procreation is a religious duty. 'Be fruitful and multiply,' they taught, is the first commandment proclaimed by God, and voluntary abstention from it is tantamount for murder.

Were the Qumran sectaries Pharisees? The answer is no.

3 The Zealots

The theory claiming that the Qumran sectaries were Zealots, i.e. members of the revolutionary movement initiated at the beginning of the Christian era by Judas the Galilean, was advanced in Oxford in the late 1950s by the late Sir Godfrey Driver and the late Cecil Roth.

A proper assessment of this idea is made the more difficult in that academic opinion concerning the Zealots is confused. There are two principal reasons for this. Firstly, the evidence of the main source, Josephus, is tendentious. He hated the Zealots and held them fully responsible for the disaster of AD 70. For him they were nothing but brigands and murderers. Secondly, the title 'Zealot' is an umbrella notion under which all sorts of revolutionaries sheltered. Recently, however, matters have become even more chaotic as a result of attempts to supplement Josephus's meagre information on Zealot teaching with a concatenation of data borrowed from later rabbinic sources. On the other hand, while admitting the fluidity of both the terminology and the historical realities, enough essential information undoubtedly exists for a basic outline of the 'philosophical school', or religious party, of the Zealots to be reconstructed.

Josephus writes that in AD 6, after complaints lodged against him by Jewish and Samaritan dignitaries had resulted in the banishment of Herod Archelaus, ethnarch of the Jews, Judaea was converted into a Roman province. This administrative change was preceded by a registration or *census* for purposes of taxation ordered and executed by the legate of Syria, Publius Sulpicius Quirinius. (The Gospel of Luke wrongly places this event in the reign of Herod the Great, who died ten years earlier.) To Judas the Galilean and to a Pharisee called Zadok, such a *census* appeared intolerable, and they advocated rebellion and launched a patriotic movement. Their manifesto was short: God is the one Lord, therefore no tribute must be paid to the emperor of Rome. Apart from these two dogmatic points, one positive and the other negative, Josephus has little to add to their Zealot 'philosophy', and even that seems to be contradictory. As an illustration, in his earlier account (*War* ii. 118) he asserts that the Zealots are unlike anything else in Judaism; then some twenty years later (*Antiquities* xviii. 23) he represents them as a group indistinguishable from the Pharisees except for their burning passion for freedom. He does not give a name to the movement started by Judas, but makes it clear in sundry references that Judas's rebellious spirit was shared by other members of his family. Judas himself was killed (Acts 5:37); two of his sons, Jacob and Simon, were crucified by Tiberius Julius Alexander, procurator of Judaea (AD 46–8); more relations took part in the first war against the Romans, as will be indicated presently. The title 'Zealot' definitely existed earlier in the first century: one of the apostles of Jesus was called Simon the Zealot (Lk. 6:15; Acts 1:13), or *Kananaios* (Mt. 10:4 – a garbled Greek transliteration of the Aramaic *qannai* = Zealot) – but positive evidence for its use by the revolutionaries dates only to the time of the war of AD 66–70 (*War* iv. 160). A few years earlier, a faction associated with the family of Judas the Galilean had been active, known as *Sicarii*, men armed with a *sica*, a curved dagger (*War* ii. 254). These had supported Menahem, the last surviving son of Judas the Galilean, in his attempt to seize the leadership of the uprising. When he was murdered in Jerusalem (*War* ii. 433–48), they established themselves in the fortress of Masada under the command of Eleazar the son of Jairus, probably a grandson of Judas, and from there carried on the fight with the Romans until AD 74 (see chapter 1, pp. 19–20).

A few arguments can be adduced in favour of identifying the Qumran sect as Zealots. The final adversaries mentioned in the War Rule are Kittim/Romans led by a 'king'. More support comes from the discovery of a Qumran sectarian writing (the Angelic liturgy), first attested in Cave 4, in the ruins of the Zealot stronghold of Masada. But as proofs they are hardly convincing. Archaeological evidence shows in any case that the Qumran establishment was occupied from about 140 BC while the Zealot party did not come into being until AD 6. If it were identical with the Community of the Scrolls, there would have been visible changes at one point in the Qumran settlement which the excavations have in fact not confirmed. Besides, the general description of the Community as it emerges from its literature has nothing in common with the Zealots and their aims and aspirations; though no real comparison can be made because nothing is known of the Zealot organization, the reason perhaps being that as an underground movement they could not afford to possess an identifiable structure.

As for the discovery of a Qumran writing at Masada, it does not *ipso facto* equate the inhabitants of the Dead Sea establishment with the garrison of Masada. It is more likely to mean, either that some of the Qumran sectaries made common cause with the revolution during the last stage of the Community's history and brought their manuscripts to Masada with them, or that the Masada rebels considered the Qumran Community politically unreliable and seized its settlement as the Romans advanced towards the Dead Sea.

In short, identification of the Qumran sectaries as Zealots is without any solid basis, and the attempt made by Driver and Roth to expound various cryptic historical allusions in the Scrolls as pointing to events that took place during the first

Jewish revolution is without recognizable substance. The most convincing testimony to the precariousness of the Zealot-Qumran hypothesis is perhaps that since the death of its two eminent but extravagant proponents it has been allowed to sink into obscurity.

4 The Essenes

The Essenes, unmentioned in the New Testament, are extensively described by Josephus and his older contemporary, the Jewish philosopher Philo of Alexandria. Another first century author, the Roman geographer and naturalist Pliny the Elder, devotes only one paragraph to them, but those few lines include information of inestimable value.

Unlike the three other religious parties discussed here, the Essenes formed a sect proper. They lived on the fringes of Jewish society as an esoteric community and imposed a lengthy initiation on aspiring candidates. Chronologically, Josephus first introduces them as one of three groups – the other two being the Pharisees and the Sadducees – in the middle of the second century BC under Jonathan Maccabaeus (*Antiquities* xiii. 171), and continues to attest their existence until his own time. Indeed, he himself experimented with the Essene way of life when he was sixteen years old (he was born in AD 37–8): (*Life* 10–11). Josephus and Philo locate the sect in Palestine (*War* ii. 124; *Probus* 75–6; *Hypothetica* 11.1), and both estimate that it numbered over four thousand souls (*Antiquities* xviii. 21; *Probus* 75). Pliny places the Essenes by the Dead Sea on the western shore (*Natural History* v. 73).

The sect was rigorously organized. Its superiors were elected. Reception into its ranks proceeded by degrees; every novice had to undergo a year of probation before being permitted to take part in the ritual ablutions and, following this, a further two years of training. He had then to make his vows as a full member and was accepted at the common table. If he subsequently offended against the rule in grave matters, he was excommunicated by a community tribunal composed of one hundred judges.

The Essenes practised a kind of communism. The fully professed members were required to hand over their belongings and earnings to stewards, and all their needs were met. Buying and selling was thereby excluded among themselves, and if Philo is to be believed, even with outsiders. Pliny also asserts that the Essenes lived *sine pecunia*, without money.

All three ancient witnesses are unanimous in their testimony that the Essenes shunned marriage and chose celibacy. Josephus, however, adds that there was in addition a branch of married Essenes.

Another Essene feature was their critical attitude to the Temple. Philo alludes to their rejection of animal sacrifice. Josephus is more equivocal; on the one hand he reports that they sent offerings to the sanctuary, but in the next sentence we are told that they kept away from its precincts and substituted their own worship for that in Jerusalem. Also, instead of the ritual washing of hands, they took purificatory baths before eating like the priests in the Temple. Their meals, according to Josephus, were special and solemn, and were eaten in refectories open, like sanctuaries, to initiates only. Sacred white garments were worn, and priests – who also prepared the simple food – recited grace before and after the meal.

The Essenes were opposed to slavery. They were also against taking vows, except of course the formidable oath sworn on reception into the sect by which they undertook, among other obligations, not to divulge their peculiar doctrines to non-members. They observed the Sabbath and obeyed the laws of purity more punctiliously than the rest of Jewry. Another of their specialities, one that would appear to argue the derivation of their Greek name *Essaioi* from the Aramaic *asayya*, 'healers', was an interest in healing implied by Josephus's reference to their expert knowledge of the medicinal properties of roots and stones.

In view of the undeniable similarities and overlaps between the sect of the Scrolls and the Essenism of the classical accounts, it is not surprising that ever since the early days of Qumran a strong school of thought has regarded the two as identical.

Its case is as follows:

Josephus's testimony concerning the Essenes, and the archaeological finds made at Qumran, point to the same chronological context: from the middle of the second century BC to the first Jewish war (AD 66–70).

Likewise, Pliny's location of the Essene village appears to correspond to the Qumran site; but here some explanation is called for. Pliny first mentions Jericho, then the Essenes by the Dead Sea, then Engedi 'below them' (*infra hos Engada*), a town situated twenty-eight miles south of Jericho; and finally Masada, south of Engedi. The general direction of his description is therefore from north to south. But what does the phrase 'below them' mean? It may be interpreted in two senses. Literally, it could indicate that the Essenes lived in the vicinity of Engedi, on some place high above the town. If so, the Qumran site is excluded since it lies twenty miles north of Engedi. But the likelihood of an Essene establishment near Engedi is anyway slender. A thorough exploration of the area by Benjamin Mazar and his team of Israeli archaeologists in the early 1960s revealed no ruins remotely connected with Pliny's account. On the other hand, if 'below them' means 'south of them', or 'further down', or 'downstream', in the context of Pliny's journey southward, then Qumran fits perfectly: travelling eight miles south of Jericho we come to Qumran; twenty miles south of Qumran, to Engedi; and eleven miles south of Engedi, to Masada. In the absence of a rival archaeological site, Pliny's evidence offers a powerful argument in favour of the Essene thesis.

Then there is the information contained in the Scrolls themselves, which on many points coincides with the Greek and Latin reports on the Essenes; though there are also differences. Thus Essenes and Qumran desert sectaries both favoured the common ownership of property, both refused to participate in Temple worship, both had purificatory baths, both partook of a sacred meal blessed by a priest. Both furthermore were opposed to taking vows apart from the vow of entry, and both appear to have been interested in healing (in the Scrolls it figures at the head of the spiritual blessings). As for celibacy, although it is not positively referred to in the Qumran Community Rule, its probability in the monastic brotherhood has been shown to be great.

Geography, chronology, and especially organization and customs, therefore militate in favour of a close relationship between Essenism and Qumran: at the very least they both belong to the same general movement. But before suggesting that we have here something more, the conflicting evidence must also be honestly confronted.

Some of the difficulties arise from internal contradictions. For instance, the Community Rule envisages common ownership, but the Damascus Rule legislates also in matters of private property. Or while Pliny, Philo and Josephus emphasize that the Essenes were celibate, Josephus admits elsewhere that there were also married sectaries. Again, Philo, and Josephus in his later work (*Antiquities*), state that the Essenes were opposed to slavery; but Josephus in his earlier and much more detailed account (*War*) says nothing of this. The Damascus Rule, on the other hand, implies, by its ban on the sale to a Gentile of a slave converted to Judaism, that such slaves may have been owned by members of the Dead Sea sect.

Other points of difference exist between the Scrolls and the Graeco-Latin documents. In the latter, the sectaries are called Essenes, a title completely absent from the Hebrew-Aramaic sources. At Qumran, the oath is the first act in the initiation procedure; among the Essenes of Josephus it is the last.

Apart from the possibility that some of the discrepancies may represent various stages of development, this lack of conformity between the classical evidence and the Scrolls may be attributed to two causes: the varying reliability of the witnesses and the diversity of the readership addressed.

Pliny, Philo and Josephus are not fully trustworthy. This is not to say that they deceive deliberately, though Philo in particular is apt to force his story so that it illustrates some cherished philosophical principle. For example, he mentions in *Probus* 76 that the Essenes avoided the cities, a habit of which he approved. Yet in *Hypothetica* 11.1, he writes that they lived 'in many towns of Judaea'. But even if all three had intended to tell the whole unadulterated truth, it would not have been in their power. Neither of them was a full member of the Essene sect so neither was privy to its secret teachings. Nor as non-initiates would they have understood in any depth the Essene customs with which they were superficially familiar.

As far as the readership of the two types of literature is concerned, the fact that the Scrolls were directed to internal use among the sectaries themselves, whereas Philo, Josephus and Pliny wrote for non-Essenes and even largely for non-Jews, is bound to have affected the presentation of their material. Thus Josephus reports on the Essene abstinence from vows (though he knows of the vow taken on admission), and from animal sacrifice, and also on their frequent purificatory baths, with a view to presenting the sectaries as Jewish equivalents to the Pythagoraeans, a much admired Hellenistic philosophico-religious group renowned for such practices. That this is not speculation, and that Josephus actually intended to portray his Jewish 'philosophies' as comparable to Greek schools of thought, is patent to anyone familiar with his description of the Pharisees as quasi-Stoics (*Life* 12), and of the Essenes as 'a group which follows a way of life taught to the Greeks by Pythagoras' (*Antiquities* xv. 371).

When these observations are borne in mind, most of the conflicts can be solved without difficulty. The contradictions between celibacy and marriage (Josephus testifies unwillingly, as it were, to the same duality of practice) and between communism and private ownership, are to be seen in the context of the difference between the strict discipline imposed on the members of the Council at Qumran and the less demanding regulations followed by the other members of the Covenant. The discrepant information about when the oath was sworn may be due to Josephus's desire to emphasize the secret character of the Essene association. Similarly the Scrolls impart a new meaning to the confused classical information in that the War Rule makes it plain that, where it existed, the ban on Temple worship was not absolute but temporary, and valid only while the Temple was in the hands of the wicked priests.

As for the absence of the word 'Essene' from the Scrolls, the title 'Pharisee' is likewise generally avoided in rabbinic sources. Both names appear to have been coined and used by outsiders. So the non-employment of the Hebrew/Aramaic word for 'Essene' cannot be used as an argument against the Essene thesis.

The final verdict must therefore be that of the proposed solutions the Essene theory is relatively the soundest. It is even safe to say that it possesses a high degree of intrinsic probability. The only remaining alternative is that the archaeologists have uncovered relics of a hitherto totally unknown Jewish sect almost identical to the Essenes: which reminds one of the story of the Old Testament scholar who would not accept that Joshua led the Israelites in the conquest of Canaan and argued that the real leader was a cousin who happened to bear the same name.

BIBLIOGRAPHY TO CHAPTER 5

Among the many general works devoted to inter-Testamental Judaism the following are particularly recommended: Schürer–Vermes–Millar, *The History of the Jewish People in the Age of Jesus Christ* I (Clark, Edinburgh, 1973) [Political history from 175 BC to AD 135]; II (to appear in 1978) [Institutions and movements]. On a less technical level see *The Jewish People in the First Century*, ed. S. Safrai and M. Stern (Van Gorcum, Assen and Fortress, Philadelphia, I [1974]; II [1977]). See also M. Simon, *Les sectes juives au temps de Jésus Christ* (Presses Universitaires de France, Paris, 1960) and J. Jeremias, *Jerusalem in the Time of Jesus* (S.C.M., London and Fortress, Philadelphia, 1969). For the reconstruction of Judaism at Jamnia, cf. J. Neusner, *A Life of Yohanan ben Zakkai* (Brill, Leiden, ²1970).

For the organization of the synagogue and its worship, including the Eighteen Benedictions, see Schürer–Vermes–Millar–Black II, §27.

The identification of the Qumran sect as a Christian community was first advanced in a series of articles by J. L. Teicher in JJS 2–5 (1950–4). The same view has been expressed by Y. Baer, '*Serekh ha-Yaḥad* – The Manual of Discipline. A Jewish-Christian Document from the Beginning of the Second Century CE', *Zion 29* (1960), 1–60 in Hebrew. For a more recent theory, see B. E. Thiering, *Redating the Teacher of Righteousness* (Theological Explorations, Sidney, 1979).

1 The Sadducees
For a general discussion, see Schürer–Vermes–Millar–Black II, §26 with full bibliography. J. Le Moyne, *Les Sadducéens* (Gabalda, Paris, 1972) [a comprehensive survey]. See also R. Meyer, art. 'Sadducee', TDNT VII (1971), 35–54.

The only endeavour to identify the Qumran sectaries and

Sadducees is that of R. North, 'The Qumran Sadducees', CBQ 17 (1955), 164–88.

2 The Pharisees

Once again see Schürer–Vermes–Millar–Black II, §26 for a general examination of the subject and bibliography. The following are a few of a large number of monographs: R. T. Herford, *The Pharisees* (Allen & Unwin, London, 1924); L. Finkelstein, *The Pharisees* I–II (Jewish Publication Society of America, Philadelphia, ³1962); A. Michel – J. Le Moyne, 'Pharisiens', *Dict. de la Bible, Suppl.* VII (1966), 1022–1115; J. Neusner, *The Rabbinic Traditions about the Pharisees before 70* I–III (Brill, Leiden, 1970) [a pioneering form-critical examination of the rabbinic sources]; *From Politics to Piety: The Emergence of Pharisaic Judaism* (Prentice-Hall, Englewood Cliffs N.J., 1973); R. Meyer – H. F. Weiss, 'Pharisee', TDNT IX (1974), 11–48; E. Rivkin, 'Pharisees', IDBS (1976), 657–63. The constitution of the *ḥaburoth* is outlined in Schürer–Vermes–Millar–Black II §26. The relationship of the Qumran sect to the *ḥaburah* has been discussed by S. Lieberman, 'The Discipline of the so-called Manual of Discipline, JBL 71 (1952), 199–206 [= *Texts and Studies* (Ktav, New York, 1974), 200–7]; C. Rabin, *Qumran Studies* (O.U.P., Oxford, 1957).

For the rabbinic attitude towards celibacy, see G. F. Moore, *Judaism* II (Harvard U.P., Cambridge, 1927), 119–20, 270; G. Vermes, *Jesus the Jew* (Collins, London, 1973 and Fortress, Philadelphia, 1981), 101–2; E. Rivkin, *The Hidden Revolution* (Abingdon, Nashville, 1978).

3 The Zealots

Schürer–Vermes–Millar–Black II contains an Appendix on the Zealots compiled by C. T. R. Hayward.

The most important and extensive monograph is by M. Hengel, *Die Zeloten* (Brill, Leiden, 1961, ²1976); cf. also 'Zeloten und Sikarier', *Josephus-Studien* (O. Michel Festschrift), ed. O. Betz *et al.* (Vandenhoeck & Ruprecht, Göttingen, 1974), 175–96. The following general studies are available in English: W. R. Farmer, *Maccabees, Zealots, Josephus* (Columbia,

New York, 1956); S. G. F. Brandon, *Jesus and the Zealots* (Manchester U.P., Manchester, 1967); M. Stern, 'Zealots', *Encyclopaedia Judaica Yearbook* (Keter, Jerusalem, 1973), 135–52; E. M. Smallwood, *The Jews under Roman Rule* (Brill, Leiden, 1976), 153–5, 312–69; D. M. Rhoads, *Israel in Revolution 6–74 CE* (Fortress Press, Philadelphia, 1976).

Among the learned articles published in recent years the most important are: M. Smith, 'Zealots and Sicarii: their Origins and Relations', HTR 64 (1971), 1–19; M. Borg, 'The Currency of the Term Zealot', JTS 22 (1971), 504–12; S. Applebaum, 'The Zealots: the Case for Revaluation', JRS 61 (1971), 1956–70; V. Nikiprowetzky, 'Sicaires et Zélotes – une reconsidération', *Semitica* 23 (1973), 51–64.

The results of the archaeological excavations at Masada referred to on p. 19 are summarized and illustrated in Y. Yadin, *Masada: Herod's Fortress and the Zealots' Last Stand* (Weidenfeld & Nicolson, London, 1966).

The theory identifying the Qumran sect with the Zealots was the creation in the mid-1950s of my greatly missed colleague G. R. (later Sir Godfrey) Driver and my predecessor Cecil Roth. Their plan for a joint publication misfired when Roth released his thesis unilaterally in *The Historical Background of the Dead Sea Scrolls* (Blackwell, Oxford, 1958), claiming the theory as his own and that he was the first to voice it in seminars in early 1957. 'At the same time,' Roth explains in the Introduction, 'I communicated my views to my colleague Professor G. R. Driver, who accepted them generously . . .' (p. vii). Driver's much more substantial book (624 pages against Roth's 87) had to wait another seven years before completion: *The Judaean Scrolls: the Problem and a Solution* (Blackwell, Oxford, 1965). In the Preface, Driver's version of the same incident reads: '. . . in 1953 I showed that the same document (the Commentary on Habakkuk) alluded to an event which took place in AD 70 . . . When . . . early in 1957 . . . Dr C. Roth, who knew my views, drew my attention to the same solution, I saw at once that a fresh investigation would be required, and I invited him to join me in carrying it out' (p. ix).

4 The Essenes

As a preamble to an Essene bibliography a few notes are called for on the ancient writers who serve as primary sources.

Flavius Josephus, originally called Joseph son of Mattathias before adopting a Roman name, was a Jewish priest. He was born in AD 37-8 and died *c.* 100. During the war against the Romans he was the rebel commander-in-chief of Galilee, but surrendered, and afterwards settled in Rome. He wrote four works in Greek. (1) *The Jewish War*, mostly devoted to the history of the revolution, was completed in the late 70s. Book ii. 119-61 discusses the Essenes. (2) *Jewish Antiquities*, concluded in AD 93-4, relates the history of the Jewish people from its beginning to AD 66, the outbreak of the first revolution. The two main but brief notices on the Essenes appear in xii. 171-2 and xviii. 18-22. (3) *The Life* deals mainly with Josephus's activities in AD 66-7 as commander of Galilee. It was written in the second half of the 90s. Sections 11-12 allude to Josephus's association with the Essenes. (4) *Against Apion*, a vindication of Judaism, was composed after *Antiquities*, which it cites. A bilingual Greek-English edition of the whole of Josephus is available in the Loeb Classical Library in ten volumes. For an introduction see Schürer–Vermes–Millar I, 43-63.

Philo of Alexandria, the Jewish philosopher and interpreter of the Bible, was probably born in the 20s BC. The date of his death is unknown, but he was still alive in AD 40, for in that year he led an Alexandrian Jewish embassy to the emperor Gaius Caligula. His principal treatise on the Essenes is entitled, *Every Good Man is Free*, or, *Quod omnis probus liber sit* 75-91. Extracts from a shorter account contained in his *Hypothetica* or *Apology for the Jews* have been saved for posterity by the Church historian Eusebius in his *Praeparatio evangelica* viii, 11.1-18. Philo is also the author of *On the Contemplative Life*, where he describes the Therapeutae, a Jewish group of ascetics living in Egypt. Like Josephus, Philo wrote in Greek. His writings, with an English translation, fill twelve volumes of the Loeb Classical Library.

Pliny the Elder (AD 23/4-79) is the author of a famous

Natural History in Latin. Consisting of thirty-seven books, it was completed two years before his death in the eruption of Vesuvius which also buried Pompeii and Herculaneum. His paragraph on the Essenes appears in a geographical description of Judaea (v. 73). The same Loeb Library includes *Naturalis Historia* in a Latin-English edition.

All the Greek and Latin texts are assembled in a handy booklet by A. Adam and C. Burchard, *Antike Berichte über die Essener* (W. de Gruyter, Berlin, ²1972). An English translation of all the main texts is also included in A. Dupont-Sommer, *The Essene Writings from Qumran* (Blackwell, Oxford, 1961), 21-38. For a historical survey of the research into Essenism from the end of the eighteenth to the beginning of the twentieth century, cf. S. Wagner, *Die Essener in der wissenschaftlichen Diskussion* (Töpelmann, Berlin, 1960).

A comprehensive bibliography (pp. 66-88) is appended to the work of Adam and Burchard quoted above. For a general introduction with a selected book list, see Schürer–Vermes–Millar–Black II, §30.

For a full discussion of the meaning of the term Essene, see Vermes, PBJS, 8-36.

The identification of the Qumran Community as an Essene sect was first suggested by E. L. Sukenik, *Megillot genuzot* [Hidden Scrolls] I (Bialik, Jerusalem, 1948), 16, and more systematically advanced by A. Dupont-Sommer, *Aperçus préliminaires sur les manuscrits de la Mer Morte* (Maisonneuve, Paris, 1950), 105-17. His thesis is fully developed in *The Essene Writings . . .* (1961).

Pliny's evidence is examined and applied to Qumran by R. de Vaux, *Archaeology*, 133-7. For the two baths identified at Qumran, cf. ibid. 9-10, 131-2.

On the question of celibacy, see chapter 7, pp. 181-2; Vermes, *Jesus the Jew*, 99-102, 245-6.

For attempts to prove that the Qumran sectaries were not Essenes, see M. H. Goshen-Gottstein, 'Anti-Essene Traits in the Dead Sea Scrolls', VT 4 (1954), 141-7; C. Roth, 'Why the Qumran Sect cannot have been Essenes', RQ 1 (1959), 417-22;

'Were the Qumran Sectaries Essenes?', JTS 10 (1959), 87–93; G. R. Driver, *The Judaean Scrolls*, 100–21.

This bibliographical survey would remain incomplete without some reference to that other ascetic group described by Philo, the Therapeutae, i.e. Worshippers/Healers, whom he associates with the Essenes in regard to aims and inspirations. The essential difference between them as he presents it is that the Essenes were active, i.e. combined prayer and study with manual work, whereas the contemplative Therapeutae spent all their life in meditation and worship. For a bilingual Greek-English edition of *On the Contemplative Life*, see vol. IX of Philo in the Loeb Library. See also P. Geoltrain, '*Le Traité de la Vie contemplative de Philon d'Alexandrie*', *Semitica* 10 (1960), 5–67; F. Daumas-P. Miquel, *Les Oeuvres de Philon d'Alexandrie* vol. 29 (Cerf, Paris, 1963).

For a link between Therapeutae, Essenes and Qumran, see Vermes, 'Essenes-Therapeutae-Qumran', *Durham University Journal* 21 (1960), 97–115; PBJS, 30–6; Schürer–Vermes–Millar–Black II, §30.

The church historian Eusebius erroneously identified the Therapeutae as Egyptian Jewish ascetics converted to Christianity (*Ecclesiastical History* ii. 16–17). Whilst his thesis is untenable, an influence of the Therapeutae on Christian monasticism still remains a serious possibility. See F. Daumas, 'La solitude des Thérapeutes et les antécédents égyptiens du monachism chrétien', *Philon d'Alexandrie – Lyon 11–15 September 1966* (Colloques Nationaux du CNRS) (CNRS, Paris, 1967), 347–58; A. Guillaumont, 'Philon et les origines du monachisme', ibid. 361–73.

CHAPTER 6

History of the Sect

The absence from the Dead Sea Scrolls of historical texts proper should not surprise us. Neither in the inter-Testamental period, nor in earlier biblical times, was the recording of history as we understand it a strong point among the Jews. Chroniclers are concerned not with factual information about past events, but with their religious significance. In Scripture, the 'secular' past is viewed and interpreted by the prophets as revealing God's pleasure or displeasure. Victory or defeat in war, peace or social unrest, abundance of harvest or famine, serve to demonstrate the virtue or sinfulness of the nation and to forecast its future destiny. And when prophecy declined in the fifth century BC, it was still not succeeded by a growth of historiography: only the memoirs of Ezra and Nehemiah and the retelling of the age-old stories of the kings of Israel and Judah in the Books of Chronicles belong to the historical *genre*. It was followed instead by eschatological speculation, by apocalyptic visions of the end of time, with its awe-inspiring beasts and battles, and by announcements of the ultimate triumph of truth and justice in a future kingdom of God.

In the Scrolls, the apocalyptic compositions form part of this later tradition. On the other hand, most of the knowledge we possess of the sect's history is inserted into works of Bible interpretation. The Qumran writers, while meditating on the words of the Old Testament prophets, sought to discover in them allusions to their own past, present and future. Convinced that they were living in the last days, they read the happenings of their times as the fulfilment of biblical predictions.

Yet all that these non-historical sources provide are fragments.

Even with the help of the archaeological data from Qumran they cannot be made into a consistent and continuous narrative. For an understanding of the sect's history as it occurred within the larger framework of inter-Testamental Jewish history, we have to rely principally on Flavius Josephus, the Palestinian Jew who became a Greek man of letters, and on other Jewish Hellenists, such as the authors of the Greek Books of the Maccabees, and Philo of Alexandria, all of whom inherited the Greek predilection for recording and interpreting the past and set out to depict the life of the Jews of Palestine in itself, and as part of the Graeco-Roman world, from the early second century BC to the first anti-Roman war in AD 66–70. It is only with the help of the wider canvas painted by these ancient scholars that places can be found for the often cryptic historical indications contained in the Scrolls.

1 INTER-TESTAMENTAL JEWISH HISTORY: 200 BC–AD 70
At the beginning of the second century BC, Palestinian Jewry passed through a state of crisis. Alexander the Great had conquered the Holy Land in 332 BC and, after the early uncertainties which followed his death, it became part of the empire of the Greeks of Egypt, the Ptolemies. During the third century, the Ptolemies avoided, as much as possible, interfering with the internal life of the Jewish nation and, while taxes were required to be paid, it remained under the rule of the High Priest and his council. Important changes in the patterns of population nevertheless took place during this time. Hellenistic cities were built along the Mediterranean coast, such as Gaza, Ascalon (Ashkelon), Joppa (Jaffa), Dor, and Acco re-named Ptolemais. Inland also, to the south of the Lake of Tiberias, the ancient town of Beth Shean was reborn as the Greek city of Scythopolis; Samaria, the capital city of the Samaritans, was Hellenized; and in Transjordan, Rabbath-Ammon (Amman) was re-founded as Philadelphia. In other words, Greeks, Macedonians and Hellenized Phoenicians took up permanent residence on Palestinian soil and the further spread of Greek civilization and culture was merely a matter of time.

With the conquest of the Holy Land by the Seleucids, or Syrian Greeks, in 200 BC, the first signs appeared of Jews succumbing to a foreign cultural influence. In the apocryphal Book of Ecclesiasticus dated to the beginning of the second century BC, its author, Jesus ben Sira, a sage from Jerusalem, rages against those 'ungodly men' who have 'forsaken the Law of the Most High God' (41:8). But the real trouble started when Antiochus Epiphanes (175–164 BC) officially promoted a Hellenizing programme in Judaea that was embraced with eagerness by the Jewish elite. The leader of the modernist faction was the brother of the High Priest Onias III. Known as Jesus among his compatriots, he adopted the Greek name of Jason, and set about to transform Jerusalem into a Hellenistic city, building a gymnasium there and persuading the Jewish youth to participate in athletic games. As 2 Maccabees describes the situation:

So Hellenism reached a high point with the introduction of foreign customs through the boundless wickedness of the impious Jason, no true High Priest. As a result, the priests no longer had any enthusiasm for their duties at the altar, but despised the temple and neglected the sacrifices; and in defiance of the law they eagerly contributed to the expenses of the wrestling-school whenever the opening gong called them. They placed no value on their hereditary dignities, but cared above everything for Hellenic honours (2 Mac. 4:13–15).

Jason was succeeded by two other High Priests with the same Greek sympathies, Menelaus and Alcimus. In 169 BC Antiochus IV visited Jerusalem and looted the Temple. But when in 167 BC he actually prohibited the practice of Judaism under pain of death and re-dedicated the Jerusalem Sanctuary to Olympian Zeus, the 'abomination of desolation', the opponents of the Hellenizers finally rose up in violent resistance. An armed revolt was instigated by the priest Mattathias and his sons the Maccabee brothers, supported by all the traditionalist Jews, and in

140 *The Dead Sea Scrolls*

particular by the company of the Pious, the Asidaeans or
Hasidim, 'stalwarts of Israel, every one of them a volunteer
in the cause of the Law' (1 Mac. 2:42-3). Led by Judas Maccabaeus and, after his death on the battlefield, by his brothers
Jonathan and Simon, the fierce defenders of Judaism were able
not only to restore Jewish worship ·in Jerusalem, but against
all expectations even managed to eject the ruling Seleucids and
to liberate Judaea.

The Maccabaean triumph was however not simply a straightforward victory of godliness and justice over idolatry and
tyranny; it was accompanied by serious social and religious
upheavals. There was firstly a change in the pontifical succession.
With the murder of Onias III and the deposition of the usurper,
his brother Jason, the Zadokite family, from which the incum-
bents of the High Priest's office traditionally came, lost the
monopoly which it had held for centuries. Furthermore, when
Onias IV, the son of Onias III, was prevented from taking over
the High Priesthood from Menelaus, he emigrated to Egypt
and in direct breach of biblical law erected a Jewish temple in
Leontopolis with the blessing of King Ptolemy Philometor
(182-146 BC). His inauguration of Israelite worship outside
the Jerusalem sanctuary, with the connivance of some priests
and Levites, must have scandalized every Palestinian conservative, even those priests who belonged, or were allied, to the
Zadokite dynasty.

There was trouble also within the ranks of the Maccabees
themselves. The Hasidim – or part of their group – defected
when Alcimus was appointed High Priest in 162 BC. This move
on their part turned out to be naïve; Alcimus's Syrian allies
massacred sixty of them in one day (1 Mac. 7:12-20).

Lastly, a major political change came about when Jonathan
Maccabaeus, himself a priest but not a Zadokite, accepted in
153-2 BC pontifical office from Alexander Balas, a usurper of
the Seleucid throne. Alexander was anxious for Jewish support
and was not mistaken in thinking that an offer of the High
Priesthood would be irresistible. For the conservatives this was

an illegal seizure of power. But they were even more scandalized by the appointment in 140 BC, following Jonathan's execution in 143–2 BC by the Syrian general Tryphon, of Simon Maccabee as High Priest and leader of the people by means of a decree passed by a Jewish national assembly.

From then on, until Pompey's transformation of the independent Jewish state into a Roman province in 63 BC, Judaea was ruled by a new dynasty of High Priests, later Priest-Kings, known as the Hasmonaeans after the grandfather of the Maccabees, Hasmon, or Asamonaeus according to Josephus, *War* i. 36. During the intervening years, all Simon's successors, but especially John Hyrcanus I (134–104 BC) and Alexander Jannaeus (103–76 BC), for whom their political role took precedence over their office of High Priest, occupied one by one the Hellenistic cities of Palestine and conquered the neighbouring territories of Idumaea, Samaria and Ituraea.

Throughout this period of territorial expansion, the Hasmonaean rulers enjoyed the support of the Sadducees, one of the three religious parties first mentioned under Jonathan Maccabaeus (cf. chapter 5, p. 125) and regular allies of the government. They were opposed by the Pharisees, an essentially lay group formed from one of the branches of the Hasidim of the Maccabaean age. Already in the days of John Hyrcanus I there was Pharisaic objection to his usurpation of the High Priesthood, though they were willing to recognize him as national leader (*Antiquities* xiii. 288–98), but on one other occasion, at least, their opposition was overcome by force. Accused of plotting against Alexander Jannaeus in 88 BC in collusion with the Syrian Seleucid king Demetrius Eucaerus, eight hundred Pharisees were condemned by Jannaeus to die on the cross (*Antiquities* xiii. 380–3; *War* i. 96–8).

After Pompey's seizure of Jerusalem, the Hasmonaean High Priesthood continued for another three decades, but the political power formerly belonging to them passed to the Judaized Idumaean, Herod the Great, when he was promoted to the throne of Jerusalem by Rome in 37 BC. It is to the last year or two of his reign – he died in 4 BC – that the Gospels of

Matthew and Luke date the birth of Jesus of Nazareth (Mt 2:1; Lk. 1:5).

After the ephemeral rule of the successor to Herod the Great, Herod Archelaus (4 BC–AD 6), who was deposed by Augustus for his misgovernment of Jews and Samaritans alike, Galilee continued in semi-autonomy under the Herodian princes Antipas (4 BC–AD 39) and Agrippa (AD 39–41), but Judaea was placed under the direct administration of Roman authority. In AD 6, Coponius, the first Roman prefect of Judaea, arrived to take up his duties there. This prefectorial regime, whose most notorius representative was Pontius Pilate (AD 26–36), lasted for thirty-five years until AD 41, when the emperor Claudius appointed Agrippa 1 as king. He died, however, three years later, and in AD 44 the government of the province once more reverted to Roman officials, this time with the title of procurator. Their corrupt and unwise handling of Jewish affairs was one of the chief causes of the war of AD 66 which led to the destruction of Jerusalem in AD 70, and to the subsequent decline of the Sadducees, the extinction of the Zealots in Masada in AD 74, the disappearance of the Essenes, and the survival and un-contested domination of the Pharisees and their rabbinic successors.

It is into this general course of events that the history of Qumran has to be inserted. Document by document the Scrolls will be scrutinized and the literary information combined, both with the findings of Qumran archaeology and with the incidental reports provided by Josephus. In the end it is hoped that the history of the Essene sect will begin to fall reliably into place.

2 THE HISTORY OF THE ESSENES

(a) Concealed references in the Scrolls

The search for clues to the origins and story of the movement begins with the Damascus Rule because it is a document particularly rich in such hints. Here, the birth of the Community is said to have occurred in the 'age of wrath', three hundred and ninety years after the destruction of Jerusalem by

Nebuchadnezzar, king of Babylon. At that time, a 'root' sprung 'from Israel and Aaron', i.e. a group of pious Jews, laymen and priests, came into being in a situation of general ungodliness. These people 'groped for the way' for twenty years, and then God sent them a 'Teacher of Righteousness' to guide them 'in the way of His heart'. The Teacher did not meet with unanimous approval within the congregation, and a faction described as 'seekers of smooth things', 'removers of the bounds' and 'builders of the wall', all metaphors seeming to point to religious laxity and infidelity, turned against him and his followers. The leader of the breakaway party is accorded the unflattering sobriquets of 'Scoffer', 'Liar' or 'Spouter of Lies'. His associates erred in matters of ritual cleanness, justice, chastity, the dates of festivals and Temple worship; they were lovers of money and enemies of peace. In the ensuing fratricidal struggle, the Teacher and those who remained faithful to him went into exile in the 'land of Damascus' where they entered into a 'new Covenant'. There, the Teacher of Righteousness was 'gathered in', meaning that he died. In the meantime, the wicked dominated over Jerusalem and the Temple, though not without experiencing God's vengeance at the hands of the 'Chief of the Kings of Greece'.

A similar picture emerges from the Habakkuk Commentary with its explicit reference to desertion by disciples of the Teacher of Righteousness to the Liar, but also by members unfaithful to the 'new Covenant'. The allusions to the protagonists of the conflict are sharper in this document than in the Damascus Rule. We learn that the villain, known in this Scroll as the 'Wicked Priest' as well as the 'Liar' and 'Spouter of Lies', was 'called by the name of truth' before he became Israel's ruler and was corrupted by wealth and power – the implication being that for a time he had met with the sect's approval. Subsequently, however, he defiled Jerusalem and the Temple. He also sinned against the Teacher of Righteousness and his disciples, chastising him while the 'House of Absalom' looked silently on, and confronting him in his place of exile on the sect's Day of Atonement. He 'vilified and outraged the elect of

God', 'plotted to destroy the Poor', i.e. the Community, and stole their riches. As a punishment, God delivered him 'into the hand of his enemies', who 'took vengeance on his body of flesh'. At the last judgement, predicts the Commentary, the Wicked Priest will empty 'the cup of wrath of God'. His successors, the 'last Priests of Jerusalem', are also charged with amassing 'money and wealth by plundering the peoples', i.e. foreigners. But, so the commentator asserts, all their riches and booty will be snatched from them by the Kittim, the conquerors of the world commissioned by God to pay them their just deserts.

Because of lacunae, one cannot be quite sure from the Habakkuk Commentary that the Teacher was a priest. The Commentary on Psalm 37, by contrast, makes this plain. Interpreting verses 23–4, it reads: 'this concerns the Priest, the Teacher of [Righteousness]'. It further supplies a significant detail by assigning to 'the violent of the nations', that is to say to the Gentiles as opposed to the Jews, the execution of judgement on the Wicked Priest. Another point of interest is that the enemies of the sect are alluded to as 'the wicked of Ephraim and Manasseh', i.e. as of two distinct factions.

In the Messianic Anthology or Testimonia, references appear in the final section to two 'instruments of violence' who ruled Jerusalem. They are cursed for making the city a 'stronghold of ungodliness' and for committing 'an abomination' in the land. They are also said to have shed blood 'like water on the ramparts of the daughter of Zion'. The relationship of the two tyrants to one another cannot be established with certainty because of the fragmentary nature of the manuscript. They could be father and son. On the other hand, the expression, 'instruments of violence', depends on Genesis 49:5, where it describes the brother murderers, Simeon and Levi, the destroyers of Shechem.

The Nahum Commentary moves on to an age following that of the Teacher of Righteousness and the Wicked Priest. The principal character here is the 'furious young lion', a Jewish ruler of Jerusalem. He is said to have taken revenge on the 'seekers of smooth things', whom he reproached for having invited 'Demetrius' the king of Greece to Jerusalem. The attempt failed; no foreigner entered the city 'from the time of Antiochus until the coming of the rulers of the Kittim'. The enemies of the 'furious young lion' were 'hanged alive on the tree', a Hebrew circumlocution for crucifixion. As in the Commentary on Psalm 37, the sobriquets 'Ephraim' and 'Manasseh' are attached to the Community's opponents. 'Ephraim' is said to 'walk in lies and falsehood', but because of gaps in the manuscript, the description of 'Manasseh' is less clear. It seems nevertheless that this party included 'great men', 'mighty men', 'men of dignity'.

The Nahum Commentary was the first of the Qumran Scrolls to disclose historical names: those of two Seleucid kings, Antiochus and Demetrius. But their identity has still to be determined because nine monarchs in all bore the first name, and three the second. Apparently, three additional names figure in an unpublished liturgical calendar: 'Shelamzion', the Hebrew name of Queen Alexandra-Salome, widow of Alexander Jannaeus, who reigned from 76 to 67 BC; 'Hyrcanus', probably John Hyrcanus II, son of Alexandra and High Priest from 76 to 67 and again from 63 to 40 BC; and 'Emilius', no doubt M. Aemilius Scaurus, the first Roman governor of Syria from 65 to 62 BC.

In the Commentaries on Habakkuk and Nahum, the Kittim are represented as instruments appointed by God to punish the ungodly priests of Jerusalem. The War Rule, however, testifies to a changed attitude towards them on the part of the sect by making the Kittim appear as the chief allies of Satan and the final foe to be subjugated by the hosts of the sons of Light.

Several Qumran Hymns reflect the career and sentiments of a teacher, possibly of the Teacher of Righteousness himself. According to them, he was opposed by 'interpreters of error', 'traitors', 'deceivers', by 'those who seek smooth things', all of whom were formerly his 'friends' and 'members of (his) Covenant', bearers of the 'yoke of (his) testimony'. In one of them, the reference to a 'devilish scheme' is reminiscent of the allusion in the Habakkuk Commentary to the visit of the Wicked Priest to the Community's place of exile in order to cause them 'to stumble':

> Teachers of lies [have smoothed] Thy people with words
>   and false prophets have led them astray . . .
> They have banished me from my land
>   like a bird from its nest . . .
> And they, teachers of lies and seers of falsehood,
>   have schemed against me a devilish scheme,
> to exchange the Law engraved on my heart by Thee
>   for the smooth things [which they speak] to Thy people.
> And they withhold from the thirsty the drink of knowledge,
>   and assuage their thirst with vinegar,
> that they may gaze on their straying,
>   on their folly concerning their feast-days,
>   on their fall into their snares (1QH 4:7–12 – DSSE 161).

Another Hymn appears to hint at the Teacher's withdrawal from society and to announce with confidence his eventual glorious justification:

> For Thou, O God, has sheltered me
>   from the children of men,
> and hast hidden Thy Law within me
>   against the time when Thou shouldst reveal
>   Thy salvation to me (1QH 5:11–12 – DSSE 165).

It would be unrealistic, taking into account the vagueness of all these statements, the cryptic nature of the symbolism and the entire lack of any systematic exposition of the sect's history, to expect every detail to be identified. We can however attempt to define the chronological framework of the historical references and thus be in a position to place at least some of the key events and principal personalities within the context of Jewish history as we know it.

(b) The chronological framework

The chronological setting of Qumran history as it emerges from archaeological and literary evidence has been outlined in chapter 2 (pp. 37–9). The excavations of 1951–6 date the beginning, the *terminus a quo*, of the sectarian establishment to 150–140 BC, and its end, the *terminus ad quem*, to the middle of the first war against Rome, AD 68. The literary allusions, particularly the identifiable historical names, confirm this general finding. It goes without saying, however, that the initial phases of the Community's existence must have preceded by some years or decades the actual establishment of the sect at Qumran. The first task therefore is to examine the Scrolls for indications of its origins. The Nahum Commentary implies that a king by the name of Antiochus was alive at the beginning of the period with which the documents are concerned. This Antiochus, although one among several so called, can only have been Antiochus IV Epiphanes, notorious for his looting of Jerusalem and the profanation of the Temple in the early 160s BC.

More significant as a chronological pointer is the dating, in the Damascus Rule, of the sect's beginnings to the 'age of wrath', three hundred and ninety years after the conquest of Jerusalem by Nebuchadnezzar in 586 BC. This should bring us to 196 BC but, as is well known, Jewish historians are not very reliable in their time-reckoning for the post-exilic era. They do not seem to have had a clear idea of the length of the Persian domination, and they were in addition not free of the theological influence of the Book of Daniel, where a period of seventy weeks of years, i.e. 490 years, is given as separating the epoch of Nebuchadnezzar from that of the Messiah. As it happens, if to this figure of three hundred and ninety years is added, firstly twenty (during which the Community 'groped' for its way until the entry on the scene of the Teacher of Righteousness), then another forty (the timespan between the death of the Teacher and the dawn of the messianic epoch), the total stretch of years arrived at is four hundred and fifty. And if to this total is added the duration of the Teacher's ministry of, say, forty years – a customary round figure – the final result is the classic seventy times seven years.

Yet even if the literal figure of three hundred and ninety is rejected, there are still compelling reasons for placing the 'age of wrath' to the opening decades of the second century BC. Only the Hellenistic crisis which occurred at that time, and which is recalled in various Jewish literary sources from the last two centuries of the pre-Christian era, provides a fitting context for the historical allusions made in the sectarian writings (cf. Daniel 9–11; 1 Enoch 90:6–7; Jubilees 23:14–19; Testament of Levi 17; Assumption of Moses 4–5). Also, it is the Hasidim of the pre-Maccabaean and early Maccabaean era who best correspond to the earlier but unorganized group as it is described there (cf. pp. 139–40).

As for the *terminus ad quem* of Qumran history, as this is linked to the appearance of the Kittim, we have to determine who these people were. In its primitive sense, the word 'Kittim' described the inhabitants of Kition, a Phoenician colony in Cyprus. Later, the name tended to be applied indiscriminately to those living in 'all islands and most maritime countries' (Josephus, *Antiquities* i. 128). But from the second century BC, Jewish writers also used 'Kittim' more precisely to denote the greatest world power of the day. In 1 Maccabees (1:1; 8:5) they are Greeks; Alexander the Great and Perseus are called kings of the 'Kittim'. In Daniel 11:30 on the other hand, the 'Kittim' are Romans; it was the ambassador of the Roman senate, Poppilius Laenas, brought to Alexandria by 'ships of Kittim', who instructed the 'king of the North', the Seleucid monarch Antiochus Epiphanes, to withdraw at once from Egypt. The term 'Romans' is substituted for 'Kittim' already in the old Greek or Septuagint version of Daniel 11:30. None of these texts is critical of the 'Kittim'. They are seen as the ruling force of the time, but not as hostile to Israel. In fact, in Daniel they humiliate the enemy of the Jews. It is not till a later stage, especially after AD 70, that they come to symbolize oppression and tyranny.

In the Habakkuk Commentary, the portrait of the Kittim is neutral, as in Maccabees and Daniel. (In the Damascus Rule they play no part; the alien adversary there is the 'Chief of the Kings of Greece'.) Feared and admired by all, they are seen to be on the point of defeating the 'last Priests of Jerusalem' and confiscating their wealth, as they have done to many others before. Such a representation of a victorious and advancing might would hardly apply to the Greek Seleucids of Syria, who by the second half of the second century BC were in grave decline. But it does correspond to the Romans, whose thrust to the east in the first century BC resulted in their triumphs over Pontus, Armenia and Seleucid Syria, and finally, with the arrival of Pompey in Jerusalem in 63 BC, in the transformation of the Hasmonaean state into a province of the Roman republic.

Since the identification of the 'Kittim' as Romans is nowadays generally accepted, it will suffice to cite a single, but very striking, feature in the Habakkuk Commentary to support it. Interpreting Hab. 1:14–16 as referring to the 'Kittim', the commentator writes: 'This means that they sacrifice to their standards and worship their weapons of war' (1QpHab. 6:3-5 – DSSE 238). Now this custom of worshipping the *signa* was a characteristic of the religion of the Roman armies, as Josephus testifies in his report of the capture of the Temple of Jerusalem by the legionaries of Titus in AD 70.

The Romans, now that the rebels had fled to the city, and the Sanctuary itself and all around it were in flames, carried their standards into the Temple court, and setting them up opposite the eastern gate, there sacrificed to them (*War* vi. 316).

It is also worth noting that the 'Kittim', the final opponents of the eschatological Israel, are subject to a king or emperor (*melekh*).

In brief, the time-limits of the sect's history appear to be at one extreme, the beginning of the second century BC, and at the other, some moment during the Roman imperial epoch, i.e., after 27 BC. And this latter date is determined by Qumran archaeology as coinciding with the first Jewish war, and even more precisely, with the arrival of the armies of Vespasian and Titus in the neighbourhood of the Dead Sea in June AD 68.

(c) Decipherment of particular allusions

The 'age of wrath' having been identified as that of the Hellenistic crisis of the beginning of the second century BC, the 'root' as the Hasidim of the pre-Maccabaean age, and the 'Kittim' as the Romans, the next major problem is to discover who was, or were, the principal Jewish enemy or enemies of the sect at the time of the ministry of the Teacher of Righteousness variously known as 'the Scoffer', 'the Liar', 'the Spouter of Lies' and 'the Wicked Priest'.

It is not unreasonable to conclude that all these insults are directed at the same individual. It would appear from the Damascus Rule that the 'Scoffer' and the 'Liar' were one and the same ('when the Scoffer arose who shed over Israel the waters of lies', CD 1:14 – DSSE 97). And we read of the 'Wicked Priest' that he was called 'by the name of truth' (1QpHab 8:8–9 – DSSE 240) at the outset of his career, the inference being that later he changed into a 'Liar'.

Another basic premise must be that the person intended by the fragments of information contained in the Scrolls became the head, the national leader, of the Jewish people. For although biblical names are often used symbolically, including that of 'Israel', the actions attributed to the 'Wicked Priest' make little sense if the person in question did not exercise pontifical and secular power. He 'ruled over Israel', He 'robbed . . . the riches of the men of violence who rebelled against God', probably Jewish apostates, as well as 'the wealth of the peoples', i.e. the Gentiles. He built 'his city of vanity with blood', committed 'abominable deeds in Jerusalem and defiled the Temple of God'. Taken separately, these observations might be understood allegorically, but considered together, they constitute a strong argument for recognizing the 'Wicked Priest' as a ruling High Priest in Jerusalem.

The 'Wicked Priest', then, was a Pontiff who enjoyed good repute before he assumed office. He was victorious over his adversaries at home and abroad. He re-built Jerusalem. And he was eventually captured and put to death by a foreign rival.

The chronological guide-lines established in the preceding section locate the period in which this individual flourished between the reign of Antiochus Epiphanes (175–164 BC) and the probable date of the foundation at Qumran (150–140 BC). During that time, five men held the office of High Priest. Three of them were pro-Greek: Jason, Menelaus and Alcimus. The remaining two were the Maccabee brothers, Jonathan and Simon. All the Hellenizers can be eliminated as candidates for the role of 'Wicked Priest' since none can be said to have enjoyed anything like good repute at the beginning of their ministry. Jason and Alcimus fail also because neither was killed by an enemy: Jason died in exile (2 Mac. 5:7–9) and Alcimus in office (1 Mac. 9:54–56). The Maccabee brothers, by contrast, meet all the conditions. The careers of both men fall easily into two stages marked, in the case of Jonathan, by his acceptance of the High Priesthood from Alexander Balas, and in the case of Simon, by his willingness to become a hereditary High Priest. Both were also 'instruments of violence' and both died by violence. Jonathan is nevertheless to be chosen rather than Simon because he alone suffered the vengeance of the 'Chief of the Kings of Greece' and died at the hands of the 'violent of the nations', whereas Simon was murdered by his son-in-law (1 Mac. 16:14–16). A gallant defender of Jewish religion and independence, Jonathan succeeded the heroic Judas in 161 BC when the latter fell in battle. But he qualified for the epithet 'Wicked Priest' when he accepted in 153–2 BC, from Alexander Balas, a heathen usurper of the Seleucid throne who had no right to grant them, the pontifical vestments which Jonathan was not entitled to wear. Captured later by Tryphon, a former general of Alexander and protector of his son, he was killed by the Syrian at Bascama in Transjordan (1 Mac. 13:23).

Concerning the identity of the 'last Priests of Jerusalem', the passion for conquest, wealth and plunder for which they are reproached points to the Hasmonaean priestly rulers, from Simon's son, John Hyrcanus I (134–104 BC), to Judas Aristobulus II (67–63 BC). There can in particular be little doubt that the 'furious young lion', designated also 'the last Priest' in a badly damaged Commentary on Hosea (4QpHos 2:2–3), was one of them, namely Alexander Jannaeus. The application to him of the words of Nahum, 'who chokes prey for its lionesses', and the report that the 'young lion' executed the 'seekers of smooth things' by 'hanging men alive', accord perfectly with the known story that Jannaeus crucified eight hundred Pharisees whilst feasting with his concubines (cf. above, p. 114).

From this it follows that 'Ephraim', equated in the Commentary on Nahum with the 'seekers of smooth things', symbolizes the Pharisees, and that if so, 'Manasseh' and his dignitaries must refer to the Sadducees. In other words, the political and doctrinal opponents of the Essene community were the Pharisees and the Sadducees.

This division of Jewish society into three opposing groups corresponds to the conformation described by Josephus as existing from the time of Jonathan Maccabaeus, but the new insight provided by the Scrolls suggests that the united resistance to Hellenism first fell apart when the Maccabees, and more precisely Jonathan, refused to acknowledge the spiritual leadership of the Teacher of Righteousness, the priestly head of the Hasidim. From then on, the sect saw its defectors as 'Ephraim' and 'Manasseh', these being the names of the sons of Joseph, associated in biblical history with the apostate North of the kingdom, and referred itself as the 'House of Judah', the faithful South.

Unfortunately, on the most vital topic of all, the question of the identity of the Teacher of Righteousness, we can be nothing like as clear. If the 'Wicked Priest' was Jonathan Maccabaeus, the Teacher would, of course, have been one of his contemporaries. Yet all we know of him is that he was a priest, no doubt of Zadokite affiliation, though obviously opposed to Onias IV since he did not follow him to Egypt and to his unlawful Temple in Leontopolis. He founded or refounded the Community. He transmitted to them his own distinctive interpretation of the Prophets and, if we can rely on the Hymns, of the laws relating to the celebration of festivals. The 'Liar' and his sympathizers in the congregation of the Hasidim disagreed with him, and after a violent confrontation between the two factions in which the 'Liar' gained the upper hand, the Teacher and his remaining followers fled to a place of refuge called 'the land of Damascus': it has been suggested that this is a cryptic designation of Babylonia, the original birthplace of the group, or that 'Damascus' is a symbolical name for Qumran. The 'House of Absalom' gave the Teacher of Righteousness no help against the 'Liar', writes the Habakkuk commentator (1QpHab 5:9–12 – DSSE 238), the implication being that this was support on which he might have relied. If 'Absalom' is also a symbol, it doubtless recalls the rebellion of Absalom against his father David, and thus points to the perfidy of a close relation or intimate friend of the Teacher. On the other hand, since the 'House of Absalom' is accused, not of an actual attack but simply of remaining silent during the Teacher's 'chastisement', this allegorical solution may not be convincing. The allusion may then be a straightforward one. A certain Absalom was an ambassador of Judas Maccabaeus (2 Mac. 11:17), and his son, Mattathias, was one of Jonathan's gallant officers (1 Mac. 11:70). Another of his sons, Jonathan, commanded Simon's army which captured Joppa (1 Mac. 13:11).

Meanwhile, even in his 'place of exile' the Teacher continued to be harassed and persecuted by the Wicked Priest. In this connection, the most important and painful episode appears to have been the Priest's pursuit of the Teacher to his settlement with the purpose of confusing him 'with his venomous fury'. Appearing before the sectaries on 'their sabbath of repose', at the 'time appointed for rest, for the Day of Atonement', his intention was to cause them 'to stumble on the Day of Fasting'. It is impossible to say, from the evidence so far available, precisely what happened on this portentous occasion, or whether it was then or later that the Wicked Priest 'laid hands' on the Teacher 'that he might put him to death'. The wording is equivocal. For example, the verb in 1QpHab 11:5, 7. translated 'to confuse' can also mean 'to swallow up', and some scholars have chosen to understand that the Teacher was killed by the Wicked Priest at the time of the visit. On the other hand, we find recounted in the imperfect tense (which can be rendered in English into either the future or the present tense): 'The wicked of Ephraim and Manasseh . . . seek/will seek to lay hands on the Priest and the men of his Council . . . But God redeems/will redeem them from out of their hand' (4QpPs. 37 2:17–19). In other words, we neither know who the founder of the Essenes was, nor how, nor where, nor when he died.

It has been argued that this inability to identify the Teacher of Righteousness in the context of the Maccabaean period undermines the credibility of the reconstruction as a whole. Is it conceivable, it is asked, that a figure of the stature of the Teacher should have left no trace in the literature relating to that time? The answer to this objection is that such writings are to all intents and purposes restricted to the Books of the Maccabees, sources politically biased in favour of their heroes and virtually oblivious of the very existence of opposition movements. Josephus himself relies largely on 1 Maccabees and cannot therefore be regarded as an independent witness. But even were this not so, and he had additional material at his disposition, his silence *vis-à-vis* the Teacher of Righteousness would still not call for particular comment since he also makes no mention of the founders of the Pharisees and Sadducees. And incidentally, not a few historians hold that he has nothing to say either of Jesus of Nazareth. The so-called Testimonium Flavianum (*Antiquities* xviii. 63–64), they maintain, is a Christian interpolation into the genuine text of Antiquities, (though others, myself included, think that part of the text is authentic). Be this as it may, not a word is breathed by him about Hillel, the greatest of the Pharisee masters, or about Yohanan ben Zakkai, who re-organized Judaism after the destruction of the Temple, although both of these men lived in Josephus's own century.

Admittedly, the various fragments of information gleaned from the Dead Sea Scrolls result in an unavoidably patchy story, but it is fundamentally sound, and the continuing anonymity of the Teacher does nothing to impair it. For the present synthesis to be complete it remains now to turn to Josephus for his occasional historical references to individual Essenes and to Essenism.

Apart from the general notices analysed in chapter 5 (pp. 125–30), four members of the Community are mentioned by the Jewish historian, three of them associated with prophecy, one of the distinctive interests of the Teacher of Righteousness himself. The first, called Judas, is encountered in Jerusalem surrounded by a group of pupils taking instruction in 'fore-telling the future', which probably means, in how to identify prophetic pointers to future events. Josephus writes of him that he had 'never been known to speak falsely in his prophecies', and that he predicted the death of Antigonus, the brother of Aristobulus I (104–103 BC) (*Antiquities* xiii. 311–13). A second Essene prophet, Menahem, apparently foretold that Herod would rule over the Jews (xv. 373–8). Herod showed his grati-tude to him by dispensing the Essenes, who were opposed to all oaths except their own oath of the Covenant, from taking the vow of loyalty imposed on all his Jewish subjects. A third Essene named Simon interpreted a dream of Archelaus, ethnarch of Judaea (4 BC–AD 6), in 4 BC to mean that his rule would last for ten years (xvii. 345–8). John the Essene, the last sectary to be referred to by Josephus, was not a prophet, but the commander or *strategos* of the district of Thamna in north-western Judaea, and of the cities of Lydda (Lod), Joppa (Jaffa) and Emmaus at the beginning of the first revolution (*War* ii. 567). Said to have been a man of 'first-rate prowess and ability', he fell in battle at Ascalon (iii. 11, 19).

Finally, Josephus depicts in vivid language the bravery of the Essenes subjected to torture by the Romans.

The war with the Romans tried their souls through and through by every variety of test. Racked and twisted, burned and broken, and made to pass through every instrument of torture in order to induce them to blaspheme their lawgiver or to eat some forbidden thing, they refused to yield to either demand, nor ever once did they cringe to their persecutors or shed a tear. Smiling in their agonies and mildly deriding their tormentors, they cheerfully resigned their souls, confident that they would receive them back again (*War* ii. 152–3).

Since it would appear from this passage that the Romans were persecuting not individuals, but a group, it is tempting, bearing in mind the archaeologists' claim that the Qumran settlement was destroyed by the Romans, to associate it with the story of Essenes captured by the Dead Sea. If such a surmise is correct, the sect's disappearance from history may well have been brought about in the lethal blow suffered by its central establishment during the fateful summer of AD 68.

BIBLIOGRAPHY TO CHAPTER 6

1 INTER-TESTAMENTAL JEWISH HISTORY

The most comprehensive scholarly exposition of Jewish history from 175 BC to AD 135 is the first volume of Emil Schürer-Geza Vermes-Fergus Millar, *The History of the Jewish People in the Age of Jesus Christ* (T. & T. Clark, Edinburgh, 1973). For a less technical treatment of the epoch in question see F. V. Filson, *A New Testament History* (S.C.M., London, 1975); F. F. Bruce, *New Testament History* (Nelson, London, 1969); B. Reicke, *The New Testament Era* (Fortress, Philadelphia, 1968); S. Safrai–M. Stern (eds), *The Jewish People in the First Century* (Van Gorcum, Assen and Fortress, Philadelphia, I [1974]; II [1977]); H. H. Ben Sasson, *A History of the Jewish People* (Weidenfeld & Nicolson, London, 1976), Part III.

The reader may also consult the following monographs devoted to particular aspects of inter-Testamental history: V. Tcherikover, *Hellenistic Civilization and the Jews* (Jewish Publication Society, Philadelphia, 1959); A. H. M. Jones, *The Herods of Judaea* (Clarendon, Oxford, 1967); A. Schalit, *König Herodes* (de Gruyter, Berlin, 1969); J. Jeremias, *Jerusalem in the Time of Jesus* (S.C.M., London and Fortress, Philadelphia, 1969); M. Hengel, *Judaism and Hellenism* I–II (S.C.M., London and Fortress, Philadelphia, 1974); E. M. Smallwood, *The Jews under Roman Rule* (Brill, Leiden, 1976). The best commentary on the Books of the Maccabees is F.-M. Abel, *Les livres des Maccabées* (Gabalda, Paris, 1949). For the temple of Onias in Leontopolis see Tcherikover, op. cit. 278–80; M. Delcor, 'Le temple d'Onias en Égypte', RB 75 (1968), 188–205; Vermes, PBJS, 83–4.

2 THE HISTORY OF THE ESSENES

All the general studies on the Scrolls contain a section on historical issues, as do dictionary articles on Qumran. See most recently (1976) 'Dead Sea Scrolls' in IDBS, 210–19. Cf. also Schürer–Vermes–Millar–Black II, §30. Further important special studies of Qumran history include H. H. Rowley, 'The History of the Qumran Sect', BJRL 49 (1966), 203–32. F. M. Cross, 'The Early History of the Qumran Community', *New Directions in Biblical Archaeology*, ed. D. N. Freedman– J. C. Greenfield (Doubleday, Garden City, 1971), 70–89; H. Stegemann, *Die Entstehung der Qumrangemeinde* (Bonn Dissertation, privately published, 1971); J. Murphy-O'Connor, 'The Essenes and their History', RB 81 (1974), 215–44; H. Burgmann, 'Gerichtsherr und Generalankläger: Jonathan und Simon', RQ 9 (1977), 3–72.

For the literature on the Habakkuk and Nahum Commentaries, see pp. 75–7 above.

The phrase '390 years' in CD 1:5 requires a brief discussion. We may safely discard the idea that 390 is a symbolical figure borrowed from Ezekiel 4:4 where it corresponds to the number of days during which the prophet, lying on his left side, atoned for the 390 years of iniquity of the House of Israel. Indeed there is no indication whatever that the fate of the Northern kingdom played any part in the sect's speculation concerning its own origins. Similarly the view that the 390 years are to be counted not from, but to, the time of Nebuchadnezzar, seems to run counter to the whole logic of the account in the Damascus Rule. For the thesis in question see I. Rabinowitz, 'A Reconsideration of "Damascus" and "390 Years" in the "Damascus" (Zadokite) Fragments', JBL 73 (1954), 11–35; E. Wiesenberg, 'Chronological Data in the Zadokite Fragments', VT 5 (1955) 284–308.

The unreliability of the post-exilic chronology of ancient Jewish writers may be illustrated by two examples. The third century BC Jewish Hellenist Demetrius calculates the total number of years between the fall of Samaria (722–1 BC) and the accession of Ptolemy IV of Egypt (221 BC) to have been 573 instead of the actual 500; cf. Clement of Alexandria, *Stromateis* i. 141, 2; see N. Walter, 'Fragmente jüdisch-hellenistischer Exegeten', *Jüdische Schriften aus hellenistisch-römischer Zeit*, ed. W. G. Kümmel, III.2 (Mohn, Gütersloh, 1975), 292. Even the careful Josephus in the first century AD was unable to produce precise figures. He reckoned 481 (*Antiquities* xiii. 301) or 471 (*War* i. 70) years, instead of 435, between the return from the Babylonian exile (538 BC) and the death of Aristobulus I (103 BC), and 343 years, i.e. roughly a hundred years too many, for the duration (approximately 160 BC-AD 73) of the Leontopolis Temple (*War* vii. 436). As for the chronology contained in the Seder Olam Rabbah 30 of Rabbi Yose the Galilean (second century AD), the lapse of time from Nebuchadnezzar to the destruction of the Temple amounts there to the mystical 70 times 7, i.e. 490 years, echoing Daniel 9:24. R. Yose's data are: Babylonian rule, 70 years; Persian rule, 34 years; Greek rule, 180 years; Hasmonaean rule, 103 years; Herodian rule, 103 years. Cf. G. R. Driver, *The Judaean Scrolls* (Blackwell, Oxford, 1965), 311-16; though his use of the evidence is to be taken with a pinch of salt since he did not seem to realize that we have to deal with a theological time-schedule.

In the early years of Qumran research, some scholars argued that the Kittim were Greek Seleucids. See e.g. E. Stauffer, 'Zur Frühdatierung des Habakkukmidrasch', TLZ 76 (1951), 667-74; H. H. Rowley, *The Zadokite Fragments and the Dead Sea Scrolls* (Blackwell, Oxford, 1952). The Roman theory, strongly favoured since the beginning, has now become the dominant one. Cf. A. Dupont-Sommer, *Essene Writings*, 341-51; R. Goossens, 'Les Kittim du Commentaire d'Habacuc', *Nouvelle Clio* 2 (1952), 137-70; G. Vermes, *Discovery*, 79-84; PBJS, 215-16.

For a discussion of the 'last Priests of Jerusalem', see Vermes, *Discovery*, 78-9, and for possible allusions to the Teacher of Righteousness in the Qumran Hymns, ibid. 216-20; Dupont-Sommer, *Essene Writings*, 358-67. For a recent survey, see E. P. Sanders, *Paul and Palestinian Judaism* (S.C.M., London and Fortress, Philadelphia, 1977), 321-3.

Various views concerning the meaning of the phrase 'Land of Damascus' have been advanced. Cf. I. Rabinowitz, 'A Reconsideration of Damascus . . .', JBL 73 (1954), 11-35 (locality of the exile of the Judaeans after 586 BC), 219-23

(Damascus = Babylonia); A. Jaubert, 'Le pays de Damas', RB 65 (1958), 214–48; J. Murphy-O'Connor, 'The Essenes and their History', RB 81 (1974), 219–23; R. North, 'The Damascus of Qumran Geography', PEQ 87 (1955), 33–48 (Damascus = Qumran); R. de Vaux, *Archaeology*, 113–14. For the exegetical symbolism Damascus = Jerusalem (Qumran), cf. Vermes, *Scripture and Tradition*, 43–9.

Although in my opinion the Teacher of Righteousness is likely to remain anonymous, the following (unconvincing) identifications have been proposed: Onias III, High Priest, murdered in 170 BC (H. H. Rowley, op. cit., 67–8); Yose ben Yoezer, Priest, one of the first Pharisaic masters (E. Stauffer, 'Der gekreuzigte Thoralehrer', ZRGG 8 (1956), 250–3); an anonymous High Priest who succeeded Alcimus in *c.* 160 BC (J. Murphy-O'Connor, art. cit., 229–30; 'Demetrius I and the Teacher of Righteousness', RB 83 (1976), 400–20; cf. J. G. Bunge, 'Zur Geschichte und Chronologie der Oniaden und des Aufsteigs der Hasmonäer', JSJ 6 (1975), 27–43); the Pharisee Eleazar, a critic of John Hyrcanus I, or the Essene prophet Judas at the end of the second century BC (W. H. Brownlee, 'The Historical Allusions of the Dead Sea Habakkuk Midrash', BASOR 126 (1952), 18); Onias the Just, a miracle-worker executed in 65 BC (R. Goossens, 'Onias le Juste, le Messie de la Nouvelle Alliance, lapidé à Jérusalem en 65 avant J.-C.', *Nouvelle Clio* 1–2 (1949–50), 336–53; B. E. Thiering, *Redating the Teacher of Righteousness* (Theological Explorations, Sidney, 1979), tentatively identifies the Teacher as John the Baptist; Jesus of Nazareth (J. L. Teicher, 'Jesus in the Habakkuk Scroll', JJS 3 (1952), 53–5; Menahem son of Judas the Galilean murdered in AD 66 (C. Roth, op. cit., 60–3; G. R. Driver, op. cit., 267–81). For a brief general survey, cf. F. F. Bruce, 'Teacher of Righteousness', Enc. Jud. 15, 885–8.

Regarding the historicity of Josephus's notice on Jesus, see Schürer–Vermes–Millar I, 428–41 with a full bibliography to which should be added E. Bammel, 'Zum Testimonium

Flavianum', *Josephus-Studien . . . Festschrift für O. Michel* (Vandenhoeck & Ruprecht, Göttingen, 1974), 9–22. For the history of the Essenes consult Schürer–Vermes–Millar–Black II, §30. A succinct bibliography of the various historical theories advanced during the last three decades may appropriately conclude this section.

1 Pre-Maccabaean theory

H. H. Rowley, *The Zadokite Fragments and the Dead Sea Scrolls* (1952); 'The History of the Qumran Sect', BJRL 49 (1966), 203–32; I. Rabinowitz, 'The Meaning of the Key ("Demetrius") Passage of the Qumran Nahum Pesher' *Journal of the American Oriental Society* 98 (1978), 394–9.

2 Maccabaean theory (Wicked Priest = Jonathan or Simon)

G. Vermes, *Les Manuscrits du désert de Juda* (1953); *Discovery*, 89–97; DSSE, 61–8; J. T. Milik, *Dix ans de découvertes dans le désert de Juda* (1957); *Ten Years of Discovery*, 84–7; F. M. Cross, *The Ancient Library of Qumran* (1958), 135–53; *Canaanite Myth and Hebrew Epic* (Harvard U.P., Cambridge, Mass., 1973), 626–42; R. de Vaux, *L'Archéologie et les manuscrits de la Mer Morte* (1961); *Archaeology*, 116–17; G. Jeremias, *Der Lehrer der Gerechtigkeit* (1963); H. Stegemann, *Die Entstehung der Qumrangemeinde* (1971); M. Hengel, *Judaism and Hellenism* I (1974), 224–7; J. Murphy-O'Connor, 'The Essenes and their History', RB 81 (1974), 215–44; 'Demetrius I and the Teacher of Righteousness', RB 83 (1976), 400–20; 'The Essenes in Palestine', BA 40 (1977), 100–24; H. Burgmann, 'The Wicked Woman: Der Makkabäer Simon?', RQ 8 (1974), 323–59; 'Gerichtsherr und Generalankläger: Jonathan und Simon', RQ 9 (1977), 3–72; G. W. E. Nickelsburg, 'Simon—A Priest with a Reputation for Faithfulness', BASOR 223 (1976), 67–8; J. Starcky, 'Le Maître de Justice et la chronologie de Qumrân', *Qumrân* (ed. M. Delcor, 1978), 249–56.

3 Hasmonaean theory (a. Wicked Priest = Alexander Jannaeus)

M. Delcor, *Le Midrash d'Habacuc* (1951); J. Carmignac, *Les Textes de Qumran* II (1963), 48–55.

(*b. Wicked Priest = Hyrcanus II*)
A. Dupont-Sommer, *The Essene Writings from Qumran* (1961), 351–7.

4 Zealot theory
C. Roth, *The Historical Background of the Dead Sea Scrolls* (1958); G. R. Driver, *The Judaean Scrolls* (1965).

5 Judaeo-Christian theory
See above pp. 117, 131.

6 Medieval theory
For S. Zeitlin's persistent polemics against the antiquity of the Scrolls, see JQR from 39 (1949) onwards. On possible connections with the medieval Karaites, see N. Wieder, *The Judean Scrolls and Karaism* (East & West Library, London, 1962), and A. Paul, *Écrits de Qumrân et sectes juives aux premiers siècles de l'Islam* (Letouzey & Ané, Paris, 1969).

CHAPTER 7

The Religious Ideas and Ideals of the Community

The first essays in the 1950s on the religious outlook of the Qumran sect all suffered from a serious defect in that scholars in those days tended to envisage the Scrolls as self-contained and entitled to independent treatment. Today, with the hindsight of decades of research and a considerably increased, though still incomplete, documentation, it is easier to conceive of the theology of the Community as part of the general doctrinal evolution of ancient Judaism.

On the other hand, it is no simple task to follow that evolution itself, the reason being that the systematic exposition of beliefs and customs is not a traditional Jewish discipline. The theology of Judaism, biblical, inter-Testamental, medieval or modern, even when written by Jews, is often modelled consciously or unconsciously on Christian dogmatic structures: God, creation, human destiny, messianic redemption, judgement, resurrection, heaven and hell. Such structures may and sometimes do distort the religious concepts of Judaism. For example, the interest of the Church in the messianic role of Jesus is apt to assign a greater importance to Messianism in Jewish religion than the historical evidence justifies, and Paul's hostility to the 'legalism' of Israel obscures the Jewish recognition of the humble realities of everyday life prescribed by the law as no mere 'works' but as a path to holiness walked in obedience to God's commandments.

1 THE COVENANT

Since the key to any understanding of Judaism must be the

notion of the Covenant, it may safely be taken as an introduction to Essene religious thought. The history of mankind and of the Jewish people has seen a series of such covenants. God undertook never to destroy mankind again by a flood; in exchange, Noah and his descendants were required to abstain from shedding human blood and, on the ritual level, from eating animal 'flesh with the life, which is the blood, still in it' (Gen. 9:1–17). To Abraham, who was childless and landless, God offered posterity and country provided he led a perfect life and marked his body and that of all his male progeny with a visible reminder of the Covenant between himself and heaven, circumcision (Gen. 17:1–14). Again, in the days of Moses the Israelites were declared 'a kingdom of priests, and a holy nation' (Exod. 19:5), God's special possession, on condition that they obeyed the Torah, the divine Teaching of the religious, moral, social and ritual precepts recorded in the Pentateuch from Exodus chapter 20 and repeated in the farewell discourse addressed by Moses to his people in the Book of Deuteronomy.

After the conquest of Canaan and the distribution of the land to the tribes, the fulfilment of God's promise to Abraham, the Covenant was renewed by Joshua and the Israelites reasserted their commitment to their heavenly Helper (Jos. 24). From then on, the biblical story is one of continuous unfaithfulness to the Covenant. But God was not to be thwarted by human unworthiness and ingratitude, and for the sake of the handful of just men appearing in every generation he allowed the validity of the Covenant to endure. Though he punished the sinful and the rebellious, he spared the 'remnant' because of their fidelity to it.

From time to time, saintly leaders of the Jewish people, King David and King Josiah before the Babylonian exile (2 Sam. 7; 2 Kings 23:1–3) and Ezra the Priest after the return from Mesopotamia (Neh. 8–10), persuaded them to remember their Covenant with God with solemn vows of repentance and national re-dedication; but the promises were usually short-lived. This would no doubt account for the development of an

idea in the sixth century BC of a 'new Covenant' founded not
so much on undertakings entered into by the community as
on the inner transformation of every individual Jew for whom
the will of God was to become, as it were, second nature.

> The time is coming... when I will make a new Covenant with
> Israel... This is the new Covenant which I will make with
> Israel in those days... I will set my law within them and
> write it on their hearts... (Jer. 31:31–33; Isa. 54:13).

It was this same Covenant theology that served as the foundation of the Qumran Community's basic beliefs. The Essenes
not only considered themselves to be the 'remnant' of their
time, but the 'remnant' of all time, the final 'remnant'. In the
'age of wrath', while God was making ready to annihilate the
wicked, their founders had repented. They had become the
'Converts of Israel' (cf. CD 4:2 – DSSE 100). As a reward for
their conversion, the Teacher of Righteousness had been sent to
establish for them a 'new Covenant', which was to be the sole
valid form of the eternal alliance between God and Israel.
Consequently, their paramount aim was to pledge themselves
to observe its precepts with absolute faithfulness. Convinced
that they belonged to a Community which alone interpreted
the Holy Scriptures correctly, they devoted their exile in the
wilderness to the study of the Bible. Their intention was to do
according to all that had been 'revealed from age to age, and
as the Prophets had revealed by His Holy Spirit' (1QS 8:14–16
– DSSE 86).

Without an authentic interpretation it was not possible properly to understand the Torah. All the Jews of the inter-Testamental era, the Essenes as well as their rivals, agreed that true
piety entails obedience to the Law, but although its guidance
reaches into so many corners of life – into business and prayer,
law court and kitchen, marriage-bed and Temple – the six
hundred and thirteen positive and negative commandments
of which it consists still do not provide for all the problems
encountered, especially those which arose in the centuries

following the enactment of biblical legislation. To give but one example, the diaspora situation was not envisaged by the jurists of an autonomous Jewish society.

Torah interpretation was entrusted to the priests and Levites during the first two or three centuries following the Babylonian exile. Ezra and his colleagues, the ancient scribes of Israel, 'read from the book of the Law . . . made its sense plain and gave instruction in what was read'. In this passage from the Book of Nehemiah (8:8), Jewish tradition acknowledges the institution of a regular paraphrase of Scripture known as Targum, or translation into the vernacular of the members of the congregation. When the parties of the Pharisees, Sadducees, Essenes, etc., came into being with their different convictions, they justified them by interpretations suited to their needs.

A classic example in the Scrolls of idiosyncratic Bible interpretation concerns a law on marriage. Since no directly relevant ruling is given in the Pentateuch on whether a niece may marry her uncle, Pharisaic and rabbinic Judaism understands this scriptural silence to mean that such a union is licit. When the Bible wishes to declare a degree of kinship unlawful, it does so: thus we read apropos of marriage between nephew and aunt, 'You shall not approach your mother's sister' (Lev. 18:13). So a tradition surviving in the Talmud is able to go so far as even to praise marriage with a 'sister's daughter' and to proclaim it as a particularly saintly and generous act comparable to the loving kindness shown to the poor and needy (bYebamoth 62b). The Qumran Essenes did not adopt this attitude at all. On the contrary, they regarded an uncle/ niece union as straightforward 'fornication'. Interpreted correctly, they maintained, the Leviticus precept signifies the very opposite of the meaning accepted by their opponents; the truth is that whatever applies to men in this respect applies also to women.

Moses said, 'You shall not approach your mother's sister (i.e. your aunt); she is your mother's near kin' (Lev. 18:13). But although the laws against incest are written for men, they also apply to women. When therefore a brother's daughter uncovers the nakedness of her father's brother, she is (also his) near kin' (CD 5:7–9 – DSSE 101–2).

Again, according to the strict views of the sectaries, fidelity to the Covenant demanded not only obedience to the Law, to all that God has 'commanded by the hand of Moses', but also adherence to the teaching of 'all his servants, the Prophets' (1QS 1:2–3 – DSSE 72). Although not expressly stated, this special attention to the Prophets implies, firstly, that the Essenes subscribed to the principle incorporated into the opening paragraph of the Sayings of the Fathers that the Prophets served as an essential link in the transmission of the Law from Moses to the rabbis.

Moses received the Torah from (God on) Sinai and passed it on to Joshua; Joshua to the Elders (= Judges); the Elders to the Prophets; and the Prophets passed it on to the members of the Great Assembly (= the leaders of Israel in the post-exilic age) (mAboth 1:1).

The second inference to be drawn is that the sect believed the Prophets to be not only teachers of morality, but also guides in the domain of the final eschatological realities. But as in the case of the Law, their writings were considered to contain pitfalls for the ignorant and the misinformed, and only the Community's sages knew how to expound them correctly. Properly understood, the books of Isaiah, Hosea and the rest indicate the right path to be followed in the terrible cataclysms of the last days. A simple reading can convey only their super-ficial meaning, but not their profounder significance. The Book of Daniel sets the biblical example here when it announces that Jeremiah's prediction that the Babylonian domination would last for seventy years is not to be taken literally; the real and final message is that seventy times seven years would separate Nebuchadnezzar from the coming of the Messiah (Dan. 9:21–24). But the Qumran sectaries went even further than

Daniel. They argued that it is quite impossible to discover the meaning without an inspired interpreter because the Prophets themselves were ignorant of the full import of what they wrote. Habakkuk, for instance, was commanded to recount the history of the 'final generation', but he did so without having any clear idea of how far ahead the eschatological age lay. God 'did not make known to him when time would come to an end'. Knowledge of the authentic teaching of the Prophets was the supreme talent of the Teacher of Righteousness. The surviving Bible commentaries, whether or not the Teacher was directly responsible for them, are almost all concerned with predictions concerning the ultimate destiny of the righteous and the wicked, the tribulations and final triumph of the 'House of Judah' and the concomitant annihilation of those who had rebelled against God. But in addition to this general evidence of the subject-matter, the Scrolls directly impute to the Teacher a particular God-given insight into the hidden significance of prophecy. He was 'the Teacher of Righteousness to whom God made known all the mysteries of His servants the Prophets' (1QpHab. 7:1–5 – DSSE 239). He was 'the Priest (in whose heart) God set (understanding) that he might interpret all the words of his servants the Prophets, through whom He foretold all that would happen to His people' (1QpHab. 2:8–10 – DSSE 236). He was the Teacher who 'made known to the latter generations that which God would do to the last generation, the congregation of traitors, those who depart from the way' (CD 1:12–13 – DSSE 97). The Teacher's interpretation alone, propagated by his disciples, offered true enlightenment and guidance.

Supported in this way by the infallible teaching of the Community, the sectary believed himself to be living in the true city of God, the city of the Covenant built on the Law and the Prophets (cf. CD 7:13–18 – DSSE 104).

Again and again, the architectural metaphors used in the Scrolls suggest security and protection. The sect is a 'House of Holiness', a 'House of Perfection and Truth', (1QS 8:5, 9 – DSSE 85), a 'House of the Law' (CD 19 (B2): 10, 13 – DSSE 106–7); it is a 'sure House' (CD 3: 19 – DSSE 100) constructed on solid foundations. Indeed the language used is reminiscent of Isaiah 28:16, and of Jesus' simile about the Church built not on sand but on rock (Mt. 7:24–27; 16:18):

> But I shall be as one who enters a *fortified city,*
>   as one who seeks refuge behind a *high wall* . . .
> I will [lean on] Thy truth, O my God.
> For Thou wilt set the *foundation* on *rock*
>   and the *framework* by the *measuring cord* of justice;
> and the tried *stones* [Thou wilt lay]
>   by the *plumb-line* [of the truth],
> to [build] a mighty [wall] which shall not sway;
>   and no man entering there shall stagger
> (1QS 6:24–27 – DSSE 171)

Fortified by his membership of the brotherhood, the sectary could even carry his notions of solidity and firmness over into his own self so that he too became a 'strong tower':

> Thou hast strengthened me
>   before the battles of wickedness . . .
> Thou hast made me like a *strong tower,* a *high wall,*
>   and hast established my *edifice* upon the *rock*;
> *eternal foundations* serve for my ground,
>   and all my *ramparts* are a *tried wall* which shall not sway
> (1QH 7:7–9 – DSSE 173).

2 ELECTION AND HOLY LIFE IN THE COMMUNITY OF THE COVENANT

In the ideology of the Old Testament, to be a member of the chosen people is synonymous with being party to the Covenant. Israel willingly accepts the yoke of the Law given on Sinai, and God in his turn acknowledges her as his 'special possession' (Exod. 19:5):

> For you are a people holy to the Lord your God; the Lord your God has chosen you to be a people for his own posses-

sion, out of all the peoples that are on the face of the earth
. . . You shall therefore be careful to do the commandment,
and the statutes, and the ordinances which I command you
this day (Dt. 7:6, 11).

Theoretically, there is no distinction between election *de jure*
and election *de facto*: every Jew is chosen. But already in biblical
times a deep gulf is in fact seen to divide righteous observers
of the Covenant from the wicked of Israel. Though not deprived
of their birthright, the unfaithful are viewed as burdened with
guilt and as such excluded, provisionally at least, from the
congregation of the sons of God. The fully developed concept
of election is summarized by the third century AD Galilean
Rabbi Lazar. Expounding the words of Deuteronomy quoted
above, he comments:

> When the Israelites do the will of the Holy One, blessed by
> He, they are called sons; but when they do not do His will,
> they are not called sons (yKiddushin 61c).

Inevitably, for the Qumran Essenes such a notion of Covenant
membership was far too elastic. Consistent with their approach
to legal matters, their attitude in regard to the Covenant was
that only the initiates of their own 'new Covenant' were to be
reckoned among God's elect and, as such, united already on
earth with the angels of heaven.

> [God] has caused [His chosen ones] to inherit
>   the lot of the Holy Ones,
> He has joined their assembly
>   to the Sons of Heaven,
> to be a Council of the Community,
>   a foundation of the Building of Holiness,
>   an eternal Plantation throughout all ages to come
>   (1QS 11:7–9 – DSSE 93.)

They insisted moreover, on the individual election of each sectary. The ordinary Jew envisaged entry into the congregation of the chosen primarily through birth, and secondly through the symbolical initiation of an eight-day-old infant submitted to circumcision. An Essene became a member of his sect by virtue of the deliberate and personal adult commitment of himself. For this reason, as will be remembered, even children born to married members and brought up in their schools had to wait until their twentieth birthday before they were allowed to make their solemn vows of entry into the Covenant. Also, believing in divine foreknowledge, they considered their adherence to the 'lot of God' as the effect of grace, as having been planned for each of them in heaven from all eternity. They, the elect, were guided by the spirit of truth in the ways of light, while the unprivileged, Jew and Gentile alike, were doomed to wander along paths of darkness. The Community Rule gives a fascinating description of these two human groups, the chosen and the unchosen.

The Master shall instruct all the sons of light and shall teach them the nature of all the children of men according to the kind of spirit which they possess . . .

From the God of Knowledge comes all that is and shall be. Before ever they existed He established their whole design, and when, as ordained for them, they come into being, it is in accord with His glorious design that they accomplish their task without change . . .

He has created man to govern the world, and has appointed for him two spirits in which to walk until the time of His visitation: the spirits of truth and falsehood.

Those born of truth spring from a fountain of light, but those born of falsehood spring from a source of darkness. All the children of righteousness are ruled by the Prince of Light and walk in the ways of light, but all the children of falsehood are ruled by the Angel of Darkness and walk in the ways of darkness.

The Angel of Darkness leads all the children of righteousness astray, and until his end, all their sins, iniquities, wickednesses, and all their unlawful deeds are caused by his dominion in accordance with the mysteries of God . . .

But the God of Israel and His Angel of Truth will succour all the sons of light. For it is He who created the spirits of Light and Darkness and founded every action upon them and established every deed (upon) their (ways).

And He loves the one everlastingly and delights in its works for ever; but the counsel of the other He loathes and for ever hates its ways (1QS 3:13–4:1 – DSSE 75–6).

Convictions of this kind, with their theories of individual election and predestination, coupled with a precise knowledge of the boundary dividing right from wrong, can lead to self-righteousness and arrogant intolerance of the masses thought to be rejected by God. The Essenes, however, appear to have concentrated more on the blessedness of the chosen than on the damnation of the unjust. Besides, they could always argue that Jews who refused to repent and remained outside the new Covenant were responsible for their own doom.

But the spiritual masters of the Community were doubtless aware of the danger of the sin of pride to which their less enlightened brothers were exposed and attacked it on three fronts. The Qumran Hymns, unlike certain biblical Psalms (e.g. Psalm 26) which testify to an acute form of sanctimoniousness, never cease to emphasize the sectary's frailty, unworthiness and total dependence on God.

> Clay and dust that I am,
>   what can I devise unless Thou wilt it,
>   and what contrive unless Thou desire it?
> What strength shall I have
>   unless Thou keep me upright
> and how shall I understand
>   unless by (the spirit) which Thou hast shaped for me?
>   (1QH 10:5–7 – DSSE 182).

Not only is election itself owed to God's grace, but perseverance in the way of holiness cannot be counted on unless he offers his continuous help and support.

> When the wicked rose against Thy Covenant
>   and the damned against Thy word,
> I said in my sinfulness,
>   'I have been forsaken by Thy Covenant'.
> But calling to mind the might of Thy hand
>   and the greatness of Thy compassion,
> I rose and stood . . .
>   I lean on Thy grace and on the multitude of Thy mercies
>   (1QH 4:34–37 – DSSE 164).

Another theme constantly stressed in Essene teaching is that not only is God's assistance necessary in order to remain faithful to his Law; the very knowledge of that Law is a gift from heaven. All their special understanding and wisdom comes from God.

> From the source of His righteousness
>   is my justification,
> and from His marvellous mysteries
>   is the light in my heart.
> My eyes have gazed
>   on that which is eternal,
> on wisdom concealed from men,
>   on knowledge and wise design
>   (hidden) from the sons of men;
> on a fountain of righteousness
>   and on a storehouse of power,
> on a spring of glory
>   (hidden) from the assembly of flesh.
> God has given them to His chosen ones
>   as an everlasting possession,
> and has caused them to inherit
>   the lot of the Holy Ones (1QS 11:5–8 – DSSE 92–3).

The sentiments expressed in the Hymns, of love and gratitude and awareness of God's presence, represent a true religiousness and must have helped the sectary not to allow his life – governed as it was by laws and precepts – to slide into one of mere religious formalism.

Thou hast upheld me with certain truth;
   Thou hast delighted me with Thy Holy Spirit
   and [hast opened my heart] till this day . . .
The abundance of Thy forgiveness is with my steps
   and infinite mercy accompanies Thy judgement of me.
Until I am old Thou wilt care for me;
   for my father knew me not
   and my mother abandoned me to Thee.
For Thou art a father
   to all [the sons] of Thy truth,
and as a woman who tenderly loves her babe,
   so dost Thou rejoice in them;
and as a nurse bearing a child in her lap,
   so carest Thou for all Thy creatures
                   (1QH 9:32–36 – DSSE 181–2).

Whether the average Essene actually succeeded in fulfilling his high ideals, we cannot of course know: experience past and present has shown that paths to sanctity devised by organized religion are beset with snares. But there can be no doubt of their intention. The aim of a holy life lived within the Covenant was to penetrate the secrets of heaven in this world and to stand before God forever in the next. Like Isaiah, who beheld the Seraphim proclaiming 'Holy, holy, holy', and like Ezekiel, who in a trance watched the winged Cherubim drawing the divine Throne-Chariot, and like the ancient Jewish mystics who consecrated themselves, despite official disapproval by the rabbis, to the contemplation of the same Throne-Chariot and the heavenly Palaces, the Essenes, too, strove for a similar mystical knowledge, as one of their number testifies in a description of his own vision of the ministers of the 'Glorious Face'.

The [ministers] of the Glorious Face in the Abode of [the gods] of knowledge fall down before Him [and the Cherubim] utter blessings. And as they rise up, there is a divine small voice . . . and loud praise; [there is] a divine [small] voice as they fold their wings.

The Cherubim bless the image of the Throne-Chariot above the firmament and they praise the [majesty] of the fiery firmament beneath the seat of His glory. And between the turning wheels, Angels of Holiness come and go, as it were a fiery vision of most holy spirits; and about them [flow] seeming rivulets of fire, like gleaming bronze, a radiance of many gorgeous colours, of marvellous pigments magnificently mingled.

The spirits of the Living God move perpetually with the glory of the wonderful Chariot. The small voice of blessing accompanies the tumult of their depart, and on the path of their return they worship the Holy One. Ascending, they rise marvellously; settling, they [stay] still. The sound of joyful praise is silenced and there is a small voice of blessing in all the camps of God. And a voice of praise [resounds] from the midst of all their divisions . . . and each one in his place, all their numbered ones sing hymns of praise (Angelic Liturgy 2:9 – DSSE 212–13).

3 WORSHIP IN THE COMMUNITY OF THE COVENANT

In addition to the worship of God offered through a life of holiness, the Qumran sectary had more particularly to perform the ritual acts prescribed by Moses in the correct manner and at the right times. The earthly liturgy was intended to be a replica of that sung by the choirs of angels in the celestial Temple.

To judge from the many references to it, the time element both calendric and horary was crucial. The Community Rule lays down that the Community was not to 'depart from any command of God concerning their appointed times; they shall be neither early nor late for any of their appointed times, they shall stray neither to the right nor to the left of any of His true precepts' (1QS 1:13–15 – DSSE 72). This injunction asks for exact punctuality in regard to the two daily moments of prayer meant to coincide with and replace the perpetual burnt-offering sacrificed in the Temple at sunrise and sunset (Exod. 29:30; Num. 28:4), but it demands in addition a strict observance of the sect's own liturgical calendar.

To understand the peculiarity of Essenism in this respect, a few words need to be said about the calendar followed by non-sectarian Judaism. Essentially, this was regulated by the move-ments of the moon; months varied in duration from between twenty-nine and thirty days and the year consisted of twelve months of 354 days. Needless to say, such a lunar year does not correspond to the four seasons determined by the movements of the sun, by solstices and equinoxes. The shortfall of about ten days between the lunar and the solar year was therefore compensated for by means of 'intercalation', i.e. by inserting after Adar (February/March), the twelfth month of the year, a supplementary 'Second Adar' at the end of every thirty-six lunar months.

The Qumran sect rejected this seemingly artificial system and adopted instead a chronological reckoning, probably of priestly origin, based on the sun, a practice attested also in the Book of Jubilees and 1 Enoch. The outstanding feature of this solar calendar was its absolute regularity in that, instead of 354 days, not divisible by seven, it consisted of 364 days, i.e. fifty-two weeks precisely. Each of its four seasons was thirteen weeks long divided into three months of thirty days each, plus an additional 'remembrance' day (1QS 10:5 – DSSE 89) linking one season to another $(13 \times 7 = 91 = 3 \times 30 + 1)$. In tune in this way with the 'laws of the Great Light of heaven' (1QH 12:5 – DSSE 188) and not with the 'festivals of the nations' (4QpHos 2:16 – DSSE 230), Qumran saw its calendar as corresponding to 'the certain law from the month of God' (1QH 12:9 – DSSE 189). Its unbroken rhythm meant further-more that the first day of the year and of each subsequent season always fell on the same day of the week. For the Essenes this was Wednesday, since according to Genesis 1:14–19 it was on the fourth day that the sun and the moon were created. Needless to add, the same monotonous sequence also implied that all the feasts of the year always fell on the same day of the week: Passover, the fifteenth day of the first month, was always celebrated on a Wednesday; the Feast of Weeks, the fifteenth day of the third month, always on a Sunday; the Day of Atonement, the tenth day of the seventh month, on a Friday; the Feast of Tabernacles, the fifteenth day of the seventh month, on a Wednesday, etc. This solar calendar with its eternal regularity cannot of course stand up to the astronomical calculation of 365 days 5 hours 48 minutes and 48 seconds to the year, but the Scrolls so far published give no indication of how the Essenes proposed to cope with this inconvenience, or whether indeed they were even aware of it.

One practical consequence of the sect's adherence to a calendar at variance with that of the rest of Judaism was that its feast-days were working days for other Jews and vice versa. The Wicked Priest was thus able to travel (journeys of any distance being forbidden on holy days of rest) to the place of exile of the Teacher of Righteousness while he and his followers were celebrating the Day of Atonement (cf. above, p. 143). In fact, it is likely that the persecutors of the sect deliberately chose that date to oblige the sectaries to attend to them on what they considered to be their 'Day of Fasting' and 'Sabbath of repose', and thus 'confuse them and cause them to stumble'. The same sort of story is told of the Patriarch Gamaliel II, who endeavoured to humiliate Rabbi Joshua ben Hananiah by requiring him to visit him, carrying his stick and purse (also forbidden in the circumstances), on what Joshua reckoned to be the Day of Atonement (mRosh Ha-shanah 2:9).

Another peculiarity of the liturgical calendar of the Community was the division of the year into seven fifty-day periods – hence the name pentecontad calendar – each marked by an agricultural festival, e.g. the Feast of New Wine, the Feast of Oil, etc. A similar system is mentioned by Philo in connection with the Therapeutae (cf. above, pp. 135–6). One of these festivals, the Feast of the New Wheat, coincided with the Feast of

Weeks and was for the Essenes/Therapeutae also the principal
holy day of the year, that of the Renewal of the Covenant, the
importance of which is discussed in chapters 4 and 5 (p. 107).
From the Book of Jubilees, where as has been said, the same
calendar is followed, it is clear that Pentecost (the Feast
of Weeks), together with the Feast of the Renewal of the
Covenant, were celebrated on the fifteenth day of the third
month (Jub. 6:17–19). An outline of the ceremony performed
on this holy day, with its acknowledgements of sin and its
blessings and curses, is preserved in the Community Rule
(1QS 1:16-2:25 – DSSE 72–4). The sectaries assemble in the
service in strict hierarchical order: the priests first, ranked in
order of status, after them the Levites, and lastly 'all the people
one after another in their Thousands, Hundreds, Fifties and
Tens, that every Israelite may know his place in the Community
of God according to the everlasting design' (1QS 2:22–23 –
DSSE 74). Blessing God, the priests then recite his acts of loving-
kindness to Israel and the Levites, Israel's rebellions against
him. This recognition of guilt is followed by an act of public
repentance appropriate to a community of converts.

> We have strayed! We have [disobeyed]! We and our fathers
> before us have sinned and acted wickedly in walking [counter
> to the precepts] of truth and righteousness. [And God has]
> judged us and our fathers also; but He has bestowed His
> bountiful mercy on us from everlasting to everlasting (1QS
> 1:24-2:1 – DSSE 73)

After the confession, the priests solemnly bless the converts of
Israel, calling down on them in particular, the gifts of wisdom
and knowledge.

> May he bless you with all good and preserve you from all
> evil! May He lighten your heart with life-giving wisdom and
> grant you eternal knowledge! May He raise His merciful
> face towards you for everlasting bliss (1QS 2:2–4 – DSSE
> 73).

This paraphrase of the blessing of Israel which God commanded Moses to transmit to Aaron and his sons in Numbers 6:24–26, and which recalls the fourth of the daily Eighteen Benedictions of traditional Judaism, is accompanied by a Levitical curse of the party of Satan and a special malediction directed by both priests and Levites at any sectary whose conversion may be insincere:

> Cursed be the man who enters this Covenant while walking among the idols of his heart, who sets up before himself his stumbling-block of sin so that he may backslide! Hearing the words of this Covenant, he blesses himself in his heart and says, 'Peace be with me, even though I walk in the stubbornness of my heart' (1QS 2:11–12 – DSSE 73).

Each benediction and curse is approved by the whole congregation with a twice repeated 'Amen'.

The ceremony of the Renewal of the Covenant is the only rite described in any detail among the Scrolls so far published, but as the Essenes laid so much emphasis on the full and punctilious observance of the Law of Moses it may be taken for granted that they did not omit the many other basic acts of Jewish religion and worship. Circumcision for example, was certainly practised, though it is referred to only figuratively in the context of severing the 'foreskin of the evil inclination' (1QS 5:5 – DSSE 78), or possibly as the 'Covenant of Abraham' (CD 12:11; 16:6 – DSSE 114, 109). The laws of purity were also assuredly essential to the sect, despite the absence of any practical guidance on them. The same applies to the dietary laws, though a glimpse of information on these comes from the Damascus Rule declaring the eating of 'live creatures' prohibited (e.g. larvae of bees, fish and locusts – CD 12:11–15 – DSSE 114), and from Josephus's remark that an Essene was forbidden to eat food prepared by people not belonging to the brotherhood (*War* ii. 143).

On three other topics, the Qumran sources are less taciturn: ritual ablutions, Temple worship and the sacred meal. Discussed in chapters 4 and 5 as part of the life of the sect, it remains now to consider the doctrinal significance of these rites.

Josephus, as will be recalled, observes that the Essenes took a ritual bath twice daily before meals (cf. above p. 126). To this the Scrolls add that the minimum quantity of clean water required for a valid act of purification was to be the amount necessary to cover a man (CD 10:12–13 – DSSE 111–12). This is not of course an Essene invention, but typically, where the Mishnah prescribes a minimum of forty seahs (about 120 gallons), the sect's teaching concentrates on the practical purpose of the Mishnaic rule, namely that 'in them men may immerse themselves' (mMikwaoth 7:1) and eliminates the obligation of having carefully to measure out what that quantity should be. Of greater interest, however, is the theological aspect, with its insistence on a correlation between the inner condition of a man and the outer rite. The wicked, according to the Community Rule, 'shall not enter the water . . . for they shall not be cleansed unless they turn from their wickedness' (1QS 5:13–14 – DSSE 79). True purification comes from the 'spirit of holiness' and true cleansing from the 'humble submission' of the soul to all God's precepts.

> For it is through the spirit of true counsel concerning the ways of man that all his sins shall be expiated . . . He shall be cleansed from all his sins by the spirit of holiness . . . and his iniquity shall be expiated by the spirit of uprightness and humility. And when his flesh is sprinkled with purifying water and sanctified by cleansing water, it shall be made clean by the humble submission of his soul to all the precepts of God (1QS 3:6–9 – DSSE 75).

The second issue has to do with the sect's attitude towards the Temple and Temple sacrifice. While some Essenes, notwithstanding their vow of total fidelity to the Law of Moses, rejected the validity of the sanctuary and refused to participate (temporarily) in its rites (cf. above pp. 129–30), they evaded the theological dilemma in which this stand might have placed them by contending that until the re-dedication of the Temple, the only true worship of God was to be offered in their establishment. The Council of the Community was to be the 'Most Holy Dwelling for Aaron' where, 'without the flesh of holocausts and the fat of sacrifice', a 'sweet fragrance' was to be sent up to God, and where prayer was to serve 'as an acceptable fragrance of righteousness' (1QS 8:8-9; 9:4-5 – DSSE 85, 87). The Community itself was to be the sacrifice offered to God in atonement for Israel's sins (1QS 8:4-5 – DSSE 85).

Besides this evidence in the Community Rule, the same equation of Council of the Community = the Temple appears in the Habakkuk Commentary (12:3-4) in a most interesting interpretation of the word 'Lebanon'. Traditionally, 'Lebanon' is understood by ancient Jewish interpreters to symbolize 'the Temple'. For example, Deuteronomy 3:25, 'Let me go over . . . and see . . . that goodly mountain and Lebanon', is rendered in Targum Onkelos as, 'Let me go over . . . and see . . . that goodly mountain and the Temple'. The Qumran commentator, explaining the Habakkuk text, 'For the violence done to Lebanon shall overwhelm you' (Hab. 2:17), proceeds from the belief that the Council of the Community is the one valid Temple. He then sets out to prove it by directly associating Lebanon with the Council in the conviction that the traditional exegesis will be familiar to all his readers: Lebanon = Temple. Temple = Council of the Community, *ergo* Lebanon = Council of the Community.

The symbolical approach of the sect to sacrificial worship may account for Essene celibacy (where it was practised). Sexual abstinence was imposed on those participating in the Temple services, both priests and laymen; no person who had sexual intercourse (or an involuntary emission, or even any contact with a menstruating woman) could lawfully take part. More importantly still, bearing in mind the central place occupied by prophecy in Essene doctrine, clear indications exist in inter-Testamental and rabbinic literature that a similar renunciation was associated with the prophetic state. Thus Moses, in order always to be ready to hear the voice of God, is said by Philo to have cleansed himself of 'all calls of mortal nature, food, drink, and intercourse with women' (*Life of Moses* ii. 68–9). Consequently, despite the attempt made by this writer and by Josephus to attribute the sect's celibacy to misogyny, a more reasonable explanation would be that it was thought that lives intended to be wholly consecrated to worship and wholly preoccupied with meditation on prophecy should be kept wholly and not intermittently, pure.

The Common table of the Essenes, the third special cultic subject to be examined, has already been discussed in previous chapters (pp. 94, 126), but one remaining point needs to be mentioned, namely that since the rules relating to the daily meal and the messianic meal are the same, it is not unreasonable to infer from the New Testament parallel that the former was thought to prefigure the latter. As is well known, the evangelist Matthew portrays the Last Supper as the prototype of the great eschatological feast, quoting Jesus as saying:

> I tell you, I shall not drink again of this fruit of the vine until that day when I drink it new with you in my Father's kingdom (Mt. 26:3).

4 FUTURE EXPECTATIONS IN THE COMMUNITY OF THE COVENANT

The Essene sect was born into a world of eschatological ferment, of intense expectation of the end foretold by the prophets. Using biblical models as vehicles for their own convictions, the Teacher of Righteousness and the Community's sages projected an image of the future which is detailed and colourful, but which cannot always be fully comprehended by us, partly because some of the associations escape us, and partly because of gaps in the extant texts and the incompleteness of the documentation in general. They foresaw their Community as fulfilling the prophetic expectations of the salvation of the righteous. It was from their ranks, swollen by the reconversion of some of the 'Simple of Ephraim' (4QpNah 3:4–5 – DSSE 233) who had caused such distress by their previous apostasy, and by other Jewish recruits (1QSa 1:1–5 – DSSE 118), that the sons of Light would go to battle against the sons of Darkness. The Community, the 'exiles of the desert', would after a preliminary attack on the 'army of Satan' symbolized by the 'ungodly of the Covenant' and their foreign allies from the environs of Judaea, followed by an assault on the Kittim occupying the Holy Land, move to Jerusalem. These events were expected to cover a period of six years. The seventh, the first sabbatical year of the War would see the restoration of the Temple worship.

Of the remaining thirty-three years of its duration, four would be sabbatical years, so the War would be waged during twenty-nine: against the 'sons of Shem' for nine years, against the 'sons of Ham' for ten years, and against the 'sons of Japheth' for another ten years (1QM 1–2 – DSSE 124–6). The final conflict would end with the total defeat of the 'King of the Kittim' and of Satan's hosts, and the joyful celebrations of the Hero, God, by the victorious sons of Light.

> Rise up, O Hero!
> Lead off Thy captives, O Glorious One!
> Gather up Thy spoils, O Author of mighty deeds!
> Lay Thy hand on the neck of Thine enemies
>   and Thy feet on the pile of the slain!
> Smite the nations, Thine adversaries,
>   and devour flesh with Thy sword!
> Fill Thy land with glory
>   and Thine inheritance with blessing!
> Let there be a multitude of cattle in Thy fields,
>   and in Thy palaces silver and gold and precious stones!
>
> O Zion, rejoice greatly!
>   Rejoice all you cities of Judah!
> Keep your gates ever open
>   that the host of the nations may be brought in!
> Their kings shall serve you
>   and all your oppressors shall bow down before you;
>   they shall lick the dust of your feet.

Shout for joy, O daughters of my people!
Deck yourselves with glorious jewels
    and rule over the kingdom of the nations!
Sovereignty shall be to the Lord
    and everlasting dominion to Israel
                            (1QM 19:2-8 – DSSE 147-8).

Such was to be the course of the War in its earthly dimensions.
But it would possess in addition a cosmic quality. The hosts of
the sons of Light, commanded by the 'Prince of the Congregation', were to be supported by the angelic armies led by the
'Prince of Light', also known in the Scrolls as the archangel
Michael or Melchizedek. Similarly, the 'ungodly of the Covenant' and their Gentile associates were to be aided by the demonic forces of Satan, or Belial, or Melkiresha. These two opposing
camps were to be evenly matched, and God's intervention
alone would bring about the destruction of evil (1QM 18:1-3
– DSSE 146). Elsewhere the grand finale is represented as a
judgement scene in which the heavenly prince Melchizedek
recompenses 'the holy ones of God' and executes 'the vengeance
of the judgements of God' over Satan and his lot (11QMelch
2:9, 13 – DSSE 267).

    The role of the priests and Levites in this imaginary ultimate
grappling of good with evil emerges as that of non-combatants,
but it is difficult to determine the function of the commander-
in-chief, the so-called 'Prince of the Congregation'. We learn
that on his shield will be inscribed his name, the names of
Israel, Levi and Aaron, and those of the twelve tribes and their
chiefs (1QM 5:1-2 – DSSE 130); but little room appears to be
left in the War Rule for him to act as the royal Messiah. God
himself is the supreme agent of salvation and after him in
importance is Michael.

    In the other Scrolls, by contrast, the theme of Messianism is
prominent. Complex and *sui generis*, it envisages everywhere
except in the Damascus Rule not one, but two, and possibly
even three, messianic figures. The Lay King-Messiah, otherwise
known as the 'Branch of David', the 'Messiah of Israel', the

'Prince of [all] the Congregation' and the 'Sceptre', was to usher in 'the Kingdom of his people' and 'bring death to the ungodly' and defeat '[the kings of the] nations' (1QSb 5:21, 25, 28 – DSSE 208-9). As befits a priestly sect, however, the Priest-Messiah comes first in the order of precedence, the 'Messiah of Aaron', the 'Priest', the 'Interpreter of the Law' (cf. 1QSa 2:20 – DSSE 121). The King-Messiah was to defer to him and to the priestly authority in general in all legal matters: 'As they teach him, so shall he judge' (4QpIsa 8-10: 23 – DSSE 227). The 'Messiah of Aaron' was to be the final Teacher, 'he who shall teach righteousness at the end of days' (CD 6:11 – DSSE 103). But he was also to preside over the battle liturgy (1QM 15:4; 16:13; 18:5 – DSSE 143-7) and the eschatological banquet (1QSa 2:12-21 – DSSE 121).

The third figure, 'the Prophet', is mentioned directly though briefly only once: we are told that his arrival was expected together with that of the Messiahs of Aaron and Israel (1QS 9:11 – DSSE 87). Viewed in the context of inter-Testamental Jewish ideas, the Prophet was to be either an Elijah returned as a precursor of the Messiah (Mal. 4:5; 1 Enoch 90:31, 37; Mt. 11:13; 17:12), or as a divine guide sent to Israel in the final days (1 Mac. 4:46; 14:41; Jn. 1:21) no doubt identical with 'the Prophet' promised by God to Moses ('I will raise up for them a prophet like you . . . He shall convey all my commands to them', Deut. 18:15-18; cf. Acts 3:22-23; 7:37). An identification of 'the Prophet' with a 'new Moses' is supported by the inclusion of the Deuteronomy passage in the Messianic Anthology or Testimonia from Cave 4 as the first of three messianic proof texts, the second being Balaam's prophecy concerning the Star to rise out of Jacob (Num. 24:15-17), and the third, the blessing of Levi by Moses (Deut. 33:11), prefiguring respectively the royal Messiah and the Priest-Messiah.

If it is proper to deduce from these not too explicit data that the messianic Prophet (or prophetic Messiah) was to teach the truth revealed on the eve of the establishment of the Kingdom, it would follow that his part was to all intents and purposes to be the same as that attributed by the Essenes to the Teacher of Righteousness. In consequence, it would not be unreasonable to suggest that at some point of the sect's history the coming of the Prophet was no longer expected; he was believed to have already appeared in the person of the Teacher of Righteousness.

The evidence so far published does not permit categorical statements on the sectaries' views of what was to follow the days of the Messiahs. Some kind of metamorphosis was awaited by them, as is clear from the Community Rule – 'until the determined end, and until the Renewal' (1QS 4:25 – DSSE 78). But one cannot be sure that it was understood as synonymous with the new creation of the Apocalypses of Ezra (7:75) and Baruch (32:6). Similarly, the 'new Jerusalem' described in various manuscripts (cf. chapter 3, p. 72) does not match by definition the Holy City descending from above of 1 Enoch (90:28–29) or Revelation 21, but could be an earthly city rebuilt according to the plans of angelic architects. The Temple Scroll when it is published will probably settle this issue.

As for the after-life proper, and the place it occupied in Essene thought, for many centuries in the biblical age Jews paid little attention to this question. They believed with most peoples in antiquity that after death the just and wicked alike would share a miserable, shadowy existence in Sheol, the underworld, where even God is forgotten: 'Turn, O Lord, save my life' cries the psalmist, 'for in death there is no remembrance of thee; in Sheol who can give thee praise?' (Ps. 6:5. Cf. Isa. 38:18; Ps. 88:10–12, etc.) The general hope was for a long and prosperous life, many children, a peaceful death in the midst of one's family, and burial in the tomb of one's fathers. Needless to say, with this simple outlook went a most sensitive appreciation of the present time as being the only moment in which man can be with God.

Eventually, the innate fear of death, and the dissatisfaction of later biblical thinkers with a divine justice that allowed the wicked to flourish on earth and the just to suffer, led to attempts in the post-exilic era to solve this fundamental dilemma. The idea of resurrection, or rather of the reunification of body and soul after death, first appears as a metaphor in Ezekiel's vision of the rebirth of the Jewish nation after the Babylonian captivity as the re-animation of dry bones (Ezek. 37). Later, after the historical experience of martyrdom under the persecution of Antiochus Epiphanes, resurrection was expected to be the true reward of individuals who freely gave their lives for God – i.e., for their religion (Dan. 12:2; 2 Mac. 7:9; 12:44; 14:46, etc.). At the same time, the notion of immortality also emerged, the idea that the righteous are to be vindicated and live for ever in God's presence. This view is developed fully in the Greek apocryphal Book of Wisdom (3:1 – 5:16).

Josephus tells us that the Essenes subscribed to this second school of thought. According to him, they adopted a distinctly Hellenistic concept of immortality, holding the flesh to be a prison out of which the indestructible soul of the just escapes into limitless bliss 'in an abode beyond the ocean' after its final deliverance (*War* ii. 154–8). Resurrection, implying a return of the spirit to a material body, can thus play no part in this scheme.

The Scrolls themselves, however, are not particularly helpful because they never confront the issue as such. We encounter statements such as, 'Hoist a banner, O you who lie in the dust! O bodies gnawed by worms, raise up an ensign . . .!' (1QH 6:34–35; cf. 11:10–14 – DSSE 172, 186), which may connote bodily resurrection. On the other hand, the poet's language may just be allegorical. Immortality as distinct from resurrection, is better attested. The substance of Josephus's account is confirmed, though not surprisingly without any typically Hellenistic colouring (no doubt introduced by him to please his Greek readers). The Community Rule, discussing the reward of the righteous and the wicked, assures the just of 'eternal joy in life without end, a crown of glory and a garment of majesty in unending light' (1QS 4:7–8 – DSSE 76), and sinners of 'eternal torment and endless disgrace together with shameful extinction in the fire of the dark regions' (1QS 4:12–13 – DSSE 77).

It is interesting to observe that immortality was not conceived of as an entirely new state, but rather as a direct continuation of the position attained on entry into the Community. From that moment, the sectary was raised to an 'everlasting height' and joined to the 'everlasting Council', the 'Congregation of the Sons of Heaven' (1QH 3: 20–22 – DSSE 158).

In sum, the portrait of the sectary as it is reflected in his religious ideas and ideals bears the marks of a fanatical observance of the Mosaic Law, an overwhelming assurance of the correctness of his beliefs, and certainty of his own eventual salvation. But whereas these characteristics may make little appeal to modern man, we would do well not to overlook other traits conspicuous in particular, in his prayers and hymns, which testify to his absolute dependence on God and his total devotion to what he believed to be God's cause.

> For without Thee no way is perfect,
>   and without Thy will nothing is done.
> It is Thou who hast taught all knowledge
>   and all things come to pass by Thy will.
> There is none beside Thee to dispute Thy counsel
>   or to understand all Thy holy design
> or to contemplate the depth of Thy mysteries
>   and the power of Thy might.
>
> Who can endure Thy glory,
>   and what is the son of man
> in the midst of Thy wonderful deeds?
> What shall one born of woman
>   be accounted before Thee?
> Kneaded from the dust,
>   his abode is the nourishment of worms.
> He is but a shape, but moulded clay,
>   and inclines towards the dust (1QS 11:17–22 – DSSE 94).

BIBLIOGRAPHY TO CHAPTER 7

Monographs devoted to biblical theology could fill a whole library but since they are not directly relevant in this study, only the most recent works, both translations from the German, are listed: G. Fohrer, *History of Israelite Religion* (S.P.C.K., London, 1973) and G. von Rad, *Old Testament Theology* I–II (S.C.M., London, 1975).

For the religious ideas of inter-Testamental Judaism the reader may consult R. Travers Herford, *Talmud and Apocrypha* (Soncino, London, 1933); W. Bousset-H. Gressmann, *Die Religion des Judentums im späthellenistischen Zeitalter* (Mohr, Tübingen, ⁴1966) and E. Schürer-G. Vermes-F. Millar-M. Black, *The History of the Jewish People in the Age of Jesus Christ* II (Clark, Edinburgh, 1979).

The standard works on rabbinic theology are: G. F. Moore, *Judaism in the First Centuries of the Christian Era* I–III (Harvard U.P., Cambridge, Mass., 1927–30); J. Maier, *Geschichte der jüdischen Religion* (W. de Gruyter, Berlin, 1972); E. E. Urbach, *The Sages: Their Concepts and Beliefs* I–II (Magnes, Jerusalem, 1975). For a modern attempt, see L. Jacobs, *A Jewish Theology* (Darton, Longman & Todd, London, 1973).

For the New Testament see R. Bultmann, *Theology of the New Testament* I–II (S.C.M., London, 1952-5); H. Conzelmann, *An Outline of the Theology of the New Testament* (S.C.M., London, 1969); J. Jeremias, *New Testament Theology* I–II (S.C.M., London, 1971-7). Readers well versed in Hebrew and Greek are recommended to use G. Kittel-G. Friedrich, *Theological Dictionary of the New Testament* I–X (Eerdmans, Grand Rapids, 1963-76). The work deals also with biblical, inter-Testamental and rabbinic religion as well.

There is no comprehensive study of the theology of the Scrolls. Most general works on Qumran include a chapter on doctrines and beliefs and the bibliographies given on pp. 231-2 list all the publications on the subject. The following books deserve special mention: F. Nötscher, *Zur theologischen*

Terminologie der Qumran-Texte (Hanstein, Bonn, 1956); *Gotteswege und Menschenwege in der Bibel und Qumran* (Hanstein, Bonn, 1958); H. Ringgren, *The Faith of Qumran: Theology of the Dead Sea Scrolls* (Fortress, Philadelphia, 1963); J. Jeremias, 'Qumrân et la théologie', NRT 85 (1963), 474–90; A.-M. Denis, *Les thèmes de connaissance dans le Document de Damas* (Publications universitaires, Louvain, 1967); P. von der Osten-Sacken, *Gott und Belial: Traditionsgeschichtliche Untersuchungen zum Dualismus in den Texten aus Qumran* (Vandenhoeck & Ruprecht, Göttingen, 1969); G. Klinzing, *Die Umdeutung des Kultus in der Qumrangemeinde und im Neuen Testament* (Vandenhoeck & Ruprecht, Göttingen, 1971); E. H. Merrill, *Qumran and Predestination* (Brill, Leiden, 1975); E. P. Sanders, *Paul and Palestinian Judaism* (S.C.M., London and Fortress, Philadelphia, 1977), 239–321; P. Garnet, *Salvation and Atonement in the Qumran Scrolls* (Mohr, Tübingen, 1977); M. Delcor (ed.), *Qumrân: Sa piété, sa théologie et son milieu* (Duculot, Paris–Gembloux, 1978).

1 THE COVENANT

For a recent discussion of the biblical notion, see M. Weinfeld, 'Covenant', Enc. Jud. 5, 1012–22; cf. also the relevant sections in works on biblical theology and in TDNT. The Qumran notion has been discussed by R. F. Collins, 'The Berith-Notion of the Cairo Damascus Covenant and its Comparison with the New Testament', *Ephemerides Theologicae Lovanienses* 39 (1963), 555–94; J. G. Harris, 'The Covenant Concept among the Qumran Sectaries', *Evang. Quarterly* 39 (1967), 86–92; J. A. Huntjens, 'Contrasting Notions of Covenant and Law in the Texts from Qumran', RQ 8 (1974), 361–80.

On the function of Bible interpretation in ancient Judaism and Qumran, see the following studies: F. F. Bruce, *Biblical Exegesis in the Qumran Texts* (Tyndale, London, 1959); O. Betz, *Offenbarung und Schriftforschung in der Qumransekte* (Mohr, Tübingen, 1960); G. Vermes, *Scripture and Tradition in Judaism* (Brill, Leiden, 1961, ²1973); *Post-Biblical Jewish Studies* (Brill, Leiden, 1975); 'Interpretation (History of) at

Qumran and in the Targums', IDBS (1976), 438–43; S. Lowy, 'Some Aspects of Normative and Sectarian Interpretation of the Scriptures', ALUOS 6 (1969), 84-163; W. H. Brownlee, 'The Background of Biblical Interpretation at Qumran', *Qumrân* (ed. M. Delcor, 1978), 183-93; M. P. Horgan, *Pesharim: Qumran Interpretation of Biblical Books* (Catholic Biblical Association, Washington, 1979); H. Gabrion, 'L'interprétation de l'Ecriture dans la littérature de Qumrân', *Aufstieg und Niedergang der römischen Welt* (ed. H. Temporini and W. Haase) XIX/1 (W. de Gruyter, Berlin, 1979), 779-848.

2 ELECTION AND HOLY LIFE IN THE COMMUNITY OF THE COVENANT
On the doctrine of the two spirits, see J. Licht, 'An Analysis of the Treatise of the Two Spirits in DSD', *Scripta Hierosolymitana* 4 (1958), 88–100; H. W. Huppenbauer, *Der Mensch zwischen zwei Welten* (Zwingli, Zurich, 1959); P. Wernberg-Møller, 'A Reconsideration of the Two Spirits in the Rule of the Community', RQ 3 (1962), 433–41; J. H. Charlesworth, 'A Critical Comparison of the Dualism in 1QS III, 13 – IV, 26 and the "Dualism" contained in the Fourth Gospel', NTS 15 (1969), 389–418.
On the *Merkabah* doctrine, see chapter 3, pp. 63-4.

3 WORSHIP IN THE COMMUNITY OF THE COVENANT
A considerable literature is devoted to the problem of the Qumran calendar. For a general survey in the context of the Jewish calendar as such see Schürer–Vermes–Millar I, 587–601. The most important special studies are by Annie Jaubert, 'Le calendrier des Jubilés et de la secte de Qumrân: ses origines bibliques', VT 3 (1955), 250–64; S. Talmon, 'The Calendar Reckoning of the Sect from the Judaean Desert', *Scripta Hierosolymitana* 4 (1958), 162–99; A. R. C. Leaney, *The Rule of Qumran and its Meaning* (S.C.M., London, 1966), 80–90; J. M. Baumgarten, '4Q Halakah°5, the Law of Ḥadash and the Pentecontad Calendar', JJS 27 (1976), 36–46.
The regularity of the system will appear from the following table.

	Months		
	I, IV, VII, X	II, V, VIII, XI	III, VI, IX, XII
Wednesday	1 8 15 22 29	6 13 20 27	4 11 18 25
Thursday	2 9 16 23 30	7 14 21 28	5 12 19 26
Friday	3 10 17 24	1 8 15 22 29	6 13 20 27
Sabbath	4 11 18 25	2 9 16 23 30	7 14 21 28
Sunday	5 12 19 26	3 10 17 24	1 8 15 22 29
Monday	6 13 20 27	4 11 18 25	2 9 16 23 30
Tuesday	7 14 21 28	5 12 19 26	3 10 17 24 *31*

The 31st day in the last column corresponds to the additional day linking one season of three months to the next.

For a detailed bibliography, including a section on the issue of the date of the Last Supper in the Gospels, see Fitzmyer's bibliography (cf. p. 45 above), 131–7.

Dawn as marking a specific moment of prayer in heaven appears in the ancient Aramaic paraphrases of Gen. 32:25 and 27, the story of Jacob's struggle with an angel, Sariel according to Targum Neofiti I. The biblical text, 'Let me go for the day is breaking' is interpreted as, 'Let me go for the rising of the column of the dawn has come; for the time has come for the angels on high to praise, and I am the chief of those who praise'. Cf. G. Vermes, 'The Archangel Sariel', in *Christianity, Judaism and other Greco-Roman Cults*, ed. J. Neusner (Brill, Leiden, 1975), 159–66.

The ritual of the Renewal of the Covenant is treated in the commentaries on the Community Rule. Cf. in particular, A. R. C. Leaney, *The Rule of Qumran*, 95–107. See further M. Weise, *Kultzeiten und kultischer Bundesschluss in der 'Ordensregel' vom Toten Meer* (Brill, Leiden, 1961); M. Delcor, 'Das Bundesfest in Qumran und das Pfingstfest' *Bibel und Leben* 4 (1963), 188–204; 'Pentecôte', DB Suppl. VII, 858–79.

For Jewish notions of purification, see J. Neusner, *The Idea of Purity in Ancient Judaism* (Brill, Leiden, 1973); O. Betz. 'Die Proselytentaufe der Qumransekte und die Taufe im Neuen Testament', RQ 1 (1959), 213–34; E. F. Sutcliffe, 'Baptism and

Baptismal Rites at Qumran', *Heythrop Journal* 1 (1960), 69–101; J. Gnilka, 'Die essenischen Tauchbäder und die Johannestaufe', RQ 3 (1961), 185–207; A. Dupont-Sommer, 'Culpabilité et rites de purification dans la secte juive de Qoumrân', *Semitica* 15 (1965), 61–70; J. A. Fitzmyer, *Essays on the Semitic Background of the New Testament* (Chapman, London, 1971), 469–73. On Jewish and Christian baptizing sects, see J. Thomas, *Le movement baptiste en Palestine et Syrie (150 a. J. – C. – 300 apr. J. – C.)* (Duculot, Gembloux, 1935).

Regarding the spiritualization of Temple and worship, see in addition to the monograph of Klinzing quoted above (p. 190), B. Gärtner, *The Temple and the Community in Qumran and the New Testament* (C.U.P., Cambridge, 1965) and G. Vermes, PBJS, 83–5. Cf. also *Scripture and Tradition in Judaism* (Brill, Leiden, 1961, ²1973) concerning the symbolism Lebanon = Council of the Community = Temple (pp. 26–39). On various Jewish and Christian attitudes to the Temple, see J. Neusner, *Early Rabbinic Judaism* (Brill, Leiden, 1975), 34–49.

On the question of celibacy, see H. R. Moehring, 'Josephus on the Marriage Customs of the Essenes', *Early Christian Origins. Studies in Honor of H. R. Willoughby* (Quadrangle Books, Chicago, 1961), 120–7; A. Marx, 'Les racines du célibat essénien', RQ 7 (1970), 323–42; A. Guillaumont, 'A propos du célibat des Esséniens', *Hommages à A. Dupont-Sommer* (Maisonneuve, Paris, 1971), 395–404; G. Vermes, *Jesus the Jew* (Collins, London, 1973 and Fortress, Philadelphia, 1981), 99–102; J. Coppens, 'Le célibat essénien', *Qumrân* (ed. M. Delcor, 1978), 295–303.

For the Qumran meal and its New Testament associations see J. van der Ploeg, 'The Meals of the Essenes', JSS 2 (1957), 163–75; K. G. Kuhn, 'The Lord's Supper and the Communal Meal at Qumran', *The Scrolls and the New Testament*, ed. K. Stendahl (S.C.M., London, 1958), 65–93; J. Gnilka, 'Das Gemeinschaftsmahl der Essener', *Bibl. Zeitschr.* 5 (1961), 39–55; J. F. Priest, 'The Messiah and the Meal in 1QSa', JBL 82 (1963), 95–100; M. Delcor, 'Repas cultuels esséniens et thérapeutes', RQ 6 (1969), 401–25.

4 FUTURE EXPECTATIONS IN THE COMMUNITY OF THE COVENANT

On Jewish eschatology and apocalyptic in general see P. Volz, *Die Eschatologie der jüdischen Gemeinde im neutestamentlichen Zeitalter* (Mohr, Tübingen, ²1934); D. S. Russell, *The Method and Message of Jewish Apocalyptic* (S.C.M., London, 1964); M. Delcor, 'Le milieu d'origine et le développement de l'apocalyptique juive', *La littérature juive entre Tenach et Mischna*, ed. W. C. van Unnik (Brill, Leiden, 1974), 101–17. For a useful bibliography, see J. H. Charlesworth, *The Pseudepigrapha and Modern Research* (Scholars Press, Missoula, 1976), 66–8.

For Essene and Qumran eschatology, the reader may turn to P. Grelot, 'L'eschatologie des Esséniens et le livre d'Énoch', RQ 1 (1958), 112–31; I. Hahn, 'Josephus und die Eschatologie von Qumran', *Qumran-Probleme*, ed. H. Bardtke (Akademie Verlag, Berlin, 1963) 167–91; J. Licht, 'Time and Eschatology in Apocalyptic Literature and Qumran', JJS 16 (1967), 117–82; J. Pryke, 'Eschatology in the Dead Sea Scrolls', *The Scrolls and Christianity*, ed. M. Black (S.P.C.K., London, 1969), 45–57.

For the eschatological function of angels, see in particular, Y. Yadin *The Scroll of the War of the Sons of Light against the Sons of Darkness* (O.U.P., Oxford, 1962), 229–42; J. T. Milik, '*Milkî-ṣedeq* et *Milkî-resha*' dans les anciens écrits juifs et chrétiens', JJS 23 (1972), 95–114; G. Vermes, 'The Archangel Sariel. A Targumic Parallel to the Dead Sea Scrolls', *Christianity, Judaism and other Greco-Roman Cults* III (Brill, Leiden, 1975), 159–66. See also the Melchizedek document: cf. Chapter 3 pp. 82–3, and F. L. Horton, *The Melchizedek Tradition* (C.U.P., Cambridge, 1976), 64–82.

Among the general works dealing with Messianism, see in particular S. Mowinckel, *He that Cometh* (Blackwell, Oxford, 1956); J. Klausner, *The Messianic Idea in Israel* (Allen & Unwin, London, 1956); M. de Jonge, 'The Use of the Word "Anointed" in the Time of Jesus', NT 8 (1966), 132–48; E. Schürer–G. Vermes–F. Millar–M. Black, *The History of the*

Jewish People in the Age of Jesus Christ II (Clark, Edinburgh, 1978), §29.

For New Testament Messianism, see W. Grundmann, F. Hesse, M. de Jonge, A. S. van der Woude, '*Christos*', TDNT IX (1974), 493–580. Cf. G. Vermes, *Jesus the Jew* (Collins, London, 1973 and Fortress, Philadelphia, 1981), 129–59, 250–6.

For a comprehensive list of studies in Qumran Messianism, see the various bibliographies (Jongeling, Fitzmyer). The following titles may be of special interest: A. S. van der Woude, *Die messianischen Vorstellungen der Gemeinde von Qumrân* (Van Gorcum, Assen, 1957); 'Le Maître de Justice et les deux messies de la communauté de Qumrân', *La secte de Qumran et les origines du Christianisme*, ed. J. van der Ploeg (Desclée de Brouwer, Bruges, 1959), 121–34; J. Liver, 'The Doctrine of the Two Messiahs in the Sectarian Literature in the Time of the Second Commonwealth', HTR 52 (1959), 149–85; J. Starcky, 'Les quatre étapes du messianisme à Qumrân', RB 70 (1963), 48–505; R. E. Brown, 'The Teacher of Righteousness and the Messiah(s)', *The Scrolls and Christianity*, ed. M. Black (S.P.C.K., London, 1969), 37–44, 109–12; J. A. Fitzmyer, *Essays on the Semitic Background of the New Testament* (Chapman, London, 1971), 127–60; J. R. Villalón, 'Sources vétéro-testamentaires de la doctrine qumrânienne des deux Messies', RQ 8 (1972), 53–63; A. Caquot, 'Le messianisme qumrânien', *Qumrân* (ed. M. Delcor, 1978), 231–47.

On the messianic Prophet, see Vermes, *Jesus the Jew*, 94–7; 137–9. In earlier publications I have suggested that the role of *Geber* (Man) in the Community Rule, i.e. the teacher of the elect at the end of time (1QS 4:20–22 – DSSE 77–8), corresponds to that of the Prophet, and that in the Commentary on Psalm 37 *Geber* is identified as the Teacher of Righteousness. Cf. *Discovery*, 220–2; *Scripture and Tradition*, 56–66; DSSE 50. See also W. H. Brownlee, 'The Servant of the Lord in the Qumran Scrolls', BASOR 135 (1954), 36–8; *The Meaning of the Qumran Scrolls for the Bible* (O.U.P., New York, 1964), 261–70.

Two particular problems, one raised by the Damascus Rule,

the other by the Messianic Rule, need further comment. Instead of the plural form, 'Messiahs of Aaron and Israel' attested in 1QS 9:11 (DSSE 87), the Damascus Rule regularly uses the singular, 'Messiah of Aaron and Israel' (CD 12:23 – 13:1; 14:19; 19 (B1):10; 20 (B2):1 – DSSE 115, 117, 104, 106). This is apparently not a doctrinal correction introduced by the medieval copyists of the Cairo Geniza manuscripts, since unpublished fragments from Cave 4 are said to confirm the singular reading. Nevertheless, if on the one hand the language of the Damascus Rule appears to exclude belief in several Messiahs, the same document speaks also of the coming of the 'Interpreter of the Law' and the 'Prince of the whole Congregation' (CD 6:7; 7:18–20 – DSSE 102, 104). Thus it cannot be argued that CD ignores the doctrine of multiple Messianism. Perhaps it should further be pointed out that CD 7:18–20 discovers in the single verse of Num. 24:17 (A *star* shall come forth out of Jacob and a *sceptre* shall rise out of Israel') the announcement of the coming of both the 'Interpreter of the Law' (= the Star) and the 'Prince of the whole Congregation' (= the Sceptre), while the same passage of Numbers cited in 4QTest is usually understood to refer to the king Messiah only.

There has also been much discussion concerning an obscure and badly preserved passage in the Messianic Rule about God's 'begetting' the Messiah. In 1QSa 1:11–12 the *editio princeps* (DJD I, 110, 117–18) contains the reading, 'when (God) shall beget (*ywlyd*) the Messiah'. The editor of the text, however, J. T. Milik, suggests that it should be replaced by 'when (God) shall lead (*ywlyk*) the Messiah'. I myself interpret the phrase in a completely different sense and see in the passage a sectional heading: '[This shall be the ass]embly of the men of renown [called] to the meeting of the Council of the Community when [the Priest-] Messiah shall summon (*yw'yd*) them'. If this is right, the issue of the divine origin of the Messiah does not arise. Cf. DSSE 121; *Jesus the Jew*, 198–9, 262–3. See for various views, Y. Yadin, 'A Crucial Passage in the Dead Sea Scrolls', JBL 78 (1959), 240–1; M. Smith, 'God's Begetting the Messiah in 1QSa', NTS 5 (1959), 218–24; O. Michel, O. Betz, 'Von Gott gezeugt', *Judentum-Urchristentum-Kirche. Festschrift für J. Jeremias* (Töpelmann, Berlin, 1960), 3–23; W. Grundmann, 'Die Frage nach der Gottessohnschaft des Messias im Lichte von Qumran', *Qumran-Probleme*, ed. H. Bardtke (Akademie Verlag, Berlin, 1963), 86–111.

The question of an after-life in inter-Testamental Judaism has been the subject of a full monograph by G. W. E. Nickelsburg, *Resurrection, Immortality and Eternal Life in Inter-testamental Judaism* (Harvard U.P., Cambridge, Mass. 1972). For the Qumran doctrine see M. Delcor, 'L'immortalité de l'âme dans le Livre de la Sagesse et les documents de Qumrân', NRT 77 (1955), 614–30; R. B. Laurin, 'The Question of Immortality in the Qumran *Hodayot*', JSS 3 (1958), 344–55; K. Schubert, 'Das Problem der Auferstehungshoffnung in der Qumrantexten und in der frührabbinischen Literatur', *Wiener Zeitschrift für die Kunde des Morgenlandes* 56 (1960), 154–67; J. van der Ploeg, 'The Belief in Immortality in the Writings of Qumran', *Bibliotheca Orientalis* 18 (1961), 118–24.

Recalling Josephus's description of the Essene concept of immortality, the late first century BC epitaph of a young Egyptian Jewish woman, Arsinoe, written in Greek verse, speaks of her soul as having departed towards the holy ones (*eis hosious*). Cf. J. B. Frey, *Corpus Inscritionum Iudaicarum* II (Rome, 1952), 421.

The absence of emphasis on bodily resurrection in the Scrolls may be due to the Essenes' hope for the arrival of God's kingdom during the lifetime of the current generation. Their attitude may have been similar to that of the early Christians, who did not expect to die but only to be transformed (1 Cor. 15:51). Cf. G. Vermes, *Discovery*, 119; G. W. E. Nickelsburg, 'Future Life', IDBS (1976), 350.

CHAPTER 8

Qumran and Biblical Studies

In the opening phases of Scrolls research, the adjective 'revolutionary' was on everyone's lips. Today, such an emotive word is out of place and our initial enthusiasm has given way to a more mature assessment.

The opinion at present is that our greatest gain has been, first and foremost, an acquaintance with the life customs, history and beliefs of the Dead Sea Community itself. It should never be forgotten that before 1947 the very word Qumran was known only to geographers.

The second great benefit derived from the Judaean documents, supplemented by the Masada and Bar Kokhba finds, is that they have brought into being two new fields of scholarship: the study of Hebrew manuscripts and of Hebrew script and orthography from the third century BC to the second century AD. To appreciate what this means it should be recalled that, prior to the discovery, these years were represented by one single scrap of the Nash papyrus (cf. above, pp. 35–6, 43).

Besides these contributions, three other domains have been profoundly affected by the Judaean discoveries: the text of the Old Testament and the Apocrypha; non-biblical Jewish religious literature of the inter-Testamental period, i.e. the Pseudepigrapha; and finally the New Testament.

1 THE TEXT OF THE OLD TESTAMENT

Before 1947, the non-scholarly editions of the Hebrew Bible reproduced the text first printed in Venice in 1524–5, from late medieval manuscripts, by Jacob ben Hayyim. We also had a critical edition in the *Biblia Hebraica* issued in 1937 by Paul Kahle. Kahle worked from a biblical codex dated to AD 1008 which was copied 'from correct and clear manuscripts prepared by the master Aaron ben Moses ben Asher'. This Aaron, and his father Moses, the leading Palestinian Bible scholars of the ninth and tenth centuries, were responsible for putting the final touches to the established text of the Hebrew Scriptures known as *Masoretic*, i.e. the version prepared by *Masoretes* or guardians of tradition. Before that time, all Hebrew manuscripts, biblical scrolls included, were unvocalized; they consequently left the way open to mispronunciation and misinterpretation. The Masoretes met the need for an undisputed pronunciation, and the popular success of their reform led to a rejection of all the older manuscripts and their replacement by codices furnished with vowel signs. Only some sixth to eighth century fragments from the Cairo Geniza, and the already cited Nash papyrus with its few lines from Deuteronomy, survived by chance. For instance, before the discovery in Cave 1 of the complete text of Isaiah, the oldest extant Hebrew specimen of this book was the Cairo Codex of the Prophets copied by Moses ben Asher in AD 895.

The unvocalized version on which the Ben Ashers worked, the so-called proto-Masoretic text, had been stabilized for hundreds of years. It is reflected in the various translations and transcriptions of the Old Testament made in the early centuries of the Christian era: Jerome's Latin Vulgate (*c.* AD 400), the somewhat earlier Syriac rendering, the partial transliteration of the Hebrew text with Greek letters published by the great Christian biblical expert, Origen, in the first half of the third century, and extracts from the second century revisions or retranslations of the Greek Bible by Aquila, Symmachus and Theodotion, also preserved by Origen and other Church Fathers. Their convergent testimony, reinforced by biblical quotations in the writings of the rabbis in the second to the fifth centuries, suggests that the consonantal skeleton of this Bible existed already in around AD 100.

Further corroboration comes from the Mishnah and the

Talmud, which attest that it was at about the same time that the teachers assembled at Jamnia agreed on the exact contents of Holy Scripture; that is, on a list of books to be reckoned henceforth as authoritative sources of Judaism.

Before 1947, the student needing to reach back to the pre-Masoretic and pre-Christian stage of textual development was obliged to rely on the indirect evidence of the Samaritan Pentateuch and the ancient Greek or Septuagint version of the Old Testament. The Samaritan Pentateuch, written in Hebrew and preserved in medieval manuscripts, includes variant readings, and also shows deliberate alterations, some of them thought to have been introduced into the text in antiquity. The Septuagint, produced by Greek-speaking Egyptian Jews for their own use until it was appropriated by the Christian Church, was translated from the Hebrew between the third and the first century BC. It differs in both canon and text from the Hebrew counterparts. All the apocryphal books are acknowledged as Scripture; Esther and Daniel contain supplements; and discrepant readings occur throughout, with occasionally even more noticeable changes, such as another order of chapters and an abridged text in Jeremiah. The nature of the differences pointed strongly to a Hebrew source other than that of the proto-Masoretic text, but in the absence of manuscript proof, there could be no certainty that they did not result from a wilful interference with the original (interpolation, excision, paraphrase) or even from plain mistranslation.

Today, thanks to the marvellous literary windfall of thirty years ago, our knowledge of the Hebrew Bible has been extended by another one thousand years or more (a Samuel manuscript from Cave 4 is said to date to about 225 BC). The eleven caves have yielded something from every book of the Scriptures save Esther, varying from one small scrap to a complete Scroll. Many biblical writings are represented by more than one copy, as may be seen from the following list.

Pentateuch

Genesis	15
Exodus	15
Leviticus	9
Numbers	6
Deuteronomy	25

Former Prophets		Latter Prophets	
Joshua	2	Isaiah	18
Judges	3	Jeremiah	4
Samuel	4	Ezekiel	6
Kings	3	12 Minor	8

Writings

Psalms	27
Job	4
Proverbs	2
Ruth	4
Song of Songs	4
Ecclesiastes	2
Lamentations	4
Esther	0
Daniel	8
Ezra-Nehemiah	1
Chronicles	1

It should not surprise us that of a total of one hundred and seventy-five manuscripts, seventy represent the Pentateuch. This must always be the holiest section of the Bible for all Jews. But the preponderance of Deuteronomy, with its recapitulation of the whole Mosaic legislation, is particularly indicative of Essene interests, as is the popularity of the Latter Prophets, especially Isaiah, and of the Psalms and Daniel in the Writings. A further proof of the sect's absorption in Bible study may be seen in the presence of a large number of commentaries (cf. above, pp. 66–83), and of Greek (Exodus, Leviticus, Numbers) and Aramaic (Leviticus, Job) translations of parts of Scripture.

All in all, the biblical remains amount to around two hundred manuscripts, four of them more or less complete Scrolls (two

Isaiah manuscripts from Cave 1, a Psalms Scroll and an Aramaic Job from Cave 11). And to them must be added exegetical works reproducing biblical texts, and phylacteries and *mezuzoth* (small scrolls to be affixed to door-posts), both containing extracts from the Law.

In the early years of Qumran studies, critical scholars often sought answers to questions that the manuscripts were unable to give. Did the Isaiah Scrolls from Cave 1 shed any light on the problem of the book's composition? Did they confirm that, as modern students argue, it was written by a First, Second and Third Isaiah? They did not. But neither of the Scrolls is old enough to do so, for already at the beginning of the second century BC the author of Ecclesiasticus (48:24) appears to assign the whole work to a single prophet. The Septuagint, too, in a translation roughly contemporaneous with the Scrolls, deals with all sixty-six chapters as though they form one book from one writer. Likewise, although the Qumran fragments of Daniel date to only a few decades after the text was composed (probably in the 160s BC), they reflect the traditional linguistic division which has baffled scholars for so long. Already in around 100 BC, an Aramaic section (2:4b–7:28) was sandwiched between two Hebrew sections (1:1 – 2:4a and 8:1 – 12:13).

The Scrolls are equally powerless to dispel all our uncertainties about the canon of Scripture. It is true that the whole of the Hebrew Old Testament (except Esther) is attested at Qumran; but this does not mean that the Essene canon was identical with that of traditional Judaism. Apart from passages expressly cited as Scripture in the Rules, or used as the basis of biblical commentaries, how are we to know for sure that a composition present in the caves – say Chronicles or Ruth – was held to be canonical? On the other hand we cannot assert that some of the Apocrypha were not treated by the Essenes as an integral part of Scripture. After all, the Book of Ecclesiasticus of Ben Sira was found in Caves 2 and 11 (and at Masada), five copies of Tobit have surfaced from Cave 4 (four in Aramaic and one in Hebrew) and a small Greek fragment of another of the Apocrypha, the Letter of Jeremiah, has been identified among the contents of Cave 7. The status of several major Pseudepigrapha also remains unsettled; for instance, the Book of Jubilees and the Testament of Levi are both quoted in the Damascus Rule as though they were Scripture (CD 16:3–4 and 4:16 – DSSE 109, 101). And the Psalms Scroll from Cave 11 includes a number of apocryphal poems not appended to, but interspersed among, the canonical compositions.

Have then the cave manuscripts affected in any significant way our understanding of the Bible message? The answer is once more no. Recent Old Testament translators, from 1952 (the American Revised Standard Version) onwards, have all consulted the Qumran evidence, without however introducing changes likely to impinge on religious belief. As an illustration, instead of 'lawful captives', the equivalent of the traditional Hebrew wording of Isaiah 49:24, the Revised Standard Version follows the big Isaiah Scroll and reads, 'the captives of a tyrant'. Similarly, the peculiar phrase, 'to lay bare his net', in Habakkuk 1:17, is replaced in the New English Bible (1970) by, 'to unsheath his sword', after the Habakkuk Commentary. It is not surprising in the circumstances that for biblical specialists, concerned mainly to relieve worried Christians, the Scrolls' most striking contribution to Old Testament studies has been their support of the Masoretic text. In 1955, Millar Burrows, the editor of the first Qumran Scrolls, wrote:

> We did not need the Dead Sea Scrolls to show us that the text has not come down to us unchanged . . . The essential truth and the will of God revealed in the Bible . . . have been preserved . . . through all the vicissitudes in the transmission of the text (*The Dead Sea Scrolls*, 320).

On a superficial level Burrows was right. All the same, the differences, which he did not deny, are highly significant, disclosing as they do hitherto unsuspected facets of Jewish intellectual and religious history.

When, more than twenty years ago, F. M. Cross published fragments from the Books of Samuel found in Cave 4, the student was confronted for the first time with a Hebrew text representing not the Masoretic version but the original from which the ancient Greek translation of Samuel had been made. The late third century BC Qumran manuscript (4QSam^b) contains ten passages where the Septuagint departs from the traditional Hebrew reading. In eight of these, the Cave 4 fragments reproduce the text underlying the Greek translation; the remaining two agree with the Masoretic version. For example, where in 1 Samuel 23:14 the traditional Hebrew text gives the divine name as *elohim* (God), and the Septuagint has *kurios* (the Lord, i.e. YHWH), the Qumran fragment supports the Greek version with the Tetragram.

In the case of Jeremiah, two of the three Jeremiah manuscripts from Cave 4 follow the longer recension of the Masoretes, whilst the third (4QJer^b, dated by Cross to 200 BC) attests the shorter Septuagint type of the text. In other words, two differing textual traditions co-existed in the religious library of the Essenes.

Besides texts that diverge from one another, some of the writings from Cave 4 testify to mixed versions. An unpublished fragment from Numbers (4QNum^b) displays characteristics of the Samaritan Pentateuch against the Masoretic and Septuagint evidence: e.g. Joshua's appointment by Moses as his successor (Num. 27:13) is supplemented by appropriate words borrowed from Deuteronomy 3:21. By contrast, in several cases it sides with the Septuagint against the Samaritan and Masoretic traditions. Another witness to an anti-Masoretic tendency is a Deuteronomy fragment from Cave 5. Here, the original manuscript, assigned by the editor to the first half of the second century BC, represents the Masoretic text, but a second scribe has furnished it, probably in the first century BC, with four supralinear corrections to bring it in line with the Hebrew basis of the Septuagint.

A further illustration of this sort of combination, Deuteronomy 32:8, reveals the cause of the textual variants.

In the Song of Moses we read that God established the number of the world's countries either according to the number of the 'sons of Israel' (Masoretic text), or of the 'angels of God' (Septuagint), or of the 'sons of God' (Qumran). Since 'angels of God' and 'sons of God' are synonyms, it is reasonable to conclude that the Septuagint represents the Qumran type of Hebrew. Yet why do the two differ from the Masoretic reading? The number itself, arrived at by counting the names appearing in Genesis 10, is seventy, and both traditions accept this implicitly. But whereas the Masoretic explanation of this figure is Israel-centred, that of Qumran is not. The thought underlying the former text is that the total number of Gentile countries reflects the 'seventy souls' journeying with Jacob from Canaan to Egypt, i.e. the 'seventy sons of Israel' according to Exodus 1:5. The Septuagint, and its Hebrew basis attested by a fragment from Cave 4 (4QEx^a), cannot reproduce this simile in Deuteronomy 32:8 because in their version of Exodus 1:5 the retinue of Jacob amounts to seventy-five, not seventy. Their reasoning therefore runs: the guardian angels of the various peoples were created before man, so when God divided the human race into nations, he ensured that each of the seventy pre-existent angels should have his own special client.

Thus the Masoretic 'sons of Israel' and the Septuagint-Qumran 'angels/sons of God' cannot be explained as stylistic variations: they derive from autonomous traditions. The point to be made here is that the Habakkuk Commentary from Cave 1 has revealed that a tendency to reconcile such deviant records goes back to at least as far as the inter-Testamental era itself. The commentator, quoting Habakkuk 2:16 follows a Septuagint-type text, 'Drink and stagger (*hera‘el*)'; but he shows in his exegesis that he is well aware of the Masoretic reading, 'Drink and show your foreskin' (*he‘arel*), since he writes:

For he (the Wicked Priest) did not circumcise the *foreskin* of his heart and walked in the ways of *drunkenness* (1QpHab 11:9–14 – DSSE 242).

This most ancient library of biblical manuscripts thus

testifies to a variety of textual traditions, some proto-Masoretic, some non-Masoretic, the latter being further identifiable as Samaritan or Septuagint by type. It also provides examples of conflated readings and of the reciprocal impact made by one type on another. At Qumran, in short, but no doubt also elsewhere, a plurality of textual traditions co-existed in the inter-Testamental period, a situation which stimulates us to ask how we are to account for, firstly the plurality, and secondly the unity.

Contemporary scholarship endeavours to explain the plurality, either by the theory of geographically distinct local texts (F. M. Cross), or by the hypothesis that popular recensions were succeeded by an official version (S. Talmon). It is noteworthy that neither hypothesis advocates an *Urtext*, an authentic original source from which the variants depart either intentionally or inadvertently. No doubt the reason is that it is thought that a literature, perhaps committed to writing in various places after a period during which it was transmitted orally, cannot be judged according to the norms regulating the handing down of records with a written past alone.

F. M. Cross's theory acknowledges three types of text. The first is an ancient Palestinian type, containing frequent explanatory additions and glosses and represented by the 'Samaritan'-type Qumran fragments and the later Samaritan Pentateuch. The second is an Egyptian-type text, imported from Jerusalem and related to the old Palestinian form in so far as it, too, displays the same expansionist tendency. It is this type that underlies the Septuagint. The third type is defined as 'conservative'; it is non-paraphrastic and keeps in line with the text which at Jamnia was to become the proto-Masoretic version. As it cannot be either Palestinian or Egyptian, it is assigned to Babylonia.

The alternative thesis of Shemaryahu Talmon postulates that a larger number of textual traditions were current at a stage preceding that of Qumran. Some are believed to have vanished; but it is suggested that those which have survived owe their existence not to geographically distinct centres, but to separate socio-religious groups, each of which came to adopt its own 'official' text: the Samaritans the Samaritan-type, the Hellenistic Jews (and Christians) the Septuagint-type, and the Pharisees and the rabbis the proto-Masoretic type. The fluidity manifest in the Qumran library testifies to the state of affairs obtaining prior to the standardization of the biblical text.

It is unnecessary to stress once more that no definite conclusion can be reached regarding this or any other Qumran problem until all the evidence has been published. Some of the data to be discussed presently will be seen as profoundly meaningful, but we cannot know to what extent they represent the whole truth. Bearing this reservation in mind, it is instructive to ponder on the significance of the relationship between the Qumran Samuel fragments and the parallel Masoretic text of Chronicles.

According to the traditional Hebrew, 2 Samuel 24:20 reads: 'When Araunah looked down, he saw the king and his servants coming towards him', a reading faithfully echoed by the Septuagint. The Qumran fragment (4QSam*ᵃ*), reporting the same encounter between David and the Jebusite owner of the threshing-floor on which the Temple was to be built, introduces a concrete fresh detail, '. . . and Ornan (a variant of Araunah) was threshing wheat'. Turning next to 1 Chronicles 21:20–21 in the Masoretic text, we find the identical incident told in the words of the Qumran fragment of Samuel, and with the name similarly given as Ornan: 'Now Ornan was threshing wheat . . . As David came to Ornan, Ornan looked and saw David . . .'.

This kind of correlation between the Qumran Samuel text and the Masoretic Chronicles, going hand in hand with a divergence from the Masoretic wording of Samuel itself, is not a freak occurrence: it confronts the Bible scholar again and again. He therefore has to ask himself whether the Qumran Samuel text is influenced by a Masoretic-type 1 Chronicles, or whether the Masoretic 1 Chronicles, using 2 Samuel as a source, depends on a Qumran-type text and not on a Masoretic 2 Samuel!

If the first alternative is correct, and the Qumran Samuel represents a revision of 2 Samuel (redacted in the sixth century

BC) in the light of 1 Chronicles (written in about the fourth century BC), we have in the Qumran fragment an 'updating' of the older narrative according to the more 'modern' edition. This case would then illustrate, on the level of the biblical text itself, a law which I believe to have been discovered in connection with Bible exegesis in ancient Judaism: namely, that the understanding of a composite scriptural narrative by its final redactor 'was inherited by later interpreters of the written Bible, who in turn explicitly introduced the sense of the latest tradition . . . into the former versions' (*Scripture and Tradition in Judaism*, 176). In other words, the process of harmonization detected in early post-biblical Scripture commentary was apparently preceded by a similar effort within the Bible text itself.

The second alternative, that the Masoretic Chronicles is dependent on a non-Masoretic Samuel, would be still more sensational for it would imply that the redactor of 1 Chronicles in around 400 BC was either unacquainted with the Masoretic version of 2 Samuel or discarded it deliberately in favour of the Qumran type of text.

To bring this fairly dry statement home more forcefully, let us re-phrase it in theological jargon. If we subscribe to the belief that the traditional (i.e. Masoretic) Hebrew Bible is authentic Scripture, the word of God, then we have to explain the discrepancy of the word of God preserved in 1 Chronicles from the word of God surviving in the inspired (i.e. Masoretic) text of 2 Samuel, and its conformity with a recension (attested at Qumran) which neither Synagogue nor Church recognizes as sacred. In the pre-Qumran days, Bible translators could still try, like Jerome, to reproduce the 'Hebrew truth' (*hebraica veritas*). Today, convinced that plurality antedated unity, we are compelled to ask: Which Hebrew truth?

In considering next the problem of how the text was unified, it should first be borne in mind that the Bible canonized by the rabbis in around AD 100 was not a new creation. As has been mentioned, the proto-Masoretic type is well attested at Qumran, especially for parts of the Pentateuch and the Latter Prophets. The Old Testament as we have it is not constructed from readings selected from various types of manuscripts. Nor is it a conflation of several streams of tradition. It is a one-type text that includes a few, mostly minor, variant readings preserved as marginal notes in the form of instructions that the written word (*ketib*) should be read aloud (*qere*) in a certain way.

Rabbinic tradition hints obliquely that the authentic biblical text was determined by consultation of three rolls especially esteemed and kept in the Temple. When doubts arose concerning small inconsistencies, they were settled by choosing as official and binding the reading attested by at least two of the model scrolls (Sifre on Deut. 356; yTaanit 68a). It would appear therefore that unification was the work of religious authority. Thereafter, every text which departed from the canonized Scripture was held to be an unauthorized version.

Historically, all these issues were decided by the rabbis at Jamnia in the final decades of the first century AD. In regard to the text, they confirmed one of the prevailing types; in regard to the canon, they sanctioned established custom, rejecting hesitations over the scriptural status of the Song of Songs because of its erotic overtones, and over Ecclesiastes because of its apparent agnosticism (mYadayim 3:5). And the prompt implementation of their decrees is evident from the nature of the Murabbaat and Bar Kokhba caches dating to the early second century, which consisted, in the domain of religious literature, almost exclusively of biblical fragments exhibiting the proto-Masoretic Hebrew text of Jamnia.

2 THE PSEUDEPIGRAPHA

It is not only knowledge of the Bible and the Apocrypha that has benefited so greatly from the discoveries at the Dead Sea. The same may be said of the Pseudepigrapha, Jewish religious compositions written between 200 BC and AD 100 which, although popular and influential, failed to be accepted into either the Palestinian or Hellenistic canon of Scripture. More than this, where the Apocrypha had survived in Greek as part of the Bible of the Hellenistic Church, many of the Hebrew or Aramaic Pseudepigrapha, shunned by the rabbis, had been preserved sometimes in Greek, but more often on the peripheries of Christian religious literature as secondary translations into Ethiopic, Syriac, Armenian, Slavonic, etc. Thus the main source of Jubilees, a doctrinal paraphrase of Genesis, and of 1 Enoch, is in Ethiopic, though there are also Greek and other fragments extant. The ethical Testaments of the Twelve Patriarchs can be read in full in Greek and in Armenian, but sections of the Testament of Levi from the same work, identified among the fragments of the Cairo Geniza, appear also in Aramaic.

The general absence of texts in the original languages, and the revisions or complete re-editions of these Jewish writings made by Christian copyists, had rendered their use for the study of inter-Testamental Judaism fairly complicated. Now, however, we are assured that Jubilees, for instance, was first written in Hebrew: fragments representing no less than twelve manuscripts were found in Caves 1–4 and 11. Again, the original of the Testament of Levi has proved to be Aramaic: three manuscripts from Cave 4 confirm the antiquity of the recension preserved in the medieval Geniza fragments. The Testament of Naphtali in Hebrew has emerged from Cave 4. As for the Book of Enoch, it has survived in Cave 4 in at least eleven Aramaic manuscripts.

Beyond providing definite proof of the Jewish and Semitic origin of these documents, the Qumran finds have gone some way to help solve various literary enigmas connected with them, and in particular with Enoch. This latter composition, important enough to have been quoted as an authority in the New Testament (Jude 14), is divided in its Ethiopic version into five books – like the Law and the Psalms in the Bible. The Aramaic fragments from Cave 4 testify to the same five-fold division; but the Book of Parables, the second section of the Ethiopic Enoch (chapters 37–71), does not figure among them. Instead we find a Book of Giants. Now if we accept the conclusion advanced by J. T. Milik, the editor of the Qumran Enoch, that the absence of the Parables from the Aramaic version points to a post-Qumran date for that section in the Ethiopic, the repercussions on the interpretation of the Gospels are considerable, for it is in these same Parables of Enoch that the 'Son of Man' appears, the figure formerly thought to be the prototype of the Gospels' 'Son of Man' about whom New Testament scholars have speculated so exhaustively.

In general, we can say of the Pseudepigrapha remains of Qumran that they have re-awakened scholarly interest in a potentially very rich area of studies, from which our understanding of Jewish history, religion and culture in the age immediately preceding the emergence of rabbinic Judaism and the formation of the New Testament is bound to reap enormous profit.

3 THE NEW TESTAMENT

From the beginning, the relationship between the Dead Sea Scrolls and the New Testament has been the subject of voluminous, occasionally fanciful, and frequently heated argument. As a final contribution, this review will seek to re-appraise the major aspects of the debate and summarize our conclusions.

Qumran Essenism and Palestinian Christianity can be related in three different ways. They are either identical, the Community being the Church and Jesus the Teacher of Righteousness. Or Christianity is an off-shoot of Essenism. Or Essenism and Christianity both spring from the same common stock, the Judaism of that period.

As has been anticipated in chapter 5 and confirmed by the survey of the history and teachings of Essenism, the theory of their identity is so implausible as to need no further rebuttal: the time-factor is unsuitable, the two ideologies differ fundamentally, and no New Testament fragment has been discovered in any of the Qumran Caves. In the latter respect, the claim made by the Spanish Jesuit, Jose O'Callaghan, that Greek papyrus scraps from Cave 7, almost entirely illegible, derive from manuscripts representing Mark, Acts, Romans, 1 Timothy, James and 2 Peter, has been justly rejected as totally inacceptable by all the authorities in the field.

Can Qumran then be the parent of Christianity? This view

has been advanced most forcibly by André Dupont-Sommer, who reminds us of Ernest Renan's famous dictum, 'Christianity is an Essenism that has largely succeeded' (*Essene Writings*, 13, 370). For him, the bond linking the Teacher of Righteousness to Jesus is 'quite unique' (ibid., 372), though he will not have it that Jesus was merely 'a mythical double of the Essene prophet' (ibid.). Having clarified this point, Dupont-Sommer continues:

> The documents from Qumran make it plain that the primitive Christian Church was rooted in the Jewish sect of the New Covenant, the Essene sect, to a degree none would have suspected, and that it borrowed from it a large part of its organization, rites, doctrines, 'patterns of thought' and its mystical and ethical ideas (ibid. 373).

Essenism as the mother of Christianity is of course not an impossible notion. On the other hand, the same arguments used to contest the theory of their identity operate here also: namely that the heavy emphasis on the punctilious observance of the Mosaic Law at Qumran is so greatly in contrast to the peripheral importance given to it in the Gospels that a linear descent from one to the other seems extremely improbable.

The third possibility presupposes that the Qumran sectarian writings and the New Testament represent two independent movements in pursuit of similar ideals. But even here, the question of a direct Essene influence on the early Church is possible, but arises only when their common features cannot be otherwise explained. A re-examination of some fundamental problems occurring in both literatures will help to illustrate this point.

The first concerns the part played by the Bible in the Essene and Christian theological thought. As at Qumran, Scripture is of central importance in the teaching of Jesus and of his disciples, but while the New Testament message is less directly concerned with actual observances than with their moral and religious significance, Jesus' occasional approach to the Law –

the permanent validity of which is asserted by him (Mt. 5:18) – shows similarities as well as dissimilarities with the Scrolls.

Thus in connection with marriage laws, both the New Testament and the Scrolls accentuate their inner import, though their angles of approach differ. One example of this appears in the Damascus Rule where 'Male and female created he them' (Gen. 1:27) is interpreted as forbidding polygamy (CD 4:20–21 – DSSE 101) whilst the New Testament cites the same text in support of an absolute, or conditional, ban on divorce (Mk. 10:2–12; Mt. 19:3–9). Likewise, the logic of the sectarian teachers that the biblical ban on marriage between aunt and nephew must also apply between uncle and niece, and that if one union is fornication, so must the other be, is taken even further by Jesus in his statement that one who has looked at a woman with lust has already committed adultery with her in his heart (Mt. 5:27–28).

Jesus, expounding his understanding of the Torah, lays stress on inward religiousness; he aims at combating the hypocrisy caricatured in Matthew 23, which may produce a beautiful outward appearance but conceals iniquity within (Mt. 23:27–28). The Qumran masters, addressing men accustomed to hold external observances in high esteem, also seek to do the same, but by way of preaching the necessity for those outer observances to be accompanied by corresponding spiritual attitudes.

The parallelism in the use of prophecy at Qumran and in the New Testament has often been noted. The Community and the Church were convinced that, consciously or unconsciously, the prophets were referring to the history and doctrine of their own groups when they proclaimed the final realities. The fulfilment interpretation or *pesher* is as familiar in the Gospels and Acts as at Qumran. The prophecy: 'A voice crying in the wilderness: "Prepare the way of the Lord"' (Isa. 40:3), was heard at Qumran as meaning the retirement into the desert of the Teacher of Righteousness and his followers to prepare for the coming of the Messiah. For the New Testament, the voice is that of John the Baptist carrying out a similar mission (Mk. 1:3–8; Mt. 3:1–12; Lk. 3:2–17). In both literatures, apologetic considerations often obtrude: the authors set out to prove the predestined nature of the Community or Church by demonstrating that its history conforms to prophetic prediction. The presentation of the argument varies in style. The Scrolls, addressed to initiates, can develop it summarily and even elliptically; the Gospels, with an eye on the unconverted, are inclined to make sure that they are understood: 'All this took place to fulfil what the Lord had spoken by the prophet' (Mt. 1:22), or 'For these things took place that the scripture might be fulfilled' (Jn. 19:36).

Another feature common to the Essenes and Christianity is that they both claimed to be the exclusive community of the elect, the sole beneficiaries of a new Covenant in the final age. As the sectaries saw themselves divided into twelve tribes led by twelve chiefs, so the Epistle of James is sent to 'the twelve tribes in the dispersion' (Jas. 1:1), and Jesus promises his twelve apostles that they will 'sit on twelve thrones, judging the twelve tribes of Israel' (Mt. 19:28; Lk. 22:30).

On the plane of eschatology, the outlook of the two movements was also similar in so far as each expected its founder to be ushering in the last days. The followers of Jesus were convinced that the Kingdom of God had already dawned and that their departed Master would return in glory during their own life-time to judge the world. As the coming of the end was delayed, we find both groups being exhorted to perseverance. The Qumran Habakkuk Commentary urges:

> If it (the end) tarries, wait for it, for it shall surely come and shall not be late (Hab. 2:3) – Interpreted, this concerns the men of truth who keep the Law, whose hands shall not slacken in the service of truth when the final age is prolonged. For all the ages of God reach their appointed end as He determines for them in the mysteries of His wisdom (1QpHab 7:9–14 – DSSE 239).

The writer of 2 Peter, echoing the same concern, encourages his readers likewise:

You must understand . . . that scoffers will come in the last days with scoffing . . . and saying, 'Where is the promise of his coming?' . . . But do not ignore this fact, beloved, that with the Lord one day is like a thousand years and a thousand years as one day . . . The Lord is not slow about his promise . . . but is forebearing toward you . . . that all should reach repentance (2 Pet. 3:3–9).

The attitude of the Scrolls to the Jerusalem Temple and official worship also overlaps to a large extent with that displayed in the New Testament. The Essenes, as we know, were not of one mind in this respect: some continued to participate in sacrifices while for others the Council of the Community was the sanctuary where atonement was to be offered by means of a holy life.

The New Testament is also equivocal. Jesus himself behaved in a conventionally Jewish way, visiting the Temple, teaching and no doubt praying there, and his disciples continued to do so even after his death. Paul went further: he is said to have 'purified himself' and made arrangements with the priests for a sacrificial offering in fulfilment of a vow (Acts 18:18; 21:26). Yet at the same time, he was promoting a doctrine recalling that taught at Qumran, in which Jesus and the 'apostles and prophets', like the inner Council of the Community Rule, are represented as the foundations, and the Christians as the building stones, of a new sanctuary, a 'holy Temple', a 'dwelling-place of the Lord in the spirit' (Eph. 2:20–22), where their bodies were to be presented 'as a living sacrifice, holy and acceptable' (Rom. 12:1).

Beyond this point the Scrolls and the New Testament part company in their approach to the Temple. Qumran predicts the restoration of Temple worship. The Book of Revelation dreams of a new Jerusalem where no sanctuary is needed, 'for its Temple is the Lord God the Almighty and the Lamb' (Rev. 21:22).

The organization of community life is yet another field where the customs of one movement find an echo in those of the other. The Essene superior, the *mebaqqer*, responsible for admissions, teaching, administration, distribution of charitable funds, is adjured to be the father and shepherd of his congregation. The last title is applied once to Jesus, 'shepherd and guardian of . . . souls' (1 Peter. 2:25), but the normal Pauline usage for a leader is *episkopos*, bishop. Appointed to take charge of the 'flock' and to 'feed the church' (Acts 20:28), he too was to be an 'apt teacher' and a good 'manager' (1 Tim. 3:2), 'able to give instruction in sound doctrine', a blameless 'steward of God' (Tit. 1:7, 9).

Again, the Essene rule provided for both the private ownership of property and voluntary communism. The New Testament's testimony is similar. Jesus himself exhorted his hearers to sell their belongings and to distribute the proceeds among the poor and follow him, thus proving their total reliance on God (Mt. 19:21; Mk. 10:21; Lk. 18:22), while the Fourth Gospel implies that his closest circle drew from a common purse entrusted to Judas (Jn. 12:6; 13:19). At the other extreme, however, we find the Christians of the Pauline Epistles living in community but otherwise conforming to normal secular behaviour: earning a living, caring for their families and contributing to help the poor. Thus between the two poles of an absolute renunciation of possessions and a retention of personal wealth, the early days of Christianity saw a system of religious communism or quasi-communism identical with that of Qumran in the Jerusalem Church. Jesus' command that a disciple should divest himself of all he had and pass the money to the poor was re-interpreted to advocate, as did the rule of the monastic Essenes, a common ownership of property within the brotherhood:

All who believed were together and had all things in common; and they sold their possessions and goods and distributed them to all, as any had need (Acts 2:44-45).

In this connection, an interesting parallel may be drawn between the Qumran 'lying in matters of property', punished by the relatively severe sentence of a year's exclusion from 'purity' and the reduction of food by one quarter, and the same offence and its punishment in Christian circles. When the Jerusalem couple, Ananias and Sapphira, pretended to hand over all their riches to the Church leaders but kept back part of it, God caused them both to drop dead (Acts 5:1-11)!

In regard to celibacy as it is treated in the Essene literature and the New Testament, we know that some of the sectaries were married, but learn from the classical sources that celibacy among the rest was compulsory. Similarly in the New Testament marriage is nowhere openly condemned; even Paul, who professes that 'it is well for a man not to touch a woman', concedes that married life is not ungodly (1 Cor. 7:1-7). But he, and apparently Jesus too, saw celibacy as the perfect state. Indeed, the chief difference between Paul and Jesus on this subject appears to be that Paul does not favour the severing of marital ties (1 Cor. 7:10-11), notwithstanding his advice to married men to live as though they had no wives (1 Cor. 7:29), whereas Jesus does, positively praising those who have made themselves 'eunuchs' and forsaken wives and family for the Kingdom of Heaven's sake (Mt. 19:12; Lk. 14:26; 18:29). Whether this advocation of the separation of the sexes is to be understood literally, or is a rhetorical exaggeration, is not clear. It could simply mean that if earthly bonds hinder a man in his search for God, they should be sacrificed. But it could also be intended, as was the exclusion of women from the camp of the sons of Light during the final war, as a necessary part of the preparation for the coming of the Kingdom.

It is to be doubted that celibacy was widespread among Christians of the apostolic generation. Paul declares himself to be single (1 Cor. 7:8), but he allows even his bishops to marry once (though not twice) (1 Tim. 3:2; Tit. 1:6). As for Jesus, the Gospels remain silent, though they imply that he had no wife.

If Essene and Christian motives for sexual abstinence are compared, the only element common to both groups seems to be the eschatological factor. In the Scrolls, the sectaries' association with the heavenly hosts demanded a degree of ritual purity attainable only in a life of angelic celibacy. Likewise, if Jesus was genuinely advising his disciples to renounce marriage, it was in order to stress the overriding importance of a whole-hearted quest for the Kingdom. Also, before it became an established custom in the Church, celibacy was recommended simply as a sensible measure in view of the 'impending distress' (1 Cor. 7:26) – 'Alas for those who are with child . . . in those days' (Mk. 13:17; Mt. 24:19; Lk. 21:23) – though practical Christianity continued to see it as an advantage to those desirous to devote themselves entirely to the 'affairs of the Lord' (1 Cor. 7:32–34).

Some of the parallels noticed in this survey between the Scrolls and the New Testament may be accounted for by general sectarian principles. To both the Essenes and the first Christians Scripture was central, and they both taught that their institutions fulfilled prophecy; they were both the chosen people and had inherited its privileges. Moreover, coming into being as they did in a climate of eschatological upheaval in Palestine, it is normal that they should both have awaited an imminent end of time. In their attitudes towards the Temple too, sectarian logic no doubt played a part; though not unexpectedly, the issue affected the priestly brotherhood of the Essenes more deeply than the group of Galileans, whose lack of sophistication in matters of worship and sacrifice was notorious. Nevertheless, the parallelism between Paul's theology and that of Qumran is too pronounced to be no more than a coincidence. It is very probable that he was acquainted with Qumran Temple symbolism and adapted it in shaping his own teaching on spiritual worship.

The most likely domain of Qumran influence on Christianity is that of organization and religious practice. After all, the Qumran sect was already a well-tried institution when the Judaeo-Christian Church was struggling to establish itself, and it would have been only sensible for the inexperienced men of the fellowship of Jesus to observe and imitate existing patterns. Thus the monarchic government of the Pauline churches – Jewish communities were administered not by single leaders but by a group of elders – may easily have been modelled on the Essene pattern of a Guardian as pastor of each individual camp, with Paul himself playing the part of the 'Guardian of all the camps' within the Gentile Church. It is also difficult to accept that the common life and religious communism described in Acts in regard to the Jerusalem Church owed nothing to the by then world-famous Essene life 'without money'. Finally, since lasting celibacy was completely alien to Jewish thinking, its occurrence in Christianity is likely to be an adaptation of the eschatological asceticism for which the sectaries from the Dead Sea were renowned even outside the frontiers of Palestine. 'A unique people' – to quote Pliny – 'more admirable than any other in the whole world, without women and renouncing sex altogether (*sine ulla femina, omni venere abdicata*) . . . an eternal people in which no-one is born' (*Natural History* v. 73).

In conclusion, although no Qumran impact on the primitive Church can be proved, and although the bulk of Jewish traditions incorporated into Christianity was not sectarian, a presumed Essene influence on the New Testament writers on some at least of the points mentioned explains them more satisfactorily than any other theory. The information available to us suggests that the main contact occurred, not between the sect and Jesus, a Galilean charismatic for whom a great deal of Essene doctrine would have been repugnant, but between Essenism and Judaean Christianity. Some have thought that the original channel was John the Baptist, but for this he would have to have abandoned the Essene life and its seclusion to preach to all Israel. This of course is pure speculation; John's apparently Essene characteristics can just as well be explained as the habits of a Judaean hermit devoted to ritual ablutions in the river Jordan.

It has often been remarked that the New Testament makes no mention of the Essenes. This is another mystery which we cannot yet solve. Unless we conclude from the unsubstantiated statement that the 'great many priests . . . obedient to the faith' referred to in the Acts of the Apostles (6:7) were wholly or in part Essenes, we are left with the following theories. Firstly, there is no reason whatever to suppose that Jesus, in Galilee, ever encountered any Essenes, since their establishments are attested only in Judaea. Secondly, as New Testament allusions to other religious parties (the Pharisees, Sadducees, Herodians, etc.) are made largely in the context of polemics and apologetics, silence apropos of the Essenes may be due to their known unwillingness to engage in controversy with outsiders. And if the later Church organizers followed Essene models, they probably preferred to keep this dark. This is clearly not the full answer, but those who look to find something particularly mysterious in this lacuna should bear in mind that the great mass of rabbinic literature may not mention the Essenes either, for none of its vague phrases and titles – 'the Silent', 'the Builders', 'the Holy Congregation' – can be proved to apply to them and them alone.

This brings to a close our examination of Qumran's contribution to New Testament studies. An improved comprehension of the Essene sect has opened up a new approach to the origins of Christianity. The parallelisms, established or adumbrated, will enable us more reliably to insert Jesus and the movement that arose in his wake into the historical world of Judaism. The fresh insights obtained, combined with a familiarity with the larger fields of Jewish and Gentile civilizations in the first century AD, will help not only to disclose interacting links and influences but also to single out all that is peculiar to the inspiration of two very different spiritual masters. Contrasted with the austere figure of the Teacher of Righteousness, a priest who sought to instil in his people a thorough knowledge of the Torah and urged them to combine a strict observance of the externals of the Law with inner spiritual authenticity, Jesus the Galilean holy man, who addressed not the learned or the seekers of perfection, but the simple country people, including publicans, sinners and whores, appears as a much more human person, whose concern was with other human persons and their need to be taught how to live as the children of God. At the heart of Essenism rested elements of intolerance, rigidity and exclusiveness. This, perhaps, is why it vanished, whereas Christianity and the flexible and dynamic Judaism of the rabbis were able to live on.

References to Qumran palaeography appear in chapter 2 (pp. 35–7). For matters of orthography, see M. Martin, *The Scribal Character of the Dead Sea Scrolls* I–II (Louvain, 1958).

1 THE TEXT OF THE OLD TESTAMENT

For a summary introduction to the Masoretic text, see O. Eissfeldt, *The Old Testament. An Introduction* (Blackwell, Oxford, 1966), 678–93; for the ancient versions, see ibid. 696–719. For the canon of the Bible, cf. Schürer–Vermes–Millar–Black II, §25 I. See also S. Z. Leiman, *The Canonization of Hebrew Scripture* (Transactions of the Connecticut Academy of Arts and Sciences 47, 1976).

For general information on the Samaritan Pentateuch, consult Eissfeldt, 694–5. On the Septuagint, see S. Jellicoe, *The Septuagint and Modern Study* (O.U.P., Oxford, 1968) and S. P. Brock, C. T. Fritsch, S. Jellicoe, *A Classified Bibliography of the Septuagint* (Brill, Leiden, 1973).

The most important essays dealing with the Qumran contribution to the study of the Hebrew Bible and of its Greek translations are collected in a useful single volume edited by F. M. Cross and S. Talmon, *Qumran and the History of the Biblical Text* (Harvard U.P., Cambridge, 1975). See also D. Barthélemy, *Les devanciers d'Aquila* (Brill, Leiden, 1963); W. H. Brownlee, *The Meaning of the Qumrân Scrolls for the Bible* (O.U.P., New York, 1964); J. G. Janzen, *Studies in the Text of Jeremiah* (Harvard U.P., Cambridge, 1973); E. Y. Kutscher, *The Language and Linguistic Background of the Isaiah Scroll* (Brill, Leiden, 1974); D. N. Freedman, 'Variant Readings in the Leviticus Scroll from Qumran Cave 11', CBQ 36 (1974), 525–34; P. W. Skehan, 'Qumran and Old Testament Criticism', *Qumrân* (ed. M. Delcor, 1978), 163–82.

In connection with F. M. Cross's much valued studies two reservations may be expressed. The first is provoked by a certain vagueness in his technical vocabulary. Cf. D. W. Gooding, 'An Appeal for Stricter Terminology in the Textual

Criticism of the Old Testament', JSS 21 (1976), 15–25. The second concerns the lack of clear distinction between the old Palestinian and the Egyptian types of text. Since they are both presented as possessing roughly the same characteristics, is it justified to designate them as two different *types* rather than sub-divisions within the same type?

On rabbinic traditions relating to the master copies of the Torah kept in the Sanctuary, see in particular S. Talmon, 'The Three Scrolls of the Law that were found in the Temple Court', *Textus* 2 (1962), 14–27.

2 THE PSEUDEPIGRAPHA

A brief introduction to the Pseudepigrapha is contained in Eissfeldt, 606–37. For more detailed studies see A.-M. Denis, *Introduction aux pseudépigraphes grecs d'Ancien Testament* (Brill, Leiden, 1970) and J. H. Charlesworth, *The Pseudepigrapha and Modern Research* (Scholars Press, Missoula, 1976) with full bibliography. The only English translation of the collected Pseudepigrapha remains R. H. Charles (ed.), *The Apocrypha and Pseudepigrapha of the Old Testament* II (O.U.P., Oxford, 1913). A new American edition of an enlarged collection is being prepared. A German series, directed by W. G. Kümmel, *Jüdische Schriften aus hellenistisch-römischer Zeit* is in the process of publication in separate fascicles.

On the Qumran fragments of the Pseudepigrapha, see Fitzmyer's bibliography. The Aramaic fragments of the Testament of Levi from the Cairo Geniza were first published by A. Cowley and R. H. Charles, 'An Early Source of the Testaments of the Patriarchs', JQR 19 (1907), 566–83; cf. P. Grelot, 'Notes sur le Testament araméen de Lévi', RB 63 (1956), 391–406. The fragments of 1 Enoch have been edited by J. T. Milik, *The Books of Enoch: Aramaic Fragments of Qumran Cave 4* (Clarendon, Oxford, 1976). His dating of the Parables in the Ethiopic Enoch to 'around AD 270' (p. 96) is based on a flimsy argument, and the most suitable period for these chapters appears to be the last quarter of the first century AD. For an identical dating, cf. M. A. Knibb, 'The Date of the Parables of Enoch: A Critical Review', NTS 25 (1979), 345–59.

The 'son of man' problem has been examined in G. Vermes, *Jesus the Jew*, 160–91; 256–61; cf. PBJS, 147–65. For different views, consult C. Colpe, TDNT VIII, 400–77; M. Black, 'The Christological Use of the Old Testament in the New Testament', NTS 18 (1971), 1–14; R. Leivestad, 'Exit the Apocalytic Son of Man', NTS 18 (1972), 243–67; B. Lindars, 'Re-enter the Apocalyptic Son of Man', NTS 22 (1975), 52–72; J. A. Fitzmyer, 'Methodology in the Study of Jesus' Sayings in the New Testament', *Jésus aux origines de la christologie*, ed. J. Dupont (Duculot, Gembloux, 1975), 73–102; J. Bowker, 'The Son of Man', JTS 28 (1977), 19–48. For a more recent exchange, see G. Vermes, 'The Present State of the "Son of Man" Debate', JJS 29 (1978), 123–34, and J. A. Fitzmyer, 'Another View of the Son of Man Debate', Journal for the Study of the NT (4/1979), 58–68. Cf. also M. Casey, *The Son of Man — The Interpretation and Influence of Daniel 7* (S.P.C.K., London, 1979).

3 THE NEW TESTAMENT

Among the most important general works on the relationship between the Scrolls and the New Testament are the following: K. Stendahl (ed.), *The Scrolls and the New Testament* (S.P.C.K., London, 1957); J. van der Ploeg (ed.), *La Secte de Qumrân et les origines du christianisme* (Desclée de Brouwer, Bruges, 1959); M. Black, *The Scrolls and Christian Origins* (Nelson, London, 1961); H. Braun, *Qumran und das Neue Testament* I–II (Mohr, Tübingen, 1966); J. Murphy-O'Connor (ed.), *Paul and Qumran* (Chapman, London, 1968); M. Black (ed.), *The Scrolls and Christianity* (S.P.C.K., London, 1969); J. H. Charlesworth, *John and Qumran* (Chapman, London, 1972). For a more detailed bibliography, see Fitzmyer, 124–30.

The controversy about alleged New Testament fragments at Qumran originates in J. O'Callaghan, '¿Papiros neotestamentarios en la cueva 7 de Qumrân?', Bib 53 (1972), 91–100; see further *Los papiros griegos de la cueva 7 de Qumrân* (Editorial católica, Madrid, 1974). Against O'Callaghan see P. Benoit,

'Notes sur les fragments grecs de la grotte 7 de Qumrân', RB 79 (1972), 321–4; 80 (1973), 5–12; M. Baillet, 'Les manuscrits de la grotte 7 de Qumrân et le Nouveau Testament', Bib 53 (1972), 508–16; 54 (1973), 340–50; C. H. Robert, 'On some Presumed Papyrus Fragments of the New Testament from Qumran', JTS 23 (1972), 446–7.

On the question of Bible interpretation at Qumran and the New Testament, see J. A. Fitzmyer, *Essays on the Semitic Background of the New Testament* (Chapman, London, 1971), 3–58; G. Vermes, PBJS, 37–49; 'Interpretation (History of) at Qumran', IDBS, 438–41; D. Hay, 'New Testament Interpretation of the Old Testament', ibid. 443–6.

For a variety of comparisons between the Gospels and the Scrolls, see Vermes, *Jesus the Jew*, index. A general survey may be found in Vermes, 'The Impact of the Dead Sea Scrolls on the Study of the New Testament', JJS 27 (1976), 107–16.

The first volume of H. Braun's *Qumran und das Neue Testament* lists suggested parallels from the Scrolls arranged according to book, chapter and verse of the New Testament.

Abbreviations

ALUOS	Annual of Leeds University Oriental Society
b	*babli* = Babylonian Talmud
BA	Biblical Archaeologist
BASOR	Bulletin of the American Schools for Oriental Research
Bib	Biblica
BJRL	Bulletin of the John Rylands Library
CBQ	Catholic Biblical Quarterly
CD	Cairo Damascus Rule
CRAI	Comptes rendus de L'Académie des Inscriptions et Belles Lettres
D	Damascus Rule
DBSuppl	Supplément au Dictionnaire de la Bible
DJD	Discoveries in the Judaean Desert
DSSE	G. Vermes, *The Dead Sea Scrolls in English* (Penguin, Harmondsworth, ²1975).
En.	Enoch
Enc. Jud.	Encyclopaedia Judaica
E.T.	English Translation
Flor	Florilegium
H	*Hodayoth* = Hymns
HTR	Harvard Theological Review
IDB	Interpreter's Dictionary of the Bible
IDBS	Interpreter's Dictionary of the Bible, Supplement
IEJ	Israel Exploration Journal

JBL	Journal of Biblical Literature
JJS	Journal of Jewish Studies
JQR	Jewish Quarterly Review
JRS	Journal of Roman Studies
JSJ	Journal for the Study of Judaism
JTS	Journal of Theological Studies
Jub.	Jubilees
LXX	Septuagint
M	*Milḥamah* = War Rule
MT	Masoretic Text
Melch	Melchizedek or Melkizedek
NRT	Nouvelle Revue Théologique
NTS	New Testament Studies
p	*pesher* = sectarian commentary
PBJS	G. Vermes, *Post-Biblical Jewish Studies* (Brill, Leiden, 1975).
PEQ	Palestine Exploration Quarterly
Q	Qumran (1Q, 2Q, etc. = Qumran Cave 1, 2 etc.)
RB	Revue Biblique
REJ	Revue des Études Juives
RHR	Revue de l'Histoire des Religions
RQ	Revue de Qumrân
S	*Serekh* = Community Rule
Sa	Appendix a to *Serekh* = Messianic Rule
Sb	Appendix b to *Serekh* = Benedictions
Schürer–Vermes–Millar	*The History of the Jewish People in the Age of Jesus Christ* I (Clark, Edinburgh, 1973)
Schürer–Vermes–Millar–Black	*Idem* II (1978)
TDNT	Theological Dictionary of the New Testament
Test	Testimonia
Tg	Targum

VT	Vetus Testamentum
y	*yerushalmi* = Palestinian Talmud
ZAW	Zeitschrift für die alttestamentliche Wissenschaft
ZNW	Zeitschrift für die neutestamentliche Wissenschaft
ZRGG	Zeitschrift für Religions- und Geistesgeschichte

General Bibliography

The following are standard introductions to the Scrolls. The asterisk marks volumes containing an English translation of the non-biblical documents.

*M. Burrows, *The Dead Sea Scrolls* (Viking, New York, 1955).
*G. Vermes, *Discovery in the Judaean Desert* (Desclée, New York, 1956).
*T. H. Gaster, *The Dead Sea Scriptures in English Translation* (Anchor, Garden City, 1956, ²1964).
*M. Burrows, *More Light on the Dead Sea Scrolls* (Viking, New York, 1958).
F. M. Cross, *The Ancient Library of Qumran and Modern Biblical Study* (Duckworth, London, 1958; Anchor, Garden City, 1961; rev. ed. Baker, Grand Rapids, 1980).
J. T. Milik, *Ten Years of Discovery in the Wilderness of Judaea* (S.C.M., London, 1959).
*A. Dupont-Sommer, *The Essene Writings from Qumran* (Blackwell, Oxford, 1961).
*G. Vermes, *The Dead Sea Scrolls in English* (Penguin, Harmondsworth, 1962, ²1975).
G. R. Driver, *The Judaean Scrolls* (Blackwell, Oxford, 1965).
O. Eissfeldt, *The Old Testament. An Introduction* (Blackwell, Oxford, 1966), 637–68, 775–8.

Standard works in French, German and Italian

A. Dupont-Sommer, *Les écrits esséniens découverts près de la Mer Morte* (Payot, Paris, 1959, ³1964).
J. Maier, *Die Texte vom Toten Meer* I–II (Reinhardt, Munich, 1960).

L. Moraldi, *I manoscritti di Qumrān* (Unione tipografico – Editrice Torinese, Turin, 1971).

There is a one-volume vocalized edition of the non-biblical Hebrew texts:

E. Lohse, *Die Texte aus Qumran hebräisch und deutsch* (Kösel, Munich, 1964, ²1971).

Readers requiring fuller information should consult one of the Qumran bibliographies. The most recent are:

B. Jongeling, *A Classified Bibliography of the Finds in the Desert of Judah: 1958–1969* (Brill, Leiden, 1971).
J. A. Fitzmyer, *The Dead Sea Scrolls. Major Publications and Tools for Study* (Scholars Press, Missoula, 1975, ²1977).

The latest full introductions are:

E.-M. Laperrousaz *et al.*, 'Qumrân et découvertes au désert de Juda', DBSuppl IX (1978), 737–1014.
H. Bietenhard, 'Die Handschriftenfunde vom Toten Meer (Hirbet Qumran) und die Essener-Frage. Die Funde in der Wüste Juda', *Aufstieg und Niedergang der römischen Welt* (ed. H. Temporini and W. Haase) XIX/1 (W. de Gruyter, Berlin, 1979), 704–78.

See also:

M. Delcor, ed., *Qumrân: Sa piété, sa théologie et son milieu* (Duculot, Gembloux–Paris, 1978).

Index